WARRIORS FROM ABYEI

in

The Liberation of South Sudan

Edited by Francis Mading Deng

A Note from the Publisher

The publisher wishes to acknowledge and thank Dr Douglas H. Johnson for his invaluable help and support for Africa World Books and its mission of preserving and promoting African cultural and literary traditions and history. Dr Johnson and fellow historians have been instrumental in ensuring that African people remain connected to their past and their identity. Africa World Books is proud to carry on this mission.

ISBN (Paperback) 9780645210583
ISBN (Hardback) 9780645210576

Cover design, typesetting and layout : Africa World Books

Africa
World Books
Pty Ltd

Table of Contents

ACKNOWLEDGMENTS

EVERY BOOK IS THE PRODUCT of an extensive work of collaborators, most of whom cannot be individually identified. I will mention only a few of the collaborators in the project which resulted in this book. The idea initially emanated from our response to Bona Malual Madut's book, *The Ngok Dinka of Abyei: Not Yet South Sudanese*. Rather than refute Bona Malual's assertion, a group of Ngok Dinka leaders, who had participated in the liberation of South Sudan, decided to document their experiences in South Sudanese armed struggle, based on a questionnaire I had prepared for them. Their accounts appeared in *Abyei Between the Two Sudans*, which I co-edited with Luka B. Deng Kuol and Daniel Jok M. Deng.

My son, Daniel Jok, interviewed Deng Alor for his chapter in the book. He also initiated a separate project by interviewing Gen. Pieng Deng. After a few sessions with Daniel, Pieng proceeded to record his own experiences in the liberation struggle. Daniel then transcribed the recordings into a manuscript which is planned to be published as '*War Memoirs*'. It is from that manuscript that I extracted the portions that comprise Gen. Pieng's contribution to this edited volume. I am grateful to Daniel for his invaluable contributions to this volume and earlier phases of the wider project.

My deep appreciation goes first and foremost to the five authors of the sections of the volume. I am particularly grateful to Tikley Abiem and Africa World Books for giving me the permission to reproduce the remarkable story of a ten year old warrior powerfully narrated by this talented intellectual. I am also grateful to Dengdit Ayok, who transcribed and translated the interviews with Awuor Deng. And, of course, I am profoundly grateful to Peter Lual Deng, the pioneering and dedicated publisher of Africa World Books, his staff and all those who helped in the design and production of this volume. Over the years, my cousin, Mustafa Biong, has assisted me in my numerous book projects and has been very helpful in coordinating various aspects of this book project, including the collection and provision of photographs.

While I am indebted to all these collaborators, I remain solely responsible for all the errors and shortcomings of the book. Whatever it's faults, I hope this book is a modest acknowledgment of the monumental contributions of the countless heroes and martyrs from Abyei in the long liberation struggle of South Sudan in all its varied facets and phases.

INTRODUCTION

THIS BOOK IS ABOUT FOUR sets of experiences in the liberation struggle of the people of South Sudan. Although united by the common cause of the struggle, the individuals involved were provoked into rebelling by different triggers with a common cause and purpose, demonstrating the various ways in which the grievances manifest themselves within the overall shared sense of indignation and determination to right the causal wrongs. The stories also point to the paradoxes of armed struggle and whether two wrongs make a right. Does winning the war of liberation unequivocally translate into an overall correction of the situation and a progressive march forward or does it leave the goal of liberation an unfinished business? And in a cost-benefit assessment of what is achieved, does it mean that the massive loss of lives and destruction was a sacrifice worth making or could somewhat similar results have been achieved with less sacrifices?

The individuals whose stories are narrated in this volume include one man, three women, and a child of nine years at the time of the documented experience. The man, Pieng Deng Kuol, was a brilliant student of engineering in the University of Khartoum where he was first in the class. Awuor Deng, who tells the story of her rebellion jointly with one of her half-sisters from a different mother, was a shining star in her class in secondary school in Khartoum, when she chose to leave the school and persuaded her half-sister, also called Awuor, to join her in rebelling. The two are half-sisters to Pieng from the same father and different mothers. Nyenagwek Kuol, whose story is the third in the narratives, moved to Khartoum with her family both to escape from the insecurity of the war and to seek opportunities for a better life. She diligently sought education and was a highly motivated student of information technology in college. She was fortunate enough to find good employment alongside her studies and she received recognition and successive promotions. When she became increasingly exposed to the indignities of racism in her work, she chose to join the rebellion. The fourth is the extraordinary story of Raphael Tikley Abiem, a cousin of Pieng and the sisters, a nine-year old child driven by anger to leave his education in a prestigious Catholic School in the North to join the rebellion. Abiem's first task was to carry a large sum of money in a plastic bag tightly tied, indeed plastered, to his back to take to the rebels in Congo to buy guns for the rebel army. Fortunately, after the horrors of war suffered too early in life, he returned to the Sudan and resumed his studies to the highest levels of the academic ladder.

The proximate triggers for joining the rebellion in the three cases differed significantly. Pieng witnessed a succession of horrific brutalities of his people by the security forces in his area which cumulatively developed an intense hatred of the Arab regime that was brutalizing his people. Awuor experienced a demeaning treatment in her class by her teacher, aggravated by a racist attitude by another teacher, which not only infuriated her, but reflected the broader racial discrimination against the Blacks by the Arabs that had provoked the war of liberation which she decided to join. The case of Nyenagwek was the most surprising because she was rising in her employment, which got her involved in the work of the Committee for the Eradication of Abduction of Women and Children, CEAWC, by the Arabs. She was driven into rebellion by what she witnessed in the effect of enslavement among the children, some of whom had been brainwashed into denying their identity as Dinka, identifying themselves as Arabs, and despising their own people. This contrasted sharply with the sense of pride and dignity among the rebels whom she encountered in the course of the work of the committee which made her decide to join the rebellion. For for Tikley, despite his age at the time of his rebellion, his account presents a context already ablaze in a war of resistance in the South. The reasons he gives for rebelling are the same ones that had triggered the Torit mutiny by Southern soldiers in 1955 that escalated into a full-fledged civil war that had been raging for a decade when he joined.

The experiences of these individuals had some elements in common but also differed in significant respects. Pieng, his two half-sisters and male cousin went through enormous hardship in their hazardous journey to join the struggle, while the journey for Nyenagwek was far less arduous. Their experiences in the war also differed markedly. Pieng started with establishing and managing a camp for unaccompanied children that became an astonishing success that was locally and internationally acclaimed as a virtual miracle and produced young men who were resettled in the United States, Canada, Australia and elsewhere internationally. They became well known worldwide as the Lost Boys (later, Boys and Girls) who, to this day, revere Pieng as their Father and Leader. Pieng went on from there to distinguish himself as a remarkable commander who fought battles, mostly with striking successes and some painful failures, throughout the whole South Sudan. Pieng became widely acknowledged as an exceedingly brave fighter with legendary heroism. The two Awuors witnessed the horrors of war in a mostly supportive role which eventually ended in providing medical services for the wounded in a hospital that was well supplied with equipment, medicines, and doctors from Cuba. Nyenagwek joined the rebellion at the tail end of the war and therefore did not personally experience fighting. But she saw the effect of the atrocities and destruction caused by war and eventually decided to pursue the course of peacemaking which won her the honor of appointment as Ambassador for Peace by the Universal Peace Federation. Tikley's war experience centered on his harrowing mission to deliver the money for buying guns, a process that was as hazardous as being in the battle front.

All five individuals hail from the Ngok Dinka of Abyei and were in large part provoked into rebellion by the cause of the area which they then connected with the wider cause of South Sudan. The people of Abyei, who are racially and culturally Southerners, were annexed in 1905 by the ruling British colonial rulers to the administration of the North to protect them against the persistent attacks by the Arab slave raiders from the North. Other tribes along the North–South border, notably the Twich and Ruweng Dinka, were also annexed to the North for the same reason but were later returned to the South. The Ngok Dinka remained in the North and continued to play a bridging conciliatory role between the two bordering communities of the North and the South.

While the British were in charge, they maintained a neutral and even-handed management of the relations between the two communities which ensured peaceful coexistence and cooperation. With independence, successive Arab-controlled governments in Khartoum favored the Arabs against the Ngok Dinka. And with the outbreak of the North-South conflict, that first erupted in 1955 into a civil war, the Ngok Dinka, among them Tikley Abiem, joined their kith and kin in the South in the war of liberation whose objective was the secession of the South from the North. That war continued for 17 years, was halted by the Addis Ababa Agreement in 1972 with the military regime of Jaafar Mohamed Nimeiri, through a compromise that granted the South regional autonomy within a framework of unity.

The unilateral abrogation of that agreement ten years later by President Nimeiri, the very man who had made it possible in the first place, led to the rebellion of 1983 by the Sudan People's Liberation Movement and the Sudan People's Liberation Army, SPLM/SPLA. The declared objective of the SPLM/A was not separation, but the creation of a New Sudan of full equality without any discrimination on the ground of race, ethnicity, religion or culture. That war, fought for over twenty years, was ended by 2005 Comprehensive Peace Agreement, CPA. On 9 July 2011, the South won independence from the North, and declared itself the Republic of South Sudan which was warmly received by the international community as the 193rd Member of the United Nations.

The cause of the South and the wars of liberation resulting from it led to successive changes of Government by the military overthrowing elected civilian governments for failure to end the war in the South and those regimes in turn getting ousted by popular uprising both in opposition to military dictatorship and for failure to resolve what was mis-perceived as a Southern rather than a national problem. General Ibrahim Abboud overthrew the first elected civilian government in 1958, only two years after the independence of the country on 1 January 1956. Abboud was overthrown by a popular uprising in 1964 and replaced by an elected government after one-year interim civilian government with military oversight. That democratically elected government was overthrown by the military dictatorship of Jaafar Mohamed Nimeiri in 1969. The regime of Jaafar Nimeiri was in turn overthrown by a popular uprising in 1986 in which the liberation led by the SPLM/A was a major contributing factor. Nimeiri's regime was replaced by an elected government after a year of shared civilian military rule. The failure of the elected government to end the war in the South led to another military takeover that was engineered by the National Islamic Front under the misnomer of the Revolution of National Salvation led by Omer Hassan Al-Bashir. The failure to resolve the problem of the South that became recognized as a national problem was therefore directly responsible for the instability that plagued the country since independence.

The goal of the Ngok Dinka in the struggle was both a demonstration of solidarity with their people of South Sudan and the related demand of disaffiliating themselves from the North and returning to the administration of the South. Although the 1972 Addis Ababa Agreement gave them the option to decide by a plebiscite whether to remain in the North or revert back to the South, that provision of the Agreement was never implemented. The CPA also granted them that same option through the Abyei Protocol. In the interim, the people of Abyei are to maintain dual citizenship of both the Sudan and South Sudan. In effect, Abyei is constitutionally recognized by the government of South Sudan as part of South Sudan, a status which the government in Khartoum does not recognize, by still considering Abyei as part of the Sudan, and blocking the implementation of the Abyei Protocol.

As a result of all this, the status of Abyei remains in limbo, precariously poised between the two Sudans. It is interesting that in their devoted commitment to the struggle, the people of Abyei fought as Southerners and rarely referred to the cause of their area as the reason for their joining the war. Only once, when Abyei was excluded as part of the South by the Machacos Protocol that stipulated the principles for a resolution did Pieng voice his indignation and affirmed the cause of Abyei as the primary reason for his joining the liberation struggle. Pieng's protest was registered and catered for in the Abyei Protocol.

Despite the monumental achievement of South Sudan's independence, in less than three years, specifically in December 2013, South Sudan tragically exploded in an ethnically based civil war that has continued to devastate the country ever since. Although it was halted by a precarious peace agreement in 2015, it erupted again only a year later in an even more devastating war. Regional and international efforts resulted in a Revitalized Peace Agreement that was signed in September

2018, but whose implementation has only been piecemeal and very tenuous. South Sudan has been severely shattered in a way that is negatively impacting inter-communal relations throughout the country.

Independence was the long-held goal of the people of South Sudan. Its achievement against formidable resistance in Africa and internationally was almost miraculous. Initial resistance turned into great admiration and enthusiasm with a demonstrated commitment to support the nascent country to build itself and develop into a prosperous nation. This ambition was encouraged by the vast natural, agricultural, mineral and oil resources of the country. The outbreak of the war, the failure of the country to govern itself effectively, and the rampant corruption fueled by vast oil revenues and financial mismanagement have led to deep disappointment on the part of friends and partners, regionally and internationally. Even the people of South Sudan are beginning to ask themselves whether their long struggle that had cost them millions of lives and massive destruction of the country has not been betrayed by their leaders. The Dinka have a saying that a disdain you inflict on yourself is more painful than a disdain inflicted on you by others. The conventional wisdom also holds that a feud within a family is more painful and destructive than a feud with an outside enemy.

Meanwhile, Sudan too has not been left unscathed. While Arab-Islamic agenda might have initially benefitted from the removal of the complicating factor of the competing African identity of the South and its secular demands, the SPLM/A Vision of a New Sudan of full equality, without discrimination on the ground of race, ethnicity, religion and culture, which had inspired the marginalized non-Arab communities in the Nuba Mountains in Southern Kordofan, the Angassana of the Blue Nile, and the people of Darfur to join the struggle persists. The provisions of the CPA that had stipulated 'popular consultations' for the people in these areas to decide on how they should be governed within a United Sudan had not been honored.

Armed resistance in these areas persisted. This, combined with the determined uprising against the Islamist dictatorship of President Omer Hassan Al-Beshir, led to the popular revolution that eventually culminated in the regime's downfall in August 2019. Despite the overthrow of Al-Bashir and the return of a semblance of democracy, the country remains challenged by the gross inequities that had provoked the rebellion of the SPLM/A. There is indeed now a renewed call for the SPLM/A Vision of New Sudan. On a positive side, the two Sudans have been helping one another to bring peace to their beleaguered countries. Bashir played a pivotal role in brokering the Revitalized Peace Agreement and Salva Kiir Mayardit, President of South Sudan, has been mediating between the government of Sudan and the rebel forces in the marginalized regions of the Sudan. While a comprehensive and conclusive resolution of the conflicts in the country is still to be accomplished, considerable progress has been made and piecemeal peace agreements have been reached.

The question that can legitimately be posed is whether the massive loss of lives, the devastating destruction of the country, and the chronic instability that has retarded development and aborted the process of nation-building could not have been avoided. The racist character and religious chauvinism of the North, though persistently denied, was overtly manifest. Farsightedness and enlightened self-interest should have guided the parties to enter into constructive dialogue in an earnest commitment and endeavor to address the genuine grievances of the people of South Sudan and the marginalized non-Arab regions of the North. The options which were eventually adopted or became inevitable, including autonomy for the South, federalism, and even the concept of One Country Two Systems mechanism proposed by the Washington Center for Security and International Studies, CSIS, which I was honored to co-chair, were all in sight, but were rejected, leaving partition the unavoidable last resort.

Decades of mass atrocities, physical destruction, and grave suffering of the people have led to a situation of continued violence, lack of services, economic stagnation, and retarded progress in building the nation, leaving many people who had contributed to the liberation struggle to wonder whether that was what they had fought and sacrificed for decades, going back to 1955, several months before the independence of the Sudan in 1956.

On the other hand, South Sudan as an independent country now exists and will continue to exist, which is a monumental accomplishment. The vast natural resources of the country are also there and will remain a potential, waiting to be realized. Even the area of Abyei, often described as oil rich, can look forward to the time when the people will reap the fruits of their God-given wealth. All these will need continued struggle of a different form, hopefully peaceful and determined, for ensuring peace, security, stability, development, and nation building. This requires blind faith that the sacrifices made by the heroes, many of whom have fallen as martyrs, and others of whom are still struggling through very hard times, have not been in vain and that the reward for the precious blood they have shed and the grave suffering they have endured will materialize in due course.

I now turn to their voices.

Amadi East of Mondiri.
Immediately after we captured it under my direct
command, Cdrs. Oyai Deng and Gier Chuang
came to congratulate me. General Pieng Deng Kuol.

Khor Englis, area on Juba -Torit Road.
Cdr. Mamur with General Pieng Deng Kuol.

PART ONE
NO LONGER AT PEACE

The Campaigns of General Pieng Deng

Introduction

PIENG DENG KUOL IS ONE of my many half-brothers from our father, Deng Majok, Paramount Chief of the Ngok Dinka, who had a uniquely large family of about two hundred wives and sons and daughters estimated at over five hundred. Pieng is a much younger brother, but I am delighted to say that he has emerged as a national leader, about whom we in the family and the Ngok Dinka community of Abyei, are exceedingly proud. This essay on his heroic mission is largely a commentary on his war memoirs, with the working title *From Student to Guerrilla*. I have quoted extensively extracts from the manuscript, with slight editing for language and flow, without changing the substance, to substantiate the themes of my essay. In areas where there is a close correlation between what Pieng was doing in the war theatre and what I was doing in the political and diplomatic front, I inject my own record of activities to substantiate what was in effect elements of the cumulative family service to the cause of the Nation.

It should be noted that the events cited in this essay are not presented in the sequential order in which they occurred, but are classified under the thematic order of my analysis. So, the reader should not see the order of the events as a reflection of the development or evolution of Pieng's war experience.

When I first embarked on reading Pieng Deng's memoirs of his war experience, I looked forward with great expectation to know what my brother had gone through in his heroic struggle for the cause of our people. But as I began to read the story of his struggle, several themes emerged which, though separate, are closely bound together. One was the appalling conditions of mistreatment, oppression, humiliation, denigration, and brutalization our people had gone through for centuries and were still going through under the domination of the so-called Arabs of Northern Sudan. The other was what our people were doing in their various ways and means in response to their plight. These ways and means ranged from political and military action our brothers in Southern Sudan and locally were taking. Another covered activities of political and diplomatic measures some individuals, including myself, were pursuing from some distance, at home and abroad.

Although I had no information on details, since I was outside the country, serving as Ambassador, these various strands were discretely converging at the crucial moment of my return to the country in April 1983. Our brother, Miokol Deng, who chose the Christian name Michael, presumably because it sounded very close to his Dinka name, had staged a rebellion in our Abyei area that was threatening to trigger a return to the civil war between the North and South of the country. That war, which had raged on for seventeen years, had supposedly been ended by the 1972 Addis Ababa Peace Agreement, to which I had made some contribution, albeit modest. That was when I accepted to join the Foreign Service as Ambassador. Initially, the cause of the Ngok Dinka of Abyei was addressed through a provision of the Agreement that gave the people of Abyei the right to choose between remaining in the North after joining the South. But that provision was not implemented. The Ngok Dinka responded to the situation through various forms of political and eventually military action. Michael's rebellion was the military wing of a political movement that had been formed by the Ngok Dinka leaders in the South under the chairmanship of our brother, Dr. Zacharia Bol Deng. Bol had been the Deputy Speaker of the Regional Assembly and then Regional Minister of Health. Indeed, Michael's military action was armed with weapons procured and supplied by Abyei leaders in the South working in collaboration with the Leadership of Bahr el Ghazal Province, specifically Hon Aldo Ajou Deng Akuei of Malual Dinka of

Aweil. This clearly demonstrated the solidarity of the people of South Sudan with their kith and kin in Abyei Area.

Over twenty Ngok Dinka leaders, including Bol and our brother Kuol-Adol Deng, the Paramount Chief, and a number of sub-tribal chiefs, were arrested and detained in various prisons and detention centers in Khartoum, waiting to be charged with what the central government authorities labelled treasonable offenses. I knew of course that we were all concerned about the plight of our people and were politically engaged in the search for solutions, but I had no idea what precisely all those leaders had done to deserve such serious criminal allegations. Nor did I know about the formation of the political movement under Bol's leadership and its military wing under Miokol.

What I found when I returned to Khartoum was a precarious political situation in which allegations of rebellion by my detained relatives and compatriots were being made, but without specifics of what precisely they had done. Although a prominent national personality from the South in the central government advised me to keep a distance from what was going on, and to leave the country as soon as possible to avoid getting myself implicated, there was no way I could extricate myself and leave my people in detention, awaiting the capital charges of treason. I had to do something about the situation, although it was not clear what precisely I could do.

The cause of the people of Abyei was indeed a microcosm of the cause of South Sudan. And indeed, from the inception of the South Sudanese liberation struggle, the people of Abyei had been fully involved, including in the front line of the armed struggle, and had commensurately sacrificed a great deal. That was precisely why their being left out of the Addis peace agreement was very painful to them. But that agreement too was being unilaterally abrogated, and the people of South Sudan were also agitating, verging on a return to war. In fact, leading Southern politicians too were arrested and detained at the same time the Ngok Dinka leaders were incarcerated. Their cause was also my cause to address alongside that of my people of Abyei.

Developments were unfolding which eventually led me to take the initiative to intercede and try to secure the release of the detainees, even though I still did not know the precise reasons for their arrest and what treasonous offenses they were alleged to have committed. No detailed

*General Pieng Deng Majok in the forest between Tumera and
Raja in 2001 planning to attack Deim Zubeir.*

information was given me by either side. Nor did I ask questions about
the reasons for the arrests. And although I did not plan it exactly that
way, I must have intuitively chosen to remain relatively ignorant or in
the dark about the full facts of the situation. I did however know that
our people were in conflict with their Arab neighbors and the Central
Government over Abyei. That was what I chose to focus my initiative
on. My objective was to search for a common ground on which some
compromise could be possible.

Pieng's story is therefore the story of both Abyei and South Sudan.
What is remarkable about the story is that while Pieng was initially
motivated by the egregious violations of the human rights and dignity
of his people of Abyei, his struggle became centered on the liberation
of Southern Sudan generally, of which Abyei was an integral part and
parcel. Abyei is so much taken for granted as part of the South that it is
rarely mentioned in Pieng's story. One of the occasions in which Pieng
revealed his anger was when negotiations with the North once again
seemed to leave the cause of Abyei out of a potential settlement between the South and the North. It must however be born in mind that

uniquely remarkable as Pieng's story is, he is only one of many heroic freedom fighters from Abyei who contributed with highly acclaimed bravery for the cause of South Sudan as a whole.

Several books have recently come out on the unresolved conflict between the Sudan and South Sudan over Abyei. One is *Abyei between the Two Sudans,* in which several war heroes in the armed liberation of the South recount their experiences in the struggle, with several other chapter writers coming at the struggle from a political and scholarly perspective. The book demonstrates the extent to which the people of Abyei have been fully involved throughout the historic liberation struggle of South Sudan. Another book is *Visitations: Conversations with the Ghost of the Chairman,* in which I narrate my relationship and collaboration with the late Dr. John Garang de Mabior over the entire period of his leadership of the Sudan People's Liberation Movement and its military wing, the Sudan People's Liberation Army. There have of course been many earlier works on Abyei as an integral part of the South racially, ethnically, culturally and politically. One of those is my biography of our father, *The Man Called Deng Majok: A Biography of Power, Polygyny and Change.* The other is another book by me, *Frontiers of Unity: An Experiment in Afro-Arab Cooperation.* So, reading Pieng's book as a correlative to all these documentations of the position of the Ngok Dinka, it is inconceivable that doubts are raised, as some people tend to do, about where Abyei belongs between Sudan and South Sudan.

Having said all this about the collective responsibility in the struggle for Abyei as part and parcel of South Sudan, the record of Pieng's heroism in the South Sudan liberation struggle is truly unique. The level of his commitment, the intensity of his engagement in fierce battles, and the geographical coverage of the theatre in which he fought all over the South and across the borders to the North, is truly awesome. And his linkage of war and peace, of ferocious fighting and peacemaking, his humanitarian treatment of his soldiers, civilian populations in war situations, and even his enemies, sounds more like a tale of idealism than a practically lived experience of warring.

When I reflect on what Pieng experienced, I feel both exceedingly proud and in awe. It amazes me that he still has high regard for the efforts of those who have done comparatively so much less for the cause of Abyei and indeed for the South. In many ways, this essay is a retelling

of Pieng's story by proxy in his own selected words, mostly quoted from
his book. From time to time, I inject those experiences from my own
involvement in the struggle where they supplement or complement
Pieng's account. In a sense, this demonstrates the extent to which we
have all been in this struggle together in our varying ways and means.

Context of the Rebellion

One evening, in April 1983, Pieng, then a student of engineering in the
University of Khartoum, came for dinner at our house in Khartoum. I
was Ambassador in Canada, back in Khartoum to attend the meeting of
the Central Committee of the ruling Sudan Socialist Union – SSU. I decided to bring my nuclear family with me during the children's school
break. Pieng and a number of relatives were having dinner with us.
Pieng told us that he was leaving for Southern Sudan on what I thought
was a holiday but found out later that he had gone to join a local rebellion in our area of Abyei that later joined the Sudan People's Liberation
Movement and its military wing, the Sudan People's Liberation Army,
SPLM/SPLA. The Movement, which was created two months later, was
to champion the cause of the South and indeed the Sudan as a whole for
twenty-two years before it was ended by the 2005 Comprehensive Peace
Agreement – CPA. While this essay is about Pieng's book, *From a Student
to a Guerrilla,* in which he documents his remarkable war experiences,
my objective is to place his book in a more comprehensive context that
lays the foundation for understanding the roots of the tormenting cause
that drove Pieng into taking up arms to fight such a protracted war.

Pieng was a brilliant student who had distinguished himself throughout his education up to the University of Khartoum. Sometime before
our dinner, I had a visit from a group of students from the University
of Khartoum, which included his colleagues from the Faculty of
Engineering. Pieng was not among them, but they spoke very highly
of him and how he was top of their class. I was naturally very proud,
especially because Pieng himself had never told me about his academic
performance. I had no idea at the time that Pieng was also politically active in the University, deeply concerned about the situation in the South
generally and in Abyei particularly.

The political climate in the country, particularly in the South, was

*General Pieng Deng Majok with Cdr James Hoth Mai in
Lohotok East of Torit on Lopith Mountain in 1994*

tense. The 1972 Addis Ababa Agreement between the Government and
Any-Nya One, that ended the seventeen year first civil war was unrav-
eling. President Jaafar Nimeiri, who had championed the Agreement
in the first place, was dismantling it by dividing the South into three
weakened regions, comprising the former Provinces of Bahr el Ghazal,
Equatoria, and Upper Nile, reducing the powers which had been granted the autonomous Regional Government of Southern Sudan under
the Addis Ababa Agreement, and imposing Sharia Law on the whole
country, including the non-Muslim South. The provisions of the Addis
Ababa Agreement that had granted the Ngok Dinka of Abyei the right
to decide whether to join the South or remain under the administration
of Kordofan Province in Northern Sudan, had not been implemented.

It should be recalled that Abyei was severed from the South and annexed to the North in 1905, along with other Southern tribes to provide them with better protection against slave raiders from the North. The other tribes were later returned to the South, while Abyei remained in the North.

During the meetings that were held by Southern Sudanese leaders in Khartoum in preparation for the peace talks, I happened to be in the country on my way to a UN meeting in an African country. I was then a Human Rights Officer in the United Nations Secretariat in New York. Natale Olwak Akolawin, a colleague from the Khartoum University days, invited me to attend the meeting. The precise issue being discussed was the definition of South Sudan. The definition centered on the three provinces of Bahr el Ghazal, Equatoria and Upper Nike. I raised my hand and asked the rhetorical question whether they were not omitting an area that was part of the South. A spontaneous laughter followed as I was immediately understood to be referring to Abyei. The definition was amended to include Abyei. At the Addis Ababa negotiations, in which the delegation of the Government was led by the respected statesman, Abel Alier, the compromise was that the decision for Abyei to rejoin the South should be left to the Ngok Dinka of Abyei to determine through a plebiscite. The failure to implement the relevant provisions of the Addis Ababa Agreement meant that Abyei remained in the North under the oppressive and terrorizing rule of the war era, by which people were being harassed, tortured and killed with absolute impunity.

Early in the implementation phase of the Addis Ababa Agreement, when I concluded that the Government of the Sudan was not intent on implementing the provisions of the Agreement on Abyei and that the Regional Government of the South under Abel Alier did not want to risk a return to war with the North over Abyei, I proposed an arrangement that would give the people of Abyei a 'mini' version of the autonomy granted the South. This would allow the people of Abyei to govern themselves under the direct supervision of the Presidency. They were also to be given social services and development assistance to reinforce and consolidate peace and security in the area. That would in turn promote peaceful coexistence and cooperation between and among the ethnic communities on the North–South border and enable the area to play the bridging role it had played between the North and the South.

The proposal was welcomed by both the Government in Khartoum and the leadership of the Southern Regional Government. We secured generous funding from USAID and invited the Harvard Institute for International Development, HIID, to assist with its implementation. But the project was quite controversial in the South and among both the Ngok Dinka and the Missiriya Arabs. The Ngok Dinka saw it as compromising the right of the Ngok Dinka to join the South. When Nimeiri went to Abyei to announce the policy, and I could not accompany him as originally planned in order to explain the policy to our people, as I was newly appointed Ambassador to Scandinavia and in the process of opening the Embassy, he was very aggressively received by the intellectuals who strongly stated their demand to join the South. This, together with internal divisions over traditional leadership, with a Chief, our brother Adam Kuol Deng, who was personally unpopular because of his support for the security forces, made Nimeiri abolish the position of Paramount Chief. The vacuum in traditional leadership was ironically filled by those collaborating with the Arabs and the terrorizing security forces.

I fell under intensive pressure to persuade the Government to restore Chiefship. It would take some time before I could persuade the government to reinstate one of our brothers as Paramount Chief. Kuol-Adol, a much younger brother in intermediate school, was selected to occupy the position. On their part, the Missiriya Arabs and the Kordofan Administration saw the new policy for the autonomous development of Abyei as favoring the Ngok Dinka over them and as an undue interference by the Center in the internal affairs of the state. All this had the effect of undermining the Project which was therefore not able to secure its credible implementation.

South Sudan was also politically torn apart between the so-called Kokora, comprising the regional leaders from Equatoria who favored the division of the South, and those fiercely committed to the unity of South Sudan, which comprised most of political leaders in the South. The people of Abyei were also divided between those collaborating with the government security forces in the area and those agitating for the implementation of the Addis Ababa Agreement's provisions on Abyei. Rumors of impending return to war were increasingly spreading and intensifying.

*General Pieng with Dr John Garang de Mabior Commissioning one of
the Priests as an Officer in SPLM in Ikotos South East Torit in 1995*

Although I did not know it at the time, Abyei Liberation Front
was founded in Juba in 1981 under the leadership of our brother, Dr.
Zachariah Bol who had been Minister of Health and was Deputy
Speaker of the Assembly in the Southern Sudan Regional Government.
A military wing was created in Abyei under the leadership of our broth-
er, Michael Miokol, who had started a local rebellion in the Abyei area.
That local rebellion was rapidly extending Southward. Leading person-
alities in the Regional Government, and twenty one prominent per-
sonalities from Abyei, including our brother, Paramount Chief, Kwol-
Adol Deng, Dr. Zacharia Bol, and several other members of our family,
were arrested and detained in various prisons in detention centers in
Khartoum, with one arrested and detained in Wau.

The list of those detained, recently provided by our cousin Mustafa
Biong, included the following in the order in which he listed them:

1.   Dr. Zachariah Bol Deng
2.   Silvio Rokdit Ayuak
3.   Mohamed Deng Akuei
4.   Arob Bagat Tingloth
5.   Arob Madut Arob
6.   Charles Biong Deng Majok
7.   Edward Lino Wor Abyei
8.   Edward Ayong Ngor Dholi
9.   Ring Arob Kuol
10.   Bol Manginy Malek
11.   Dominic Deng Longo
12.   Joseph Dut Paguot
13.   Awadh Row Kueth
14.   Omda Achuil Bulabek
15.   Sultan Kwol-Adol Deng Majok
16.   Sheikh Patal Biliu
17.   Aguek Ngor Kuol
18.   Alor-Jibeit Deng Majok
19.   Yusuf Deng Baar Kiir
20.   Minyiel Ayuak Guiny
21.   Kwol Arob Koor (Detained in Wau)

As I learned later, many of these individuals were members of the Abyei Liberation Front that was formed in 1981, but whose existence I did not know at the time of their arrest in 1983. During the meeting of the Central Committee of the SSU, reports from the Governors of neighboring Provinces of Bahr el Ghazal in the South and Kordofan in the North, under which Abyei was administered, were alleging that a rebellion was mounting for which they placed responsibility on Abyei, with a focus on the sons of the late Paramount Chief, Deng Majok, our father. As the abolished position of Paramount Chief had not yet been restored, the sons of Deng Majok were said to be bemoaning their loss of power over the tribe, now given to the supporters of the security forces in the area, the terrorizing force of the Arab dominated Government in Khartoum. The SSU meeting was chaired by General Omer Mohamed El-Tayeb, the First Vice President, who was also in charge of National Security. Being the only member of the family and indeed of the Ngok

Dinka attending the meeting, I passed a note to the Chairman to seek his advice on whether I should speak or not. He advised me against speaking. But we agreed that I should go to him in his office after the meeting to discuss the situation.

I went to his office after the meeting and we discussed the situations in both the South and Abyei. In the end, I offered to undertake an initiative that would try to address the crises in both situations. On the situation in the South, I intended to mediate and reconcile the conflicting parties, all of whom I knew well and I felt confident I could persuade to unify their political position to be endorsed and supported by the Central Government to avoid escalation into a return to war. On Abyei, I wanted to negotiate with the detainees a position that would be a basis for agreeing with the Government. I intended to build on a proposal that I had presented to the Government to make Abyei an autonomous area under the Presidency, which had been endorsed by the Government.

The Vice President welcomed my initiative, but wanted to first clear it with the President. The President approved both initiatives on the South and Abyei. But the aspect relating to the South was somewhat murky. I had suggested that the reconciliation talks in the South be chaired by the former First Vice President, General Mohamed Al-Baghir, whom both sides respected and trusted. But although the President ostensibly agreed, Al-Baghir himself did not believe the President was sincere, as he was convinced that Nimeiri wanted to divide and weaken the South, so that he could implement his policies of dismantling the Addis Ababa Agreement. He would mediate only if the President put his consent on paper. That never happened. On the issue of Abyei too, it took quite a while before I got the President's written authorization to his First Vice President. I decided that the approval would probably not come and decided to write a report of what I unsuccessfully tried to do and would therefore offer my resignation from the Government. I was working on the conclusion of my report when some officers came to my house with a message. The Vice President wanted to see me immediately.

I found the Vice President in a euphoric mood. The President had approved my initiative. The First Vice President showed me the President's handwritten approval and strong expression of his confidence in me. "Francis is a reasonable man; he would never do anything against the interest of the country," the President had written. So, I initiated the process in earnest. Of course, considering that the country was acutely divided, the President's reported confidence in me was a double-edged sword; to be praised by the President might signal a betrayal of the cause by my people.

For the same reason of the double-edged sword, my initiative was not supported by all the Ngok, especially among the political activists. Some people strongly opposed it, arguing that the detentions were part of the struggle. Although the government publicly stated that the detainees would be charged of, and tried for, treason, which of course, carried the death penalty. But those against my initiative took that as the ultimate price for liberation. I later learned that the activities of the Abyei Liberation Front were causing severe divisions in the area as some people saw it as a source of insecurity and terror against those who did not support the rebellion. They too did not support what I did and later came out openly against the release of the detainees. I am glad I did not know all this at the time for if I did, I might have been faced with a debilitating moral dilemma between working for the release of the detainees and concern over the negative impact of the local rebellion on our people.

I discussed at the dinner with Pieng and other family members my initiative for the release of the detainees. Both sides of the argument were presented and debated. Pieng's position, which I very clearly recall, was that it was right for me to do all I could to secure the release of my brothers and other Ngok detainees, as long as that did not compromise the cause of our people. As mentioned earlier, Pieng did announce that he was leaving for the South the next morning, which I understood to be a normal visit on leave. I eventually learned that he was on his way to join the rebellion in Abyei that was the first step toward the full-fledged rebellion in the South, which eventually led to the formation of the Sudan People's Liberation Movement and its military wing, the Sudan People's Liberation Army.

Earlier, in 1981, I had received reports from brothers about the reign of terror that was prevailing in Abyei and urging me to intercede with the President. As I was at my post as Ambassador to Canada, there was not much I could do. But then an opportunity came when I was called to Khartoum for some meeting. On arrival, I received a letter from our cousin in Abyei, Hassan Deng Arob, in which he briefly described the situation and concluded with the moving words that people were hopeful that I could intercede with the President to stop their suffering. I met with the President, with the letter in hand. After presenting the case, strongly stating the humiliating subjugation and denigration to which the citizens of Abyei were being subjected, I handed the letter to the President. He read it with a solemn impression on his face. Then he handed the letter back to me and said, "I will not allow any citizen of this country to be humiliated and denigrated." Then he said, "We can discuss the situation until tomorrow. The question now is what to do about it. Would it help if I were to form a High-Level Committee to look into the situation and recommend a course of action?" I said that it would at least tell the people that the President cared. We immediately worked on forming the Committee and the Legal Advisor in the Office of the President, Yusuf Mikhail, was to draft a Presidential Decree appointing the Committee.

The Committee was to be chaired by the Minister of State for Local Government, Sheikh Mohamed Sheikh, and comprised prominent tribal Chiefs, such as Sorror Ramley, Deputy Chief Justice, Daffalla El-Raddi, eminent personalities, and two representatives of the Southern Sudan Regional Government, Martin Majier Gai, Minister of Justice, and James Lual Deng Kuel, member of the Regional Assembly. The size of the Committee continued to grow as people lobbied for inclusion. The Paramount Chief of the Missiriya Arab tribe, Babo Nimir, and Daldoum El-Khazine, a lawyer and Regional Minister in the government of Kordofan State, were added. Daldoum, ironically from the Nuba, who were themselves among the most marginalized in the country, became more of an Arab than the Arabs.

At one point, Daldoum said to me that he could not understand why we, the Dinka, were so adamantly attached to our Dinka identity. He said that although he was a Nuba, he was married to an Arab and was in fact elected predominantly by the Arabs. I could not believe what I was hearing. It brought to mind what KDD Henderson wrote about the Nuba, that unlike the Ngok Dinka, who considered themselves at least equal and even superior to the Arabs, the Nuba had surrendered to Arab hegemony. The Nuba would eventually join the struggle against Arab domination, proving Henderson's view an underestimation. Daldoum directed his sharpest criticism against me, warning the Arabs against me as a serious danger beneath misleadingly calm waters. The work of the Committee became increasingly politicized, with the Southern Sudanese representatives demanding the implementation of the provisions of the 1972 Addis Ababa Agreement that gave the people of Abyei the right to decide whether to remain in the North or join the South, a position which was naturally opposed by the representatives of the Missiriya and the administration of Kordofan who asserted Abyei being part of the North. I found myself in a serious dilemma. I realized that we had gone far beyond what the President and I had intended to be the objective of the Committee. On the other hand, I could not contradict fellow Southern Sudanese who were fighting for our cause. Nor could I go back to Nimeiri to inform him of the deviation from our objective. I knew the President would not welcome any recommendations from the Committee. I was in a no-win position.

We went to Abyei and held a meeting with the Ngok Chiefs and leading personalities. At the start of the discussions, Mater Ayom, one of the tribal leaders who was reputed to collaborate closely with the security forces in the area and the Missiriya Arabs, got up and questioned my membership of the Committee. He asked whether I was there representing the Government of President Nimeiri or my rebel government in the forest that was seizing and executing people. He said that some of them were afraid to talk in front of me as they might be victimized by my government in the forest. The chairman reprimanded him and reaffirmed my position as a national leader against whom such a statement was unacceptable.

Then Abdalla Adam, an Arab member of the National Assembly representing the combined Dinka-Missiriya constituency, read a statement signed by all the Ngok Omdas, Chiefs of the nine sections of the tribe, declaring that the land the Ngok inhabited was Arabland into which they had been permitted by the Arabs to settle. The statement was written in Classical Arabic. Most of those who signed did not know even local Arabic, far less Classical Arabic. I was fuming with anger, but I tried to maintain my cool. I asked for the statement to be translated into Dinka. But Matet Ayom, the very elder who had alleged that I had a government in the forest, got up and protested that the statement should not be translated, unwittingly exposing his secret plot. He was overruled

by the Chairman and the statement was translated. In response, one
Chief after another, beginning with Paguot Deng, the Chief (Omda)
of Bongo Chiefdom, spoke to protest the statement they had signed,
arguing that they had been tricked into signing. Without exception, all
the Chiefs of the nine Chiefdoms said they thought they were signing
a document calling for peace and reconciliation. "How can we achieve
peace and reconciliation by treachery?" Chief Paguot Deng posed a
rhetorical question.

After the meeting, I approached Matet Ayom, the elder who had attacked me and objected to the translation of the statement. I said to him,
"Uncle Matet, as we grew up, you were among those leaders we saw in
the company of our father and about whom we were very proud as representing the dignity of our people. Has the land become so destroyed
that people like you have been reduced to the indignity of speaking
the way you did?" To my amusement, he responded, "Mading, the land
has indeed been destroyed." I could not help laughing, though with
profound sadness. As I would later learn, his accusations that I had a
government in the forest that was seizing people, were correct in that
there was a local rebellion, but wrong in alleging that I was part of that
rebellion, since I did not even know about it. Years later, in an interview
for the biography of my father, Matet was one of the elders who spoke
exhaltingly about my role in promoting the interest of the area as a continuation of the leadership of our father.

At the start of our deliberations, word reached me that two prominent leaders of Abyei in the South, Deng Alor Kuol and Edward Lino
Wuor Abyei, respectively a cousin and a relative, had come to the area
and had been arrested. There was fear for their safety. I interceded with
the members of the Committee and the Commanding Officer of the
military forces to call for their release. It was a tense and sensitive situation in which I must have come across as quite emotional and was advised by members of my Committee, in particular Chief Sorror Ramley,
not to become too partial as that would compromise my national standing. I learned later that James Lual, the Southern member of Parliament,
a son of a leading tribal Chief from Aweil, was even more vocal on the
issue. Although we thought we had averted the crisis and that the two
would safely return to the South, we learned later that there was a plot
by the security forces in Abyei to ambush them on their way back and

kill them. Ironically, it was Matet Ayom, the same elder who had attacked me in the meeting and was collaborating with the security forces, that alerted them to the plot and advised them to leave immediately and follow a different route from the one they were expected to take.

As it turned out, the work of our Committee had been made so political that it was far removed from what President Nimeiri and I had planned. I could not impose on that High-Level Committee the very limited objective President Nimeiri and I had in mind. Although Nimeiri received our report with contrived praise and Daffalla El-Raddi, the Deputy Chief Justice, told him that he and I hoped to write a book about the work of the Committee, I knew that the President would not act on our recommendations. After waiting for some time without the President acting on our report, I went to him and said that it was time for me to return to my duties abroad, but that our people were asking me about our report and whether the President was going to act upon it. The President's response was stunning to me. He told me to go back to my work abroad and that he would act on the report and give the people of Abyei their rights at the right time. He said the people of Abyei deserved the same rights as the other communities were enjoying. However, if he took the decision then, people would say that Francis had become the President. I could not believe that the President said that, and not even as a joke, for he said it solemnly, without a smile on his face. I left knowing that the President did not like our report and would not act upon it. He would indeed tell me two years later, after my initiative in ensuring the release of the detainees, that the earlier work of our Committee was 'bad.'

I did not know what precisely the detainees were suspected or accused to have done, nor did I really want to know. I knew that my brother Bol and other Ngok Dinka members in the South were promoting our cause in the region. But being abroad and removed, I had no idea about the details of their work, certainly not about the formation of the Abyei Liberation Front in the South and its military wing in Abyei. Allegations of treasonous activities were of course very serious, but I took that to be only political rhetoric about a serious crisis situation in the area.

My mediation for the release of the detainees was a very arduous venture that took several months of intensive work. All the detainees would be assembled every morning to the glamorous National Security Building, well dressed with no indication whatsoever that they were prisoners. They would spend the whole day deliberating, treated with courtesy and hospitality by the security authorities, only to be returned to their respective centers, some of them quite appalling, with the detainees sleeping on the floor. Meanwhile, the Government continued to publish statements reaffirming that they would soon be charged and tried for treason, which seemed to undermine what we were doing. But we persevered in pursuing our work with determination. It was a bizarre situation.

The agreement which we eventually reached, presented in a written and carefully scrutinized statement, endorsed the President's policy of giving Abyei a special administrative status under the Presidency, while remaining part of Kordofan as long as the principles of equality and the full rights of citizenship for the people of Abyei were respected. Should Kordofan fail to honor those principles, the people of Abyei retained their right to separate from Kordofan and join the South. I believe I kept the balance Pieng had impressed upon me, which meant securing the release of our people without compromising the core objectives of our cause. When the detainees were eventually released, the event was glamorously celebrated, with a fanfare that was akin to the way the Addis Ababa Agreement was celebrated in 1972. People who only weeks earlier had been suspected of treason and were to be tried and may be sentenced to death were being hailed as 'Ambassadors for Peace.' Those who were collaborating with the authorities were dumbfounded by their release. As I later learned, they never expected that the detainees would be released without trial.

The situation was, however, more complex than was apparent. We knew that a local rebellion had started, led by our brother Miokol. What was not known to me was that the rebellion was the military wing of a political movement led by my brother Dr. Zackariah Bol, with all the detainees as members. Indeed, the argument of the authorities was that our family should bring our brother Michael Miokol back from his rebellion. My argument with them was that Michael had already rebelled and was in the forest beyond our control or influence. Instead of antagonizing the other members of the family and risk forcing them also to rebel, the government should cooperate with them to ensure peace and security in the area.

Opponents of my efforts back home organized their joint move with their Missiriya Arab partners and sent a delegation from the area to protest the release of the detainees. When they arrived and I visited them for a courtesy call in their hotel, some of them greeted me coldly, though politely, while at least one of them, the son of Matet Ayom, refused to even acknowledge my presence. The Deputy Paramount Chief of the Missiriya, Ali Nimir, the brother and Deputy of Paramount Chief of the Missiriya, Babo Nimir, with whom I had maintained friendly relations, refused to meet me, but politely sent me a message of apology in which he explained the sensitivity of the situation. The Governor of the Province, who had been abroad during the negotiations, returned to the country as the detainees were released, which he opposed. He and I had a showdown which was very rough, but ended on a positive note. Omer Mohamed El-Tayeb also confronted the Dinka-Missiriya opposition delegation and reprimanded them for opposing an outcome that was in the interest of peace, security, and development of the area.

The Governor and I then organized a major joint rally for the community in which both sides of the political divide among the Ngok participated. The Governor began by sounding tough, but provoked an equally tough response from the audience. One of our brothers, Arob, from the University of Khartoum got up and said to the Governor that if his attitude represented the official position of the government, then Miokol would not be the only member of the family to rebel; others, including he himself, would join the rebellion. The Governor turned to Zachariah Bol and asked, "Who is that?" Bol's cautious response, which made us laugh later, was, "I think he is one of the students from the university." After an extended debate, it was agreed that a joint Committee composed of the Dinka and the Missiriya be formed to proceed to the area to promote the agreement among both the Dinka and the Missiriya Arabs. I then had to rush back to my post and take my sons back to school, where they had fallen behind because of our prolonged stay in Khartoum, in the mediation process.

Many years later, Pieng apologized to me for having kept his plan a secret from me. But far from it, having heard from so many quarters within the South the heroic role he played in the liberation struggle, and also from international partners, who interacted with him when he was the Inspector-General of Police, about the laudable work he did, I was exceedingly proud of him. Had he told me his plans, the protective instinct of an elder brother would almost certainly have prompted me to advise him against the idea, especially as I believed that there are different ways of fighting for the same cause, the non-violent means being the one I had chosen. However, in hindsight, had I done that, and succeeded, I would have deprived our people and our nation of the services of a young man, who became truly one of the shining stars of the war of liberation. As this book attests, Pieng not only demonstrated exceptional courage, which one of his comrades, the late Edward Lino Wuor, who closely observed him in the field, once described to me as 'a bravery that always took him to the face of imminent death and bordered on foolishness.' But, paradoxically Pieng also reflected the judgement of a truly wise and well-rounded leader, qualities that went beyond warfare. Pieng is a young brother, about whom I am exceedingly proud.

Pieng was not the only brother who joined the rebellion without revealing or even hinting to me the intention to rebel. Another younger brother, Luka Biong, was in Belgium on a doctoral program, sent by the University of El Gezira, where he had been appointed to the Faculty of Economics. At the request of the University, I had assisted in obtaining funding for his postgraduate program. But at precisely that point, I learned that he had joined the rebellion. He too apologized to me years later for not letting me know. I also assured him, as I did Pieng, that I fully appreciated what he did under the circumstances. And in their differing ways, both became leaders in the Movement. As I recall, our brother Zachariah Bol, too was at the verge of joining the SPLM and letting me know, but some developments within the Movement and the killing of members he knew personally made him change his mind. He nevertheless remained a de facto member of the Movement. In fact, one can say that all of us in the Family in our varying ways were virtually members of the Movement and were actively engaged to the very end.

Triggers of the Rebellion

This tortured background became for Pieng a call to arms to which he responded with vigor. His performance in the war was commensurate with the level of anger that triggered his response to this call.

Pieng's book, with the working title, *Raging Race to War,* is a record of the author's extraordinary war experience. The mission he documents is unique in its expansive geographical coverage of the war theatre, the vast number and variety of the missions accomplished, the successful execution of those missions, the moral courage of admitting failures and responsibilities, and the dignified humility in never claiming the glory that is so well deserved, except satisfaction with the success.

The book begins by answering a question I have often posed to myself without finding an answer. What triggers some people to take up arms while others opt for other means of pursuing the same goal? What factors make even brothers from the same situation choose differently from these contrasting strategies? Pieng answers this question by describing some of the horrific brutalities which he witnessed the Northern Sudanese Arab soldiers inflict on the South Sudanese. One incident involved seeing bodies of slaughtered individuals whose severed heads were dangling with a thin skin still connecting them to the bodies. This is how Pieng described some of the scenes of torture and murder that he witnessed:

"One day, we went to collect food items from our store which was near the army offices. I saw somebody tied up, with his hands behind him. I recognized that he was one of our uncles – called Acien Kuol. He had been beaten and tortured. That was my first recollection of feeling so personally angry with the army and the Government. I was very unhappy with the way he looked, but my devastation did not stop there. Three more people had been brought in front of our store; they all appeared to be dead, their necks cut from behind, almost beheaded, with only a small part of their neck remaining intact. Although I was only a small boy, I thought this was terrible."

Pieng's other experience was witnessing men being executed in a cattle camp by the Northern Sudanese soldiers who gave orders that their bodies not be buried or more people would die when they, the soldiers, returned several days later. Pieng describes the situation in these words: "In 1969, when the body of our father, the Paramount Chief, Deng Majok, was brought back home from Khartoum, where his body had been taken from Cairo where he died, we were in Abyei. The night before his body was brought, we heard shooting. The information came to us that uncle Anyiel Kuol had just been killed by the army. We ran to his house in a part of Abyei called Mading-Thon. We found that he had been tied up, made to sit against his cattle byre, and executed in that sitting position. Witnessing raw evidence of that execution, at the age of eight or nine years old, added another layer of anger. But what can a boy do? Your family – your elders – are killed without remorse and their bodies exposed for the public to see!?"

That incident was our first alert when my brother Dr. Zachariah Bol and I took the body of our father to Abyei amidst a civil war in which our people were being harassed and terrorized. Our cousins, Osman Kooc Aguer and Justin Deng Biong, were leading the Anya-Nya rebellion in the area. That was being used as a reason for targeting the civilians, and especially members of our family. Bol and I spent one month dealing with an explosive security situation with limited success which, as we will soon see in Pieng's story, would prove to be worse than the crisis we were striving to address.

Pieng continued to give accounts of more incidents that agitated him. One such incident occurred in a cattle camp: "After the death of our father, our brother Abdullah Moyak Deng was installed as Paramount Chief. In 1970, when we were on holiday, I went to the cattle camp with our brother, Arop Bar, who is now a brigadier with us here in the Sudan People's Liberation Army (SPLA) headquarters in Juba. At that time, he was still a young man. One evening, the army came to our cattle camp and gathered all of us in one place. The youth were picked out while we, the children, both girls and boys, were left. Since old people do not go to the cattle camps, it was just the mature youth who were taken away. They did not return to sleep in the cattle camp; we did not know what had happened to them and we were left alone as children. In the early morning, they were marched back with their hands tied by the Army. They selected eight from amongst them, all from Twich – and they were all shot and killed in front of us. After the soldiers killed them, they talked to us, saying, 'We are coming back after three days and if we come and find these people buried, all of you will die.'

"They left and took most of the cows with them, most of the cows belonged to the Twich. They took them back to Abyei town with them. They combined the assassination with the looting of our properties. Once they left, we all ran in disarray with our remaining cows, everyone running on his own. But they took our brother Arop with them to

Abyei. I and those with me ran to a place called Dokura. There was very heavy rain that night. When I woke up in the morning, I was extremely sick, hardly able to perceive what was real and what was not. A police officer, whom our brother, Chief Moyak, had sent to retrieve the stolen cattle, found me in that condition, and took me back to Abyei."

During the one month Bol and I spent in Abyei, one of the areas on which we focused our efforts was to improve understanding between the commanding officer of the army in the area and Abdalla Moyak, our brother who was newly installed as Paramount Chief and whom the authorities suspected of cooperation with the rebels. Our efforts seemed to improve the situation, but as Pieng's account shows, that was far from resolving the suspicion. Less than a year later, the security forces committed the gruesome murder of three brothers, including our brother Abdalla Moyak, the Paramount Chief, and three uncles in Abyei. Five of the bodies were collected from the river bank the day of the murder, and the sixth that of the Paramount Chief, was found the next day in the river. All the bodies were piled up at home in the glaring view of the children.

Pieng recounts: "After I became well, I fell back into the children's pattern, which included in the evening, sitting in the chairs of the Chiefs and elders after they would have left, pretending to be like them. But one night, sounds of many guns disturbed us, and we ran to the cattle byre, called a *luak* in our Dinka language. After some minutes, the whole family was wailing; and then bodies were brought to the luak, bodies of our brothers Chan Deng, Bulabek Deng, and two of our uncles, Arop Mahdi and Thuc Aliet. They were all brought to where we were. This tragedy got worse when we heard that Chief Moyak had also been killed, but his body was missing. In the morning, his body was discovered to have been thrown into the river. The Chief had also been assassinated. His body was brought home and we buried them all together. For me, it was too much, because I had run from the scene of the assassination of our people, and then came back to Abyei, to witness this!!"

With impressive candor, Pieng explained how those incidents built in him an extreme hatred against the Arabs and all that was Arab, including their language: "Hatred had already mounted in me. I had made up my mind that the Arabs were the most terrible people for what they kept doing to us innocent civilians. I decided to have no interest in the Arabic language. I was not good at it anyway; so, this hatred gave me all the more reason to insist on not speaking Arabic." Pieng's account of his prejudice against Arabic brings to mind an interview I had in 1973 with one of the leading Dinka Chiefs, Makuei Bilkuei of Paanaruw. It was a year after the first war ended. He explained to me his ignorance of the Arabic language: "God has forbidden me from talking Arabic", he said. I asked him, "Why?" He said, "I asked God 'Why can't I speak Arabic?' God said, 'If you speak Arabic, you will turn into a bad man.' I said, 'There is something good in Arabic'. But God said, 'No, there is nothing good in it'". A Northern Sudanese reviewer of my book, *Africans of Two Worlds: The Dinka in Afro-Arab Sudan,* focused on that statement as evidence of our shared hatred of the Arabs and their language, although Northern Sudanese often tend to spotlight with exaggeration my Arabic.

These episodes in Pieng's experience were the early seeds of anger planted in him towards the Arabs. As he puts it, "When I went to junior secondary school, I was always rough with the Arabs, as I considered them my enemies. These were initial motivations, but they would grow." In a manner I found very touching, Pieng once told me that the differences in our approaches to the Arabs were probably due to our experiences which might explain the different ways with which we see them. He said that he was well aware of his deep hatred of the Arabs because of what he saw them do to our people, including our brothers. He said that I was probably influenced by my profession as a diplomat in the way I dealt with the Arabs. He himself could never approach the Arabs the same way.

But he also said that he nevertheless respected and appreciated my approach. That reflects Pieng's remarkable combination of deep convictions with open-mindedness and respect for differences of opinion and in different means aimed at the same goal. I repeat with emphasis that his was an acknowledged prejudice of which he was well aware and for reasons that were glaringly obvious. Of course, I too was aware of the horrors committed by Arabs against our people, but not the gruesome sight of the type Pieng witnessed. This may not fully explain the reason why people choose to take up arms to fight, but it is certainly a factor. And while Pieng's anger may be strong enough to make him take up arms, a degree of that anger is certainly more widely shared within our family and community.

Sometime around 1981, we received reports of the atrocities the Arabs had committed in our area of Abyei. My wife thought we should tell our children, who were very young. Although that would not have been my spontaneous response, I agreed with her and we told our boys. After they left, our second son, Daniel Jok, who was only six or seven years old, came back to say that he wanted to go and fight the Arabs as soon as he was old enough to be allowed to fight. I told him that I deeply appreciated what he said and that I was very proud of him for thinking that way. But I told him to focus on his studies and to remember that there were different ways of fighting; you can fight with a spear or a gun, or you can fight with words and a pen.

And of course, there are always going to be exceptions among the Arabs, however few, individuals who could see the just cause of our people. Nor can hatred be absolute. In fact, I do actually believe that Pieng is being unfair in the way he overstates his feelings toward the Arabs. I remember his once telling me the compassion he felt toward those innocent civilian Arabs who found themselves in the South within the conflict zone and for whom he provided protection and even recalled the personal relations our own family had with some of the Arab Missiriya clans.

From the time Pieng left after that dinner in Khartoum in April 1983, he and other members of our family and tribe, led by our brother, Michael Miokol, and with an increasing number of volunteers from Abyei, started the rebellion that spread Southwards. They initially linked with the emerging Anya-Nya Two in Aweil and other areas in the South and eventually connected to the Nascent Movement led by Dr. John Garang. As he recalls, "At that time, we did not know what was happening across the country, but we heard that there was a rebellion in Bor and that there was a colonel called John Garang who had also rebelled. It was said that he was a PhD holder. Miokol decided around July 1983 to call for a general conference of all the forces in Bahr el Ghazal. Some forces had also rebelled in Rumbek and many intellectuals and politicians, like Lual Diing, Bol Ayoulnhom, Amon Wantok, and Mark Makiec had also run away from Wau. Miokol said we had to find them and those soldiers who rebelled in Rumbek so that we all meet and decide where to go and join the Movement because we were now locked in and could not sustain our operations isolated. He argued that joining the other forces was our only way forward. He managed to gather all of them in the Aweil area, where we all met, and there was a big conference – the first one that we organized – where all of us decided to go to Ethiopia so that we could join all those rebels from other areas."

Pieng had a touching word of praise for our brother Miokol, who had visited us in Khartoum at the beginning of 1980, and although we had discussed the deteriorating situation at home, he never indicated any plans to rebel at the time. His rebel activities must have begun with the creation of the ALF in 1981 with him as the head of the military wing in Abyei. Once he assumed the leadership of the rebellion, Miokol demonstrated impressive qualities of leadership. In Pieng's words, "The story at this stage of the rebellion makes it clear that we should be proud of Michael Miokol Deng Majok who managed to control that whole huge army without resources. He was a humble man who was loved by all of the people."

Ironically, John Garang's rebellion in Bor was announced just as I was leaving to return to my post in Canada. Our Embassy in Canada was one of the missions the government decided to close for austerity reasons and Nimeiri told me that he wanted me to be reassigned as Sudan's Permanent Representative to the United Nations. I, therefore, returned to close down our Embassy in Canada and prepare to move to New York. On a visit to Washington, First Vice President Omer Mohamed El Tayeb confirmed to me that the President had made that decision. When I returned to Khartoum for the formal reassignment, I found that the President had changed his mind only a few days before my arrival in Khartoum. He now wanted me to go to Addis Ababa where Mengistu had offered the rebels a base and was providing them with support. Nimeiri told me that Addis Ababa had become more important to us than the United Nations.

The reasons he gave me were that our bilateral relations with Ethiopia and the Organization of the African Unity were more important to us than our relations with the UN. I had served as Minister of State for Foreign Affairs for nearly five years and had wanted to resign to take more care of my eyes which were threatened with blindness by chronic childhood glaucoma that was not controlled and was not being well treated. This was in fact the advice of my ophthalmologist. Nimeiri tried to persuade me that I could go to the US for check-ups and treatment as often as my doctors required, but I argued that such an arrangement was impractical. My assignment to Canada was, therefore, a compromise. From my experience as Minister of State and having led our delegations in the negotiations with Ethiopia, I knew our bilateral relations with Ethiopia quite well.

I made my case against the assignment to Addis Ababa with candor. I also knew that Nimeiri's real reason was to confront me with our brothers who had rebelled. I told the President quite frankly that those brothers had rebelled for a cause; what was I to tell them? Besides, I knew that he and Mengistu did not see eye to eye ideologically, as Mengistu was a Marxist allied with the Soviet Union, and we were close friends with the United States, a relationship which I had personally built as Ambassador to Washington. What was I to tell Mengistu? With what I saw as either surprising naïveté or willful obliviousness, Nimeiri told me to tell our rebel brothers that although they had a cause, they should not betray their country. To Mengistu, I was to tell him that although we had our fundamental differences, we should not allow ourselves to be used by the superpowers for their own ideological interests.

After discussing the matter at length, I accepted the assignment. Later, I thought the matter over and decided to submit to the President a letter of resignation in which I said that for reasons that included what we discussed and other personal considerations, I would not be able to take the assignment, and that I was not seeking another position in the government. I assured him that whatever I did and wherever I would be, I would continue to serve the interest of my country and that I hoped our personal relations would remain cordial. His secretary wanted to make an appointment for me to meet the President. I told him that would not be necessary. Nimeiri was leaving the next morning for a trip abroad. I was told that he was very upset by my letter. He called the Foreign Minister to talk to me and find out if there was any posting I wanted and to give it to me. I reaffirmed my position that I was not looking for an alternative position.

What was interesting was that John Garang, whom I had known and befriended since his college days in the United States, came with his family to visit me in Canada on his way back to Sudan after obtaining his doctorate in development economics. He and I had discussed the developments in the country. I remember posing a question at an intimate dinner with close friends. Given the fact that the Addis Ababa Agreement, which he himself had criticized, was being dismantled, what did they think about the situation, as former rebels in Anya-Nya One, who were now part of the Army, in which he was in the rank of Colonel.

John Garang had reacted in a manner that I misread as indicative of the fact that he had been absorbed into the establishment and was no longer a revolutionary. When I later met him in Addis Ababa, our first meeting after he rebelled, I said to him, "You fooled me." He asked, "How?" I recalled our discussion in Ottawa and how I thought he had become part of the system and would no longer rebel, only to lead a rebellion shortly after. He then explained that the plan to rebel was a secret he did not share even with his wife.

That was when I told him the decision I had made to turn down the position of Ambassador because I saw it as a setup to make us come into conflict with one another. His response, obviously with a sense of humor, was, "You should have accepted and be Ambassador of both the government and our Movement." I recalled what he had said to me about double agents being the most dangerous and told him that accepting the position would have made me a double agent. With the same sense of humor, he said, "You would have been the exception."

What was noteworthy about the time I mediated the relief of the Ngok Dinka detainees was that the newly formed Abyei Liberation Front had apparently amassed weapons which were to prove critical to the fighting capacity of the nascent rebellion of John Garang. If I had known, I would have been the double agent Garang and I were talking about. According to Pieng, "The most important thing was that most of the guns that were being used by Anya-Nya Two came from Abyei, because much of the population had guns, and we used the guns from the chiefs, police and army elements that had joined us. These were the guns that we were using when we decided to go to Ethiopia. These were the guns that we brought to the revolution. The strategy was that it was the politicians and students who would go to Ethiopia and the rest of the forces would remain to deal with the Murahaleen who were still disturbing all of Bahr el Ghazal. That way, we would maintain protection on the home front while establishing ourselves within the leadership cadres of Anya-Nya Two in Ethiopia."

Treacherous March to the War Front

The journey of Pieng and his comrades from Abyei to the war front was a truly heroic adventure in a determined quest to fight for freedom. John Garang had written a letter asking them to join him. They marched for months in floods and in areas infested with ferocious animals and creeping creatures, under the persistent threat of being ambushed. They were on their way to join the liberation struggle under the leadership of John Garang. But reaching Garang was itself adventurous. It was a painstaking demonstration of determination and sacrifice that can only be explained by the level of anger against the gross injustice and humiliation the Arabs were inflicting upon a proud and dignified people. The number of recruits from Abyei kept growing until it reached thousands by the time they arrived at Bilpam, the liberation headquarters. Their group had the largest number of volunteers from any area in South Sudan. And the striking fact was not only numbers, but also the level of education among their leaders. A good number of them, including many from our own family, were university students and graduates. Their commitment and determination soon got noticed and rewarded by continuing promotions.

I quote in some detail Pieng's account of that experience: "We left with an escort to Rumbek, but along the way the Sudanese army ambushed us. They laid the ambush at one of the bridges south of Rumbek in a place called Bahr Nham, and we were scattered. Some crossed to the Yirol area and some moved towards Bentiu. I was among those who went to Bentiu because I was behind the bulk of the forces with Miokol. Those who went to Yirol crossed to Bor. For those of us who went to Bentiu, it was difficult because we had to cross the swamp full of water. It was not at all easy, but we did manage to reach a place called Leer. The enemy was there in great numbers. But fortunately, we managed to meet our comrades who were coming from Bilpam and also a part of our force that was still in Abyei and had not followed us to Rumbek.

"We decided to join that force under Bagat Aguek, who was one of our heroes. He had joined us earlier from Sudan and was a great fighter. He was moving with more than 900 soldiers from Ngok, Kuach and Ruweng. We thought his force was reliable and so we were determined to join them, but they were still ahead of us. We remained behind them

until August, when the rains were so heavy, the water level so high, and
the land so swampy that it was almost impossible to cross. We finally
managed to swim across the Nile and went to the Gawer Nuer area."

In addition to confronting the enemy, South Sudanese began to fight
among themselves, pitted along tribal lines. This forced some of the
Ngok soldiers to return to their home area. Pieng recalls: "One night,
we encountered people who were running in disarray from Bilpam, and
behind them came an army in pursuit. The force of Bagat from Bilpam
had been dispersed by Anya-Nya Two, and almost 100 of them had been
killed. Anya-Nya Two feared that if our force reached Itang we would
strengthen the force of Dr. John with whom they were having disagreements. This was the root of the southern problem of disunity that has
lasted until today."

For years later, Dr. Garang would talk about the earliest conflict over
the vision of the Movement between those who wanted the separatist
objective of the struggle to be spelt out and Dr. Garang's Vision of New
Sudan of unity with full equality. That was the early conflict between
the leaders of Anya-Nya Two and the Sudan People's Liberation Army
(SPLA). Pieng's account continues: "Seven hundred of our soldiers managed to go to where Dr. John was, and it was one of the biggest forces
that reached the SPLA. This is a fact that everyone must know. Abyei was
one of the areas that had most people in the war in 1983 under Bagat
Aguek. But those who had been ambushed and ran back had lost hope.
We met and discussed with them, asking what we could do? These people were about one hundred in number and if we were to leave them
in that desperate condition, without guns, to go back to Abyei on their
own, they would all die; they would be killed without any capacity for
self-defense."

Since they had guns and the returnees had been disarmed, they decided to escort them back to the Abyei area and then return to join the
movement after those people were secure. They were very tired from
the most exhausting journey and had almost reached Itang but had to
turn back for the sake of their comrades. After they left the dispersed
soldiers securely back, they prepared to go back. But they heard that
there was a force coming from Bilpam, sent by Dr. John. "I was one
of the first people to meet that force, which was under Kawaj Makuei
and Bol Ayuolnom. My cousin, Deng Alor, was also there as a political

commissar. Kuol Deng Abot, who was combat intelligent sergeant, and Bagat Aguek and many others had managed to reach Itang from Abyei. When I met Deng Alor, he could not recognize me, because by this time I was always moving with all my things and keeping to myself. I was very self-contained. I had my own water container, thermos for my tea, and a cup, all of which I strung along my belt with my gun and t-shirt, shorts, and a hat. I was a real guerrilla, and Deng had last seen me as a student."

This was to be a critical moment in the process of Abyei joining the struggle: "I met with them and they gave me the first written message from Dr. John to us, appreciating all that we had done, and informing us that our people had reached Itang, and were the ones who had rescued the situation, when the clashes with Anya-Nya Two started. I said, 'If that is the case, then I must go and take this written message from the SPLA chairman to Michael Miokol.' Upon receiving that message, Miokol decided that all the forces would move to Ethiopia. We were more than 15,000 that moved from Bahr el Ghazal – Mor Mor and Kazuk battalions, even before Koryom battalion, which was not as huge. We finally reached there. When we entered Ethiopia, all the leadership came. It was a big, big force being led by Miokol Deng Majok, along with his commanders, Lual Diing, Ring Madut, and Paul Malong. Dr. John shot the full magazine of his gun by himself to welcome our force and all the guns were then fired in response."

Pieng writes that over the years of the struggle, Ngok lost many of those people, not only at the hands of the enemy, but also through the tragic fratricidal internal conflicts within the movement. One of the very moving scenes in Pieng's story was when he got word about the death in action of his sibling brother, Bulabek. I myself had known Bulabek as a brilliant sprightly young man, who joined the army after graduating from the engineering faculty. He was very popular professionally and socially, and reputedly well-liked by President Nimeiri himself. He had only recently joined the rebel movement when he was killed. Pieng received the news with exceptional serenity. He said that death was to be expected as part of the struggle. His only concern was that the Family might lose another brother, Michael Miokol, who was having some problems with his senior commander:

"Dr. Riek came, driving, and said to me, 'Pieng, I am sent to inform you that your brother Bulabek was killed today.' Bulabek was my elder brother, by the same mother. I told Dr. Riek, 'Thank you very much and I don't have any problem that Bulabek died because we were expecting that anyone among us would die. But now, I am fearing that I will also lose another brother. I'm sure Miokol, if nobody is there to observe him and console him, he may commit suicide. First of all, he is not happy, and when he hears about Bulabek's death, he will enter into depression. People do not know him, but I know him because he is my brother and I lived with him. If you could give me your car, I'll go to him'. Riek said, 'No, there is no need. There are people there, including Deng Alor, they can handle the situation.'"

Michael Miokol, who had initiated the liberation in Abyei area, was having some difficulties with Kerebino Kuanyin Bol, his senior commander. He had in fact been arrested by Kerebino and although he had been released, he was embittered and disturbed. Pieng feared that since Bulabek was killed where Michael was, he might feel guilty that he had failed to prevent the death of his brother. And indeed, Bulabek died under mysterious circumstances that implicated some negligence on the part of the senior command. Pieng wanted to go to Miokol to contain the situation. But that did not happen, and his fear materialized.

"The same evening, we were moved in a car towards Bilpam, which is where Miokol was and also where Bulabek had been killed. We slept on the way and in the morning when we reached Bilpam, people came to me and I thought that it was because of the death of Bulabek, and that they were coming to console me. But instead, they informed me that unfortunately, I had also lost our brother Miokol. He had killed himself. It was one of the most depressing moments I had ever had. I could not say anything. I was definitely very seriously affected, but I tried to control myself. That was a difficult time for me. I said to myself, "My brothers have gone and there is nothing I can do."

Pieng reconstructs developments in an attempt to understand the factors that might have driven Michael to commit suicide: "When we returned in 1983 to Bahr el Ghazal from Upper Nile, there was a problem that had happened in the camp of Ring Madut, the brother of Bona Malual Madut. Ring had killed the second in command to my brother, Miokol Deng, who was organizing the forces in the area to join the Movement. That had created a problem between Ngok and Twich. We had helped to resolve the matter for a time. Later, Miokol was with us as he led that large force to join the Movement. But Kerebino arrested him and took him to Bilpam, saying that he was responsible for the man killed by Ring Madut. Now, we were about to graduate, but my brother Miokol had been under arrest in Bilpam all of that time. He was released and attended our graduation where he spoke to me bitterly.

Apparently, Miokol was still embittered by the arrest. "He said to me, 'How can Dr. John let Kerebino play around with people like this?' He believed that there was no reason for him to be arrested. But I talked to him as we were close. Although I had many brothers, maybe hundreds, Miokol was the closest to me. I cooled down his frustration, but only slightly. He was then assigned a force, called a Coy, to go to the frontline to the fight. Meanwhile, we were assigned to the headquarters and remained in the training center. Those assigned to their forces went to the frontline. Miokol was one of them.

Although Pieng had feared that Miokol might commit suicide on hearing the news of Bulabek's death, and took his alleged suicide on face value, believing that his fear had come to be, I learned that the theory of Michael's suicide was controversial among our relatives in the Movement and suspicious fingers were being pointed at some individuals.

Educating Future Warriors

One of the achievements in the liberation struggle for which Pieng became known was his care for unaccompanied children. This eventually led to his establishing a school for children who would become the so called 'lost boys' and grew up into becoming the Red Army. Again, I give Pieng's detailed account of this process: "In our movement to Bilpam, I became associated with a certain personal initiative that would influence my relationship to the Movement, its leadership and its soldiers. When I was planning to join Anya-Nya Two, I had wanted to teach at whatever local bush schools I might find, while also carrying my Kalashnikov. I had planned to be a solider and a teacher at the same time.

"So, when it happened that some schoolboys decided to join us, especially in late 1983, I decided to isolate them from the rest of the group, and to move with them and teach them as we trekked through the wilderness. When we were going to Bilpam, all of these young ones, who were between 8 and 15 years old, were put together and given to me to be responsible for them. I became both their de facto guardian and teacher, in line with the objectives I had set for myself, when I set out to join the Movement."

People were grouped into two categories that separated those who had already been part of the Sudan army and already trained and those who needed fresh training. Dr. John decided to send the new recruits where they were supposed to receive formal training. He separated the category of small children to be kept at the headquarters. "I remember him telling us, 'These children are the future Red Army.' He was amazed at how we could have thought to separate those children while trekking through this bush of South Sudan and give them educational programs on top of all the demands of survival. So, we left those two categories, the former soldiers and the 'Red Army' and went to Itang in Ethiopia.

"After one month, Dr. John came to us and said, 'I am opening the first SPLA officers' course where we will train the younger recruits, you among them. You will be given some examinations. I wish you well.' Immediately, the same day, after we finished the examinations, Dr. John marked the papers himself. He worked all day and continued through the evening, finishing late at night. In the morning, he asked us all to board a truck, about fifty of us, and sent us by road to a place called Zinc, where we became the first to establish what was called an 'Officers College'. The place where we broke ground was in the forest, without a building or any single piece of infrastructure. But he told us, 'This is the college; you must establish it."

That was the beginning of a remarkable program of self-help activities within the Movement. "We were surprised but had no option. We started to build our own accommodation in that forest. The lecture hall was under a large tree. After some time, we were joined by some former students who had been at the frontline fighting and were recalled to reinforce our efforts. Later, we were joined by some people who came from abroad, including Dr. Riek Machar and Alfred Lado. Others also came from different places.

"While we were getting our training in those early days, most of us were not happy to spend so much time, from June to December, 1984, in a place we did not choose or understand. All of us had joined with the intention of fighting and we thought we were up to the task. If training was required, we thought it would have been only for 3 months and we would then join the others to fight. Actually, we were desperate to go and fight, to the extent that many of us thought the training was not important. We held illusions that the liberation would be accomplished quickly, simply because we had guns and our morale was high. Little did we know that there was nothing simple about this liberation. Yet, the fear that our training would separate us from the glory of liberation, leaving it to those on the frontline, got us agitated and angry."

Pieng was diagnosed as having appendicitis by the Cuban doctors with them. They decided to operate, which they did very crudely under a tree with limited anesthesia. He got through that and got better. But he soon found himself given an assignment that would prove to be one of the most spectacular accomplishments of his years in the struggle. He was to take care of the children who had fled to the war from various regions of the South without parents and unaccompanied by any relatives.

As Pieng recalls: "One evening, my in-law, Deng Dau, who is now the Deputy Minister of Foreign Affairs, and who was at that time a young officer in air defense, came to my house and said, 'William Nyuon wants you.' When I went to his house, William Nyuon told me, 'Dr. John is the one that wants you and you must go to Zinc.' The technical training was there while the general training was in Bongo.

"So, I had to leave immediately, but I had no car with a working headlight, and it was night-time. William Nyuon said, 'You must go because he needs you there before 5am as he is going abroad.' So, I took the car and used torches as headlights. At 5:15am we approached Zinc, but we saw the lights of his cars leaving and we could not catch up with him. I found Arop Moyak there and he gave me a message from Dr. John. I read it and it was instructing me to go to establish a refugee camp where the young people were across the Ethiopian border. I went back to Itang and asked William Nyuon, 'This is the message I got, but I am not ready to go there because you people have refused me to go to the frontline and I joined the struggle to fight alongside my colleagues. You took me from training to Bilpam, then to Cuba, and back to Bilpam, and now you want me to go to establish a refugee camp. I will not go.'"

"William Nyuon told me, 'You are wasting your time. These are orders from Dr. John himself. You can wait for him to return from Nigeria and complain to him directly. For me, I cannot say anything.' I went to my house and thought to myself: 'I don't know when Dr. John will return. And if I stay, people will blame me.' So, I went back to William in the morning and said, 'Ok, give me a car to take me to Panyadou where the children are.'

Pieng now found himself with a very challenging assignment with nothing to build upon and no resources with which to build. His would soon prove to be one of the most remarkable accomplishments of the Movement's self-help projects. "I went in the morning to Panyadou where the children were. When I arrived, what I saw really upset me. People were in bad shape. Hunger. Disease. The worst off were the children who were without any parents. It made me wonder why Dr. John had assigned me to that Mission, with no support. No car. No food. No medicine. Nothing. I said to myself, 'For him to assign me to this, maybe he is trying to test my abilities and my capacities'. I decided I must make it possible. So, first, I went around and did my own survey. The only thing I could give at that time was sympathy and care; that was all I had."

Using self-reliance and local materials, Pieng built a school and related facilities, and recruited teachers. He soon began to show impressive progress in establishing an institution which many saw as miraculous and attracted the attention of international observers. As they say, nothing ensures success as success itself. Many international donors who observed Pieng's remarkable accomplishment offered support, providing the resources for further expansion and quality enhancement.

As he recalls, "Those local UN staff were watching the progress like a dream; they could not believe it. Even Dr. John, when he came on a visit, could not have imagined what he saw. First, the whole camp was well surveyed. Second, the buildings came up fast. The children went to school without support from anybody. The UN was amazed. Eventually, support came. And it was good support. No SPLM camp anywhere was as well supported as Panyadou. When foreign visitors came with their planes, they would see below what looked like a town. One delegation came from America composed of university professors, and one Black American. One of them said in a meeting, 'No one can convince me that this place is run by refugees. There must be a power behind it. This is not a normal accomplishment. Discipline. No fighting. No theft.'"

Obviously, such remarkable accomplishment could not have been possible without self-confidence from its leadership. But Pieng's self-confidence also grew with his success. "I started to say to myself, 'Yes, Dr.

John was right to assign me to this mission'. I started to believe in my abilities to organize people, to make people realize their own capabilities and to create groups working in teams. That was the secret of my success. There was respect, team spirit, and commitment from every person. Even those who were senior to me respected me as their boss. Whenever people from our Movement came to join us, they had to abide by all our regulations and rules. Nobody stayed without doing something assigned to him. Even though there were horrible scenes – death was all around us – in the end, we felt that we did succeed in that program."

What was also remarkable was that Pieng did all that without oversight from his superiors, not even from John who had initiated the project. "When Dr. John came back, I asked him, 'What do you want me to achieve?' He said, 'I want these children to be educated. They will be the leaders of tomorrow.' I said, 'But why me?' He said, 'I know you are capable.' I thought to myself, 'How does he know me? And why does he think that I am that capable?' The only explanation I had was that Dr. John perhaps still remembered what he saw when we arrived from Bahr el Ghazal. He saw that I had taken those children under my care, and maybe he also had a special vision for them. That thought encouraged me. So, as UNHCR came in with services and food, I thought: 'How do I develop these children to become liberators? And how do I inculcate in them a sense of nationalism, as opposed to tribal and clan identifications?' So, what I first thought was to build a team that would work with me."

Pieng did not want to lose sight of the overarching goal of preparing the children to be both leaders and fighters. He wanted them to both learn scholastically and train militarily. He recalls: "Dr. John never asked me, 'How did you do that?' But he was excited. I said, 'Dr. John, we may lose these children anytime. When they are grown up, they may choose to join the formal training of the army, since all of us desire to be of service in the struggle. So, in order to make them feel they are already part of the army, and since there must always be holidays in school, and during holidays the children should be given some options of how to spend their leave, especially those children who do not go home, I am going to open a military training center, whereby during the holidays these children will be trained. After their holiday training, they will go back to class.' Dr. John said, 'You are free. You are someone with a vision and you know what you are doing.'"

The school developed into a virtual town that flourished until 1991, when the Ethiopian regime of Mengistu that had supported the Movement was overthrown and South Sudanese refugees were forced out of the country. But perhaps the greatest experience of that phase of Pieng's contribution was the profound impact he made on the children themselves. Many were to become members of the so-called lost boys who were resettled in the United States and Canada, many of whom I later got to know. The label evolved into 'Lost Boys and Girls'. And as they became increasingly well known throughout North America, I began to call them the 'Lost and Found Boys and Girls'. Many of them have since returned to South Sudan and now occupy rising positions in the service of the country. The most remarkable thing is that virtually all of them, wherever they are, at home or abroad, and whatever positions they now hold, spoke and still speak very fondly of Pieng. For them, Pieng was not only the administrator of the school, but also the Father who held them in his arms as his children and saw them grow into warriors of varied kinds and ranks.

Pieng was not only running a school for children whose numbers rose to 30,000, but the entire camp, comprising men and women, including his comrades in the Movement. Pieng thereby proved himself not only an educator, but also an organizer, administrator, and a leader. Some of these qualities would serve him well in the War Front. Pieng made the following reflection on this first phase of his liberation struggle: "It was the first time for me to believe in myself and have confidence that I could do what might seem impossible. From the beginning, I did not think I would succeed in discharging that big responsibility. I even suspected that Dr. John was punishing me, although I did not know what wrong I had committed. I was thinking that to be in a refugee camp was nothing for someone who had decided to join the armed struggle. When I joined the struggle, I did not expect that I would be given work without fighting. But after that experience, I understood that fighting is not the only service to your people, and that there are services that are beyond fighting."

A Frontline with Porous Borders

Pieng was nevertheless aching for military action, which was the main reason for his joining the struggle. "Since I had succeeded in the management of humanitarian activities behind the fighting, I thought it was now time for me to go and experience the frontline work and see whether I would succeed or not. In terms of civilian services, I convinced myself that I had succeeded, especially when Dr. John called me to his headquarters and promoted me. It was also challenging because when I was promoted, some of my colleagues over whom I had been promoted became offended. They questioned why I was promoted over them. I was the only one who had been promoted that was not on the frontline. Some of them had been in Ethiopia in the SPLM Office, organizing foreign missions, and did not get promoted.

"I appreciated Dr. John for the promotion, but I also feared that my social relationship with Dr. John, as my brother-in-law, might be an excuse for those people to question my promotion. I knew that to manage an operation which comprised as many as 30,000 people was still not the same as their frontline work, and I acknowledged that validation of officers was typically through the frontline. So, I could not blame them for resenting my promotion over them because they did not know what I had done."

Pieng continued to pressure his superiors for an assignment at the war Front. "After the promotion, I asked Dr. John, 'Since you seem to appreciate all my efforts so far, knowing that I am a young man, I want you to do me a favor. Since the refugee camp is now established, I request that you send me to the frontline." He promised me that he would do that. He said, 'There is a force now under training. When they graduate, you will be among the officers who will command those forces.'"

I regret that I must cut a very long story short and thereby shortchange a remarkably heroic accomplishment in a theatre of war that literally covered the whole South Sudan. Pieng's battles extended beyond the entire South into the Northern frontiers of the Movement, defined as the New Sudan. He fought throughout Equatoria, Bahr el Ghazal, Upper Nile, Abyei, Raja bordering on Darfur, and in the two border regions of Southern Kordofan and Blue Nile, the Northern extensions of the New Sudan. There is really nowhere Pieng did not command a force and lead them into victorious battles, but sometimes with humiliating defeat, often through no fault of his own, but always willing to share the blame.

The first step began with the assignment after the training, when more than 12,000 graduated. Pieng and three of his colleagues were ranked as senior officers – alternate commanders. "One was an older man called Chagai Atem, who was commanding us and was responsible for the general headquarters at Bilpam; the other alternate commander was Salva Mathok, Chagai Atem's deputy, who was responsible for operations, and myself, also alternate commander. I was assigned over logistics officers because of my experience with the refugee camp and the relationships I had in that camp. As logistics officer, I had to keep the soldiers fully supplied and equipped."

Pieng's first engagement came after challenging doubts and conspiracies against him on the ground that his experience as manager of a refugee camp did not adequately prepare him for a frontline command. At the time, the enemy was on the attack and exerting much pressure on the rebels. "The attacking Sudanese army from Khartoum had reached Malakal and were threatening to go to Bor. Dr. John ordered Salva Kiir to resist that movement. And part of our force was moved to go and join Salva. The enemy was pushing hard on Salva and managed to push his forces back. So, all of our forces were ordered to move towards Bor and from there to join Salva as the enemy was moving at a high speed with a big force. When they reached Ayod, the situation became even more difficult. Even the forces that were helping me to move the food had to be deployed. I was left with only a few people to manage the challenge of moving the food."

"When we reached Bor area, Dr. John gave us orders, saying, 'Salva is under pressure; one third of the 4000 forces must move immediately to Salva under the command of Chegai Atem. The second one third is to go with Salva Mathok to James Wani, who was in Yei area'. The role of that force was to block the plan of the government to reinforce Western Equatoria, which meant preventing any supply by the government from Juba to Western Equatoria. The third one was to move with me. I was to move to Magri, 27 miles from Juba, and report to Kuol Manyang, who was responsible for all the areas east of Juba. He was based in Torit. We gave all the cars to Chegai Atem, who was going to Salva, and the rest of us were meant to move by foot to our destination. This was a new challenge, but it was normal for me, as I had long been moving with the forces by foot. So, we set off and reached Magri, east of Juba."

Pieng then began to confront the competitiveness, the rivalries and intrigues of the command: "At Magri, I wrote a message to Kuol Manyang that I had reached the destination and I was waiting for directives. There was an alternate commander, named Jok Rang, who was senior to me and commanding that front. I reported to him. Kuol Manyang wrote a message back dividing the area between Jok Rang and me – the front to Kondokoro Island was under me and Jok Rang was given Bilnyang and Mafow front. I went to Jok Rang and asked, 'Did you get the message?' He said, 'Yes.' I said, 'So then, how do we do it?' He said, 'Tomorrow, we will come and talk about how to divide the weapons.' At night, without me knowing, he took a car and went to Kuol Manyang. In the morning, I was confronted with a different situation. I got a message from Kuol Manyang in which he asked me to move immediately to Bor. I later learned that it was Jok who went to Torit at night and convinced Kuol that I could not be given the responsibility of commanding a frontline force, since I was coming from a refugee camp, and there were tanks and other artilleries in that front, which would definitely end up taken by the enemy. So, Jok Rang's perception became the basis of the decision to send me to Bor."

Pieng took the situation calmly and tried to control his temper: "I only knew Kuol Manyang rather remotely at that time because I had been taking care of his children. He was apparently convinced by what Jok Rang told him. I sent him a message explaining that I had been travelling with the new recruits, and that it was the first time for many of them to endure such movement, and some had become sick. So, I asked for one car to take the sick people and I would be ready to go back to Bor. Kuol's encoded message was not friendly. He said, 'We have no vehicles; do you think we have cars on the frontline?' This is where I started to understand the level of skepticism about us who had not served in the frontline."

Rather than allow himself to be discouraged or demoralized by the skepticism, Pieng took it as a challenge to prove them wrong. "A friend, Dut Achuek, brother of Lual Achuek, was in Mangalla. I asked him for a car. He sent a lorry and I put all the sick people in it and started moving on foot with my forces. The size of the force was more than 2000. After two days, Kuol Manyang came with many trucks. I was close to Bor, but I stopped at Pariak. The trucks of Kuol Manyang passed us on their way to Bor. He was responsible for all Central South Sudan under Bright Star Campaign One. In Bor, he asked whether I had arrived. People answered that I had not yet arrived, and that only the sick people had arrived by lorry. He sent his small car to collect me. When it arrived, I sent the sick people first and sent the message that I would come in the evening because I could not leave my sick forces behind."

The meeting with his senior commander, Kuol Manyang, would prove to be a turning point. "In the evening, I went to Kuol Manyang. We had never met in person. That was our first face to face meeting. He informed me, 'Orders are that you must move now to a place north of Bor called Poktap, where the big digging machine for Jonglei Canal is, and you will get the orders there.' I immediately ordered my forces and we moved until we reached Poktap. There, I found an officer who was junior to me, and was in command. He told me. 'You must proceed to Duk, near Ayod, which is where Salva is.' I asked, 'What about a radio?' I had been moving without radio communication all that time. He said, 'I don't know about that.'" Pieng was getting agitated. "I asked, 'Can I talk to Commander Kuol?' He said, 'Ok'. I said to Kuol Manyang, 'Comrade Kuol, you have been moving me around without asking what I have with me. I have no radio and not even a group machine gun'. He said, 'We also do not have those things.' I said, 'Ok, if that is the case, then, so it is.'"

Remarkably, the more Pieng realized the forces against him, the more determined he was to succeed in what he was doing. After all, he did not join the struggle against all odds to be frustrated by skeptics. "I continued moving until we reached Duk Padiet, where my forces rested. Some mounted cars came from the direction of Salva, under Chegai Atem. He explained, 'We have been dispersed by fighting.' I asked, 'Where is Salva?' He said, 'Salva is coming. The enemy has taken a desert route and we are going to intercept them.'" Pieng now decided to be firm and decisive. "I said, 'Commander Chegai, I think your time is over. You have been fighting for a long time; let me now take over this fight.' He said 'But Salva is coming.' I said, 'Let your soldiers come down, except for the gunners who will join my force.' He wanted to wait for Salva, but I said there was no time to waste. 'Let us go to Duk Payuel where we will intercept the enemy.' Chegai Atem agreed."

Pieng's account of his fight is a touching mix of eagerness to fight, humility of expectation in entering his first test in the battlefield, a determination to prove his ability, and a great satisfaction at his eventual success: "I knew the enemy force was huge and well equipped. But I thought that the enemy might be surprised because they would not expect us to approach from that direction. So, we went. It was almost night. The enemy might have seen the headlights of our trucks. We thought that they might head toward Bor. That was what we wanted. Their misperception would be in our favor. After travelling a long distance, we found that there was no water. So, we had to return. We met Comrade Salva at Duk Payuel. He only had seven soldiers with him. He said he had to wait for us and he moved Chegai and the rest of the soldiers to Bor. We moved with Salva to northern Bor, in a place called Yom Chir, where we made a plan of action." The battle that would vindicate him as a commander was still to come.

The first step toward recognition came from Salva Kiir. "Salva accepted that I take over the command. Our calculation was that the enemy would not come to Bor but would move through Pibor and come near Juba to Magri, where I had previously been sent. I said, 'Ok, we will go and lay an ambush at the stream called Kor Makuac, which is near to Magri towards Juba before Mangalla. I said, 'You, Comrade Salva, and Chegai, can remain here and I will go with my forces.' That would be my first experience to fight the war with me in command. At that time, no one knew about my military abilities. I actually believed that people had underestimated and even undermined me. That made me more determined to prove my capabilities at command. Perhaps Kuol Manyang sent me from that front because he knew I could help Salva, but I took it differently; I thought that he too was questioning my capacity. Chegai Atem had known me, and saw something in me. That was why he did not argue when I asked to take over the command. Salva also did not question my command to go and lay an ambush on the enemy."

Pieng then engaged in his first battle, the one whose outcome would firmly establish him as an effective commander. "I started the strategic plan, 'We will focus on the small stream – Kor Makuac – which the enemy would have to follow.' This is exactly where we lay the ambush and exactly where they came. They went with the instructions to destroy Magri, which was an SPLA base around Juba. We fought for the whole day and managed to destroy many of their vehicles so that they could not move. The commander who had told Kuol Manyang about my lack of capacity refused to join the fight, although we were near his place. My comrade, Wilson Deng Wek, came with troops and tanks, thinking they could defeat the enemy on their own. Unfortunately, they were not able to. It was in the fighting under his command that we lost two of the bravest and most famous singers of the SPLA – Fanan Magok and Fanan Magir. Still, the enemy could not move to Magri as they wanted. They had to run to Juba by the way of Kondokoro. This was an achievement, even though we did not destroy them totally."

Pieng received his first recognition as commander in the field. "I went to Magri. Salva and Kuol Manyang met me there. They both gave me congratulations and thanked me for my efforts. That was the first time that I felt I had really done something, as it was my first battle in the SPLA. Now I had my two battalions, mainly from Bahr el Ghazal, with other Dinkas and Nuers from Upper Nile and Equatorians." From this early phase of fighting, Pieng recognized the importance of close and mutually respectful relationship between the commander and his forces. "I showed them how a commander should be in solidarity with his men and their families. When the other forces from behind came to join us, we built them all up and I saw how they began to get into a cohesive group, with strong commitment to one another and a firm morale. This strengthened my belief that anyone can fight as a reliable soldier, if you build them and the group that they are a part of. Because of this, Kuol Manyang really started to build trust in me."

From this modest and yet crucial victory, battle after battle followed. With each victory, Pieng's confidence in himself increased. And so did the recognition of his abilities by his superiors; the level of the assignments given him continued to rise. This consistent progression upward is clear in Pieng's account: "Our forces would regularly shell Juba from the eastern side of the Nile River, but when I came to Sindro south of Juba, Kuol Manyang told Achuil Tito to take those guns that used to shell Juba from east to south, to where I was. He also ordered Comrade Achuil to come to join me in my place. So, together we went and established a base at Kit, which is on the stream that comes from Rejaf. There, we put the guns in place and shelled Juba. That was a surprise to the enemy because they had always expected shelling to come from the eastern side. So, the enemy advanced towards us to dislodge us. They were under the command of Thomas Cirillo."

The tide completely turned in favor of Pieng so that those who had either been skeptical or suspicious of his command capabilities became his greatest supporters. "Now Kuol Manyang began to know the differences in command style. Achuil was reporting desperately that the enemy would take the guns from us and that they should therefore be taken from our control. Comrade Kuol asked me, 'Pieng, do you agree that we have to move the guns because it seems your position is not secure in the face of this advance?' I kept calm and said, 'Comrade Kuol, it is true the enemy will try to displace us, but we are also determined to hold our position. Our forces are strong, seasoned, and have high morale. We will push the enemy back.' Kuol Manyang compared the reports, and finally told Comrade Achuil to go back to his place in Mangalla, and leave me to command the guns."

Pieng continued to fight and demonstrate his abilities as a commander, and the recognition he received continued to rise commensurately. "After seven days, we succeeded in repulsing the enemy, and took Rejaf, which is close to Juba. That new position allowed us to use our artillery to shell Juba, including the airport. From there, Kuol Manyang, for the first time, sent me a congratulatory message and ordered all the forces south of Juba, along Nimule Road all the way to Nimule, to be put under my command. This is where I realized that Kuol Manyang had now fully trusted me. I was now commander of all the forces south of Juba."

The more Pieng was recognized as commander, the more he resolved to earn even greater recognition by showing his determination to demonstrate his abilities and deepen the appreciation of his superiors: "We were informed that an enemy force was deployed from Juba to reinforce their forces. So, we took our guns and forces from the eastern side of the Nile to Jebel Bonguto to the West, which is 25 km from Juba on the western side. There, we laid our ambushes. It was the first time the enemy got such resistance. We fought for 45 days defending the front until our people captured Western Equatoria. I was very happy as it was one of the first times my command ability was truly seen."

Then came another recognition of Pieng's continuing deeds from his superiors. "I was called back to the headquarters. Comrade Oyai put me at attention and said, 'You have been promoted from Alternate Commander to Full Commander.' There were other senior officers, but I was promoted above them. Oyai went on to say, 'As an Operations Officer, you were always with the forces. Now it is time for you to join us in the headquarters. I said, 'No, let me continue coordinating with my troops close to them in the field.' I stayed in the frontline operations and joined the fight for Juba on the western side of the Nile."

What Pieng's choice meant was that instead of being in an administrative position, someone removed from the physical danger of battles, he wanted to be in the front line of war. "As we prepared for the second attack on Juba, the plan was for me to destroy Juba bridge and capture the whole eastern Juba – including such well known locations as Konyo Konyo, AFEX river camp, Bros river camp, up to the stadium, and the area where all these hotels now sit from Pyramid Hotel to Dembesh Hotel, all the way up to Hai Malakal. James Hoth was to retake the Garrison and Bior Aswad was to take the western side of Customs and Gudele." They eventually destroyed part of the bridge, not the whole bridge. "At least no cars could pass. We took all of south and east Juba according to our assignment. We reported our success and maintained our position right up to the small stream, which cuts through Hai Malakal."

While Pieng won most of the battles with shining colors, he lost some, and worse, he sometimes lost many lives under conditions in which the responsibility might be those of others, but was sometimes his. This he openly admitted and gravely regretted. Pieng was indeed very much pained by the loss of his soldiers, especially if he felt that it could have been prevented. Indeed, part of what struck me as Pieng's greatness as a war hero is his care for his soldiers. This did not only cover providing for their material needs like food, water and rest, but also their psychological and spiritual needs. Although he himself did not believe in superstition, he took the views and feelings of his soldiers very seriously. When he felt that superstitious beliefs would not cause harm, he adhered to them and when he thought it unwise to follow them, he patiently endeavored to persuade his men otherwise.

Pieng was very keen about proper planning for battle as he considered poor planning not only harmful to the military objectives of battle, but also dangerous to the fighting men. He describes one such incident:

"While we were still fighting in 1991, Dr. John ordered Commander William Nyuon to reinforce me. So, he came with his forces, mostly from the Nuba Mountains. My forces were exhausted. William Nyuon said, 'Let my forces help'. While my forces were still expecting more enemy attacks, William Nyuon said he was going to attack the enemy at Mile 40 – 40 miles from Juba, which was between my forces and theirs and along the route of their advance. The attack was a disaster; there was no plan. Many officers were involved, including Dominic Dim, who was second in command, and Isaac Tut, all senior officers. Seeing the way they were moving, I tried to caution them against the attack. But they attacked anyway and we incurred a lot of losses, including senior officers and a South Sudanese called Manyang, who was an athlete. The attack was poorly planned without proper assignment of tasks and responsibilities. The assumption that the enemy was weak and we should further disorganize them faltered as our own officers started to complain about how we were recklessly moving them. I concluded then that everything needs organization and command."

Pieng's rise led to his being given command for most of the Forces in Central South Sudan: "In early 1991, we successfully completed the operation in our area of operation and Commander Kuol Manyang ordered me to hand over the command and go to Bright Star Campaign Headquarters in Torit. I was made Chief of Operations for the whole area of what we then called Central South Sudan – the area between the eastern Nile, Ugandan border, Kenyan border, Ethiopian border and Sobat where the Sobat River meets with the Nile. This big area was under Bright Star Campaign One, and Kuol Manyang was its commander."

What impressed me about Pieng's accounts of the war is the horror of war itself. Foot soldiers are killed with little or no remorse. While Pieng himself comes across as caring about the lives of his soldiers, regrets their death, and even felt guilty if he had any personal responsibility for the loss of lives, mass atrocities are accepted as the inevitable consequence, and indeed an entangled aspect of war objectives. This account by Pieng glaringly makes the point:

"We captured Yei under direct command of Jadalla and supervised by Salva Kiir, but Gier was overwhelmed by the heavy presence of troops on the Ugandan border. They succeeded to capture some tanks while our forces that had captured Yei moved to help Gier. They captured

1,000 enemy soldiers, which was a crisis to the Khartoum regime. They abandoned their equipment because of the swiftness of our movements and were confused because they could not understand how we were able to reinforce so quickly once they had overrun Gier's forces. The terrain was against them because the forest was overgrown and they had no idea where to go because they were people brought from Khartoum and moved to the south without knowing the area. We destroyed a significant part of Khartoum's fighting capacity with more than 5000 soldiers killed and captured. We took all their equipment, tanks and artillery. So, our morale was high and they were demoralized. Thomas Cirillo was moving to Juba capturing all their positions up to a place called 40 Mile where some of our tanks were destroyed. But Thomas still managed to resist and stopped there." This relates to the enemy losses which could not have been without loss on the side of the rebel force.

Standing United or Falling Divided

1991 was the year of the internal rebellion by Dr. Riek Machar and Dr. Lam Akol against Dr. John Garang which seriously challenged the very viability of a Movement that had inspired not only the people of the South, but also significant sectors of the North. Pieng recalls: "Before I had time to get settled, we lost most of our bases in Ethiopia as the country descended into its own conflict. Our refugees, all of our families, the disabled, and the Red Army, whom I had left in Ethiopia, were on the move towards our area. Meanwhile, Riek Machar and Lam Akol declared that they were breaking away from the Movement. Action centered on our area. Riek Machar advanced the rebellion through the Nasser Declaration. But even before that, we got some papers that had been circulated saying, "Garang must go now!" While I was still around Juba, Comrade Taban Deng Gai had called me over the radio, and said, 'The two doctors seem to be planning something.' I didn't take it seriously, but he told me, 'They want to rebel against Dr. John.' I thought it wasn't possible."

According to Pieng, Riek Machar thought that because Gier and Oyai were from the same Upper Nile province as the two rebellious leaders, they would support them. So, he gave them the papers to distribute within the Movement, but Oyai shared the documents with

Pieng and other colleagues, who spoke with Dr. John and Commander Salva Kiir. The rebellion did happen. "We were in Eastern Equatoria, after having lost our headquarters, and so Torit had become our new headquarters."

Pieng elaborates on the developments: "Kuol Manyang told me, 'Riek's forces are moving towards our area, so you have to prepare. Organize the forces at the Ethiopian border and move them to our north command at Malakal.' So, I headed with vehicles to the Ethiopian border to organize them and move the logistics to our headquarters. Before I reached Boma along the border at a place called Magos, I met some senior SPLM/A officers who had been detained years back in Ethiopia. Commander Malong Awan was there. We greeted each other and I proceeded. Later, I recommended to commander Kuol, 'It's better we take them to Boma, near our headquarters.' He agreed and I moved the forces from Pakok to Boma and then on to Pibor area, near Riek's forces, and then went back to the headquarters."

Pieng tells of an instance which demonstrated the level of his commitment to the struggle and placed his sense of national duty above personal family interests. This indeed illustrates the sacrifices the families of the fighting men were making as they got separated from their loved ones for prolonged periods. "The same day I was to move to the Ethiopian border, my family arrived after almost three years without my seeing them. I had left them in 1989 in Ethiopia and now they were fleeing with the rest of our displaced people. Before I even had a chance to settle them, I received the instruction to leave. I told my family, 'I am going for a mission.' Then one of my brothers, Commander Monydhang Deng, told Kuol Manyang that our families had just arrived and Kuol Manyang said, 'Why did Pieng not tell me?' He called me and asked me the same question, to which I responded, 'This is responsibility. I will go and come back.' Kuol Manyang should remember that during those critical days of Riek's rebellion, I left my family the same evening for the call of duty."

The SPLA forces were effectively resisting the Riek-Lam rebellion. Another heroic member of our family was part of that effective resistance. According to Pieng, "The only place we were willing to advise Dr. John to let our people move from was Boma, where my cousin Kuol Deim was commanding. We asked Dr. John, 'Kuol Deim is staying at

Boma with many wounded soldiers and displaced families. We fear for them. If attacked in such a remote and hostile place, they will be annihilated.' Dr. John said, 'Ok, we agree, but you cannot decide for Kuol Deim. So, let me call him and see what he says. But you people will need to be prepared to defend our positions.' We agreed. We said, 'We cannot go from Torit to Western Equatoria to defend the area from the enemy there.'

"Dr. John talked to Kuol Deim and took notes of his communications." This casual observation of Pieng about Dr. John Garang is important for it alludes to a very significant aspect of Garang's practice for which he was well known – he always took notes of any discussion. John called them in the evening to give Kuol Deim's response. He reported that after Kuol sat with his officers and his soldiers, they said, "We cannot leave Jebel Boma. We are ready to defend it. If it is hunger, we will cultivate our food. If it is the enemy, we will fight. We are confident we will not be dislodged. But if we are, we will not be annihilated; we will go to the mountains." According to Pieng, "Kuol's message was that the soldiers were ready to die. Dr. John said, 'Since they are determined, we need not call them again; let us leave them there, while you go towards Juba with your forces.'"

The regime of Mengistu in Ethiopia, which had been the principal source of support for the SPLM/A, had been overthrown by rebel forces that were supported by Khartoum. South Sudanese refugees in Ethiopia were being forced to flee the country. Meanwhile, the Government of Khartoum was strengthening its fighting capacity with material support from the Arab world. SPLM/A was being squeezed from various fronts. Pieng writes: "When fighting began, it was serious, widespread and sustained. Riek Machar moved on Bor. I moved towards Mangalla to assess the condition of our withdrawing force. I met our people coming from Bor in a desperate condition. Families and soldiers were retreating defeated. Their conditions were horrible."

Those were very hard times for the Movement and many observers doubted that they could overcome the challenges confronting them. Salva Kiir and Kuol Manyang came from Torit and met us in Ngangala, southeast of Magri, and wanted to proceed to Bor. Oyai and I disagreed with them. We said, 'We can go to Bor; but you should not go.' Comrade Salva said, 'Juba is most dangerous; if you leave it, the enemy will go to

Torit. Soldiers are there in Bor, but they are demoralized. If we go to them, it will keep them from retreating. It will help them to stand their ground. You continue to keep the enemy at bay.'

Pieng graphically describes the depressed mood the liberators were in and their will to counter the insurgence. "We saw on their faces desperation, mixed with determination. We were happy in the way they took their leadership responsibility. The information that had come from Bor was nothing short of horrific. Riek had committed a horrible massacre of the Dinka civilians in Bor. It was one of the darkest chapters in our history as a country and a movement." And indeed, scenes of those massacres were being shown on television screens around the world. Bodies of the victims remained unburied and scattered all over, with birds and animals scavenging on them. It was a genocide that could only be surpassed by what happened in Rwanda three years later.

It was at the outset of that genocidal spree that our brother, Kuol Suuk Deng, and our cousin, Wuor Juk Abyei, promising leaders, and dedicated patriots, who were under the command of Riek Machar, and who under the command of Riek Machar refused to raise their guns against fellow South Sudanese compatriots, were gruesomely murdered by Riek's rebel forces. The horrific manner of their murders and the patriotic reason for their brutal killing make their deaths among the priceless sacrifices our family and the people of Abyei have made for the cause of South Sudan.

According to Pieng's account, with the rebels seemingly having the upper hand, "Comrades Salva Kiir and Kuol Manyang went to Mangalla and we moved some of our forces, including those under the command of Majak Agot, to try to stop our forces and civilians in Bor from running. When they saw those top leaders of the SPLA, it strengthened them and they together managed to reach Bor. We continued fighting both Machar's forces and the enemy from Khartoum. By this time, the NCP was getting support from the Arab world, including a lot of equipment. After Salva Kiir and Kuol Manyang managed to chase away Riek Machar's forces from Bor, the enemy barges were moving from Malakal toward Juba." Pieng went to prevent their barges, using explosives to block them, which he did, but that nearly killed him. In fact, some of his men thought his undertaking the use of explosives to sink the big containers was suicidal and took him for dead.

Dilemmas of Relations with the Civilians

Although Pieng had been engaged in countering the Riek-Lam rebellion, another crisis of yet another internal rebellion was in the making that called for his intervention. The situation would also confront him with the complexities of fighting, while protecting the civilians, among whom there were elements supporting the enemy. One of the senior commanders, William Nyuon, a Nuer like Riek Machar, was reported to be contemplating joining Riek. Another demonstration of Pieng's commitment was the way he wanted to go back to the front, interrupting his recovery from illness in Nairobi.

William Nyuon's rebellion posed yet another existential threat to the Movement, as the objective was to eliminate the formidable leadership of John Garang. Pieng recalls:"While we were fighting around Juba, I became seriously sick and was evacuated from around Juba to Nimule and on to Nairobi. I had an ulcer and malaria and some other problems. William Nyuon was chosen to lead the delegation of SPLM/A at the Abuja talks with the Government." But something happened that later made him join Riek Machar and Lam Akol. "They deployed him to kill Dr. John. But this information was leaked. Dr. John was on a mission abroad. When he came back, he was to meet William Nyuon. But Comrade Oyai sent James Hoth and Kuol Deng Abot to meet him as he came from Kajo Keji before he was to meet William Nyuon at Pageri. They succeeded in informing him of the plan. They all went together to Pageri, but Dr. John stopped at a distance from Pageri. Kuol Manyang was also there." Dr. John, who, in the words of Pieng, "was a brave man," seemed reluctant to accept the reports of William Nyuon's imminent rebellion. He said, "We cannot assume that William Nyuon will do this, but let us talk to him and convince him to be wise and abandon any such plan."

According to Pieng, William Nyuon was known to have said that his problem was with Kuol Manyang. Lual Diing from Bahr el Ghazal, had apparently agreed that Kuol Manyang was a problem. So, James Hoth, who was from Nuer, and was firmly loyal to Dr. John, advised that there was a danger of the areas of Bahr el Ghazal under the command of Lual Diing joining William Nyuon. He, therefore, suggested that Salva Kiir, being also from Bahr el Ghazal, be asked to help decide how to contain that front.

Dr. John agreed and he asked Salva, who was in Narus, to join him in Pageri. Since Salva had to pass through Kenya and Pieng was in Nairobi recovering, he went to meet Salva, who told him, "There is a situation in Pageri and I am going to join Dr. John there." Pieng asked, "What is happening?" Salva responded, "William Nyuon is about to rebel and he has mobilized parts of Bahr el Ghazal." Pieng said, "William is danger-ous; I must go with you." But Salva said, "No you are sick. Nothing will happen. We can contain the situation. You stay here and complete your recovery. Then you will return to the field."

Pieng recalls an incident which he saw as evidence of Salva's dedica-tion to the cause for which they were fighting: "As we took him to the airport, I saw Salva's level of commitment. The plane that was to take him was loaded with medicine and there was only one seat for a passen-ger, one for Salva, and another for the co-pilot. Salva said, 'In that seat, I must take John Koang (a Nuer), because he will help us more than my bodyguards.' He left without bodyguards. After some days we learned that William Nyuon had rebelled. So, I approached Elijah Malok who was in charge of the South Sudan Relief and Rehabilitation Agency (SRRA) in Nairobi and was taking care of my treatment. I said to him, 'Uncle Elijah,' (I called him Uncle because he was older than me and was from Bor, and therefore was my in-law.) I said, 'Since William has rebelled, he is going to cause havoc. I know Comrades Oyai and Salva are calm people; they need my help.' He allowed me to go.

It is interesting that Pieng, who is himself a very calm person, de-scribed his senior commanders as 'calm people' and argued that they needed him. This was clearly his modest way of stating his vital role. "When I reached Pageri, I said to myself, 'I must continue forward to where the forces are.' When I reached Comrade Oyai, I was informed that William had attacked where Salva was and Salva's whereabouts were not known. His radio had also been captured. We asked Kuol Manyang's radio operator who confirmed that Salva had been attacked but was still alive. We said we must talk to him. So, we managed to get Salva on the radio channel and talked to him."

Salva told them, "I am alive, but you must continue with your mis-sion where you are." Pieng told Oyai, "What we can do now is to let my forces move and I will join Salva and you continue with your mission here. While my forces move on foot, we will go in a car to see Salva and you will then go back to your command." They went to Salva and spent some hours with him. Then Salva said to Pieng, "When are you going back?" Pieng said, "Oyai will go back and I will stay with you." Salva responded, "Who gave such an order?" Pieng said, "When there is a crisis, orders are generated from the bottom up. Now my forces are almost here. I do not want you to move. I will be the one in command here with my forces." Salva said, "No this is insubordination. What will Dr. John say? He has gone to get logistics and now you are moving forces without his knowledge." Pieng insisted and Oyai joined him to convince Salva. He said, "This issue of William Nyuon will finish and Pieng will then join us."

Pieng's narrative continued: "My forces arrived. We tried to maneuver around the enemy. At night, the forces of William Nyuon recognized the threat we posed and pulled out. We pursued him. Salva was happy. My forces had both Nuer and Dinka elements. During those times of great upheaval, when tension was mounting because of Riek's rebellion, forces were killed in areas under Riek Machar and some in areas under Dr. John. But for my forces, nothing like that happened. They were still together. We did not want to lose our forces from Latuka, who could have been convinced to also rebel."

Although Pieng succeeded to keep his forces united and against the divisiveness of tribal solidarity, there were tensions within the Movement, not only due to individual differences, but also on the bases of ethnic identities and divided loyalties. "We had two Latuka commanders. Glario Modi Orinya joined William because he was in that area. We also had Obuto Mamur, who had a misunderstanding with Salva Kiir and Kuol Manyang. Salva thought Mamur had joined William Nyuon. We were in communication with Mamur and told him, 'You must meet Salva.' He said, 'No, I'll be killed.' So, we said, 'Let us all meet together at Salva's place.' When we got to Salva's place, Mamur was not there. He told us that he was on the way, but we knew that he was headed towards the direction of William Nyuon. We did not want him to join William. We knew Glario Modi would not have normally joined William. He was an old man who had become confused. Our objective was to keep the Latuka tribe as a whole from joining William because they would provide him with many forces, if they did. We didn't know that what we feared had already happened."

Pieng now faced the dilemma of fighting the rebels while protecting the civilian population in the communities within which the rebels were operating, many of whom supported them. Pieng recounts: "I had instructed my soldiers not to harass the Latuka in their areas, as we moved. We pursued William, while being careful not to cause any disturbance in Latuka area. My forward forces reported back that there were skirmishes ahead. I instructed them to send some of our Latuka officers to go and meet those people and see what was happening. We reached a hill. Some Latuka men came passing by and we took them as harmless, since we assumed that they were civilians. But then they opened fire on us and killed one of our officers." Some people began to say that the people who were shooting were Nuer in the forces of Pieng. But Pieng asserted that the allegation was not correct. His position was that if his forces believed those allegations, everything could explode from within. "I instructed all the officers to go and make sure no one killed anyone, or they, the officers, would be responsible. I was very worried, but we managed to contain the situation until morning. As no one was killed during the night, we moved ahead." But the situation got more complicated: "The enemy had mobilized some Latuka in the villages ahead of us. We took a place to rest. Armed villagers went into the Imatong mountains from where they started shooting at us. It was heavy shooting, and we found ourselves in a terrible defensive position under a hail of bullets. My soldiers could hold this against me because they had told me that those civilians were enemies and that they were leaving their homes to ambush us. They killed more than 50 of our soldiers. I started to blame myself: 'How can I continue? I've tried to respect everyone and do things the right way. But now, my soldiers have died. Will the remaining soldiers not rebel against me?' But still I told my remaining forces, 'None of you should attack civilians; let us pursue only the enemy.' I sent one officer ahead to make sure our way was clear. But he delayed from going. And when he eventually started to move, his force fell in an ambush. In that ambush, we lost another 150 soldiers. Within one day, I had lost more than 170 soldiers. I thought to myself, 'What can I possibly do?'

But Pieng did not allow the burden of guilt to weigh him down from action. "I decided to let all the cars evacuate the two hundred plus wounded and take everything heavy back. I ordered every soldier to carry whatever ammunition they could take with them. 'We don't want anything heavy to slow us down. We'll only take mounted vehicles. After giving these instructions, I convinced Mamur to come to where I was. But some soldiers insisted that if he were to come, they would kill him. After all, he was a Latuka and was respected by his people. And he was in the area when all those things were happening. It was his people who had ambushed us and killed so many of our soldiers. So, I needed to think of how to still meet Mamur without escalating the situation with my soldiers. I sought out more information on exactly who among my soldiers were intent on killing Mamur. I decided I would send them ahead when Mamur came."

Here, Pieng reveals his less known side as a peacemaker and a diplomat within his ranks. "When Mamur joined me, I asked him, 'Why are you running from us?' He said, 'I am afraid of Salva.' I then realized a paradox. Mamur was also doubting me. At any time Salva could give the orders to kill him. So, I made sure that I would move with him everywhere. One night, I was coordinating an operation where I had to climb the mountain using the Motorola. Mamur said, 'Let me go with you.' So, we left our soldiers down at the base of the mountain and proceeded by ourselves. One of his soldiers, whom we had left behind, woke up to find Mamur absent. He became concerned. He asked his colleague, 'Where is Mamur?' His colleague responded, 'He went with Pieng.. When I came back down, my radio operator approached me and informed me, 'Commander Pieng, Mamur has been coming to check the radio messages, and I know that I am not supposed to share them.' I told him, 'Let Mamur see the messages.' That let me know that he was still suspicious. But it also gave him more confidence in me. That period of trust-building at a time of so much death and suspicion around us was the basis of our friendship that has continued until now."

Pieng highlights the dilemmas of military-civilian relations in the middle of a war, which is usually acutely divisive. "Most of the people who had killed my soldiers were civilians, but I could not act harshly against the people who lived in that Latuka area. So, I kept my soldiers from taking revenge, despite their hurt and frustration. We continued to a place called Ikotos, constantly fighting and pursuing the enemy. But when we arrived in Ikotos, we found the families of SPLA soldiers, including children, had been killed. We found the body of one of William

Nyuon's soldiers and wondered what had killed him. Some civilians who were hiding came out from their hiding places and approached us. I asked them, 'What killed this man?' Those civilians informed me that the man had killed himself during the parade. He is said to have asked William, 'Why are we killing these innocent civilians? Is this what we are fighting for?' So, I knew there were revolutionaries among those who had rebelled and that the indiscipline of killing civilians would ultimately turn against them."

Nevertheless, the tension between the civilians and the army which was pursuing the rebels persisted. "We continued to a place called Lorianya, which was still in Latuka land. Mamur had told me that he had influence there. We found soldiers who had joined William Nyuon. The question was how we should treat them, as enemies or as potential allies to win over. Mamur said, 'They are still loyal to us.' But I was still suspicious. He insisted, 'I must stay here and mobilize them for SPLA.' I said, 'Mamur, these people will kill you.' He said, 'No, these are my relatives and this is my area. You can just leave some weapons with me.' I said, 'I do not believe these people are loyal.' We argued for some time and he did not back down. My strategy was never to give the enemy time but continue to aggressively pursue them."

The confusion between friends and the enemy and between fighters and civilians was a persistent feature of the fratricidal conflict. That atrocious confrontation was the result of that confusion: "I stopped my forces outside of Lofan village and said, 'Let us make our camp and defense here because we don't need to displace this village.' We sent sons from the area to call the chiefs. After two days, the chiefs came and we discussed the situation. I asked them, 'Where should we establish our base?' They gave us a school under a hill. I asked them, 'Can we put the forces on the hill?' They said, 'No, this is a spiritual place for us and also where our goats graze. I told my officers to go to the school and not the hill. They said, 'Commander, this is dangerous. How can we not take the high ground?' I said 'No, these are our friends and they will tell us if anyone comes?' Is it possible that I was more responsive to the civilians than to my own soldiers? I believed strongly that our strength as a rebellion was our relationship with our civilian populations. But perhaps I was acting more like a politician or humanitarian than a pure military officer. That was the hill from which came the atrocious attacks."

What Pieng describes is an extremely complicated situation of fratricidal conflict in which it was difficult to tell who was the foe and who
was an ally. "Meanwhile, William Nyuon had left equipment, which was
good for us. But our source also informed me that Riek Machar was
sending reinforcements. I said, 'We must meet Riek's forces at Lafon.'
Since there was no one to carry the equipment, I left them under the
command of Lokicho Lokenen, a very capable officer. I left him with
more than 140 soldiers in the school. Mamur also stayed, but in the village. I told Mamur, 'Don't stay in the village. Come and stay with us in
Lokicho in the school and make it your place. If you stay in that village,
you can be killed by Riek's forces without resistance.' Unfortunately, he
insisted on staying in the village. We left and walked for three hours in
the dark of the night. When we stopped, I called Wilson Deng Wek who
was my deputy, and told him to send back the cars to Lokicho with the
equipment. Comrade Wilson responded, 'The cars don't have lights and
cannot move at night'. I told him, 'This is an order. They must move
at night with flashlights held out of the windows, if needed.' So, they
moved and reached Lokicho and gave him the orders. He woke up the
soldiers around him."

A brutal confrontation ensued from unsuspected sources: "The reinforcements that Riek Machar had sent had already reached the area
even before we left, but the civilians had not told us. So, the place was
surrounded when we got there. It is good that the sound of the car had
awakened Lokicho's forces. So, when the enemy began shooting, they
were quick to respond. I told one of my officers, named Kuron, 'Run to
the mountain and fight whoever is there and take control of it.' I then
ordered Wilson Deng Wek to move with the soldiers and I would follow.
They managed to reach the designated point, but out of the 140 soldiers
almost 70 were killed and more than 40 were wounded, leaving only
about 30 at the headquarters of Mamur. From the enemy, more than 300
were killed. When we came back after the fighting, we found another
slaughter of Southerners killing Southerners. We chased the enemy that
was carrying out the massacre and followed them to an area between
Lafon and Lopit. We kept attacking and dislodging them until they ran
to Juba in disarray."

The war with Riek Machar continued to rage and Pieng remained
in the thick of it. Pieng's account continued: "After months of battles in

Eastern Equatoria, Riek Machar took control of the northern part of Bor. Comrade Salva told me that Kuol Manyang was passing through areas under my control on his way to Bor. He asked me to make reconnaissance of the water situation along the way. So, I sent 300 men to go to the swamps to check the water. In the evening, I intercepted enemy communications coming from Juba – 300 of our men from Bahr el Ghazal had deserted the forces from Lafon. I knew that message confirmed precisely that the enemy had infiltrated us. Either the informants were civilians, since most of them had left the village and gone to their farms, or it was some people on the hill. So, I told my officers to go up the hill. Unfortunately, they only searched the lower part of the hill and did not go to the top."

The result was that there was a surprise attack from the hill. "In the morning, those who had secretly infiltrated themselves to the hill, without our detecting them, launched an offensive position on top of the hill, without us knowing, and directed all their weapons towards us. As the onslaught began, we faced a terrible situation and did not know how to resolve the problem. I tried to send soldiers out in a wide perimeter to go up the hill from behind. But what ultimately took the hill was not my command, but the determination and independent decisions of my forces. When my soldiers saw me leave my place to go to my deputy, they all jumped up and started running directly up the hill. Minutes later, I heard them singing at the top of the hill. I apologized to them: 'I am sorry. It is my fault. I am responsible for all we lost because I did not take this hill in the first place.'" That was one of the occasions when Pieng's humility with confidence was glowingly reflected to his soldiers.

Ironically, the war in that area left a rather mixed legacy in Pieng's name. "In the history of that area, they call 1992–1993 my year. To this day, the local people still don't go to that hill. It is said that their displacement to other places has now made them healthier as they have found places that are much more productive and clean." Always one to confidently admit responsibility for any faults and learn from mistakes, Pieng comments on the experience in that area as a mixed legacy from which lessons can be learned: "They blame the destruction of the area on me, but the truth is that I lost many soldiers because I listened to what the local people were saying. I went against what my officers were saying, because I wanted to respect the traditions and norms of the local community. This balance of respect for civilians and respect for soldiers is something that every commander must face. While it may be easy to cite codes of conduct, the reality of war creates complex challenges of command that are not as easy as the theories people create and learn."

It is obvious that a remarkable thing about Pieng was how he delicately balanced pursuing the war with respecting and protecting civilians and how quickly he was ready to accept responsibility and guilt for any action in which he felt he made a mistake, whether against civilians or the objectives of the war, or where he felt he should have acted differently. However, self–scrutiny and accepting responsibility for mistakes or failures never affected the confidence Pieng enjoyed among his soldiers and superiors, who continued to assign him challenging responsibilities. After a brief period under treatment in Nairobi, Pieng was back to the field to confront the internal rebels under William Nyuon, who had now joined Riek and was conducting military operation to gain control over the areas around Chukudum. After fierce and sustained fighting, William Nyuon's forces were dislodged. A conversation between Nyuon and Peter Gadet, their commander in the area, tells of the awesome image Pieng had developed in war: "William Nyuon asked his commander, Peter Gadet, who was commanding that force, 'Gadet, where are you?' Gadet said, 'I am around the mountains, headed back. It is being said that Pieng is commanding their forces.' William Nyuon said, 'You should have told me that before. I would not have sent you because that boy cannot leave that place unless you kill him.'"

Alongside fighting the forces of William Nyuon, Pieng was tasked to organize the famous Chukudum Convention and ensure security under very treacherous circumstances. Considerable discussion was conducted on whether and where the first and most consequential convention of the SPLM should be held. Given the insecurity over the whole area of South Sudan caused by the forces of both Khartoum and Riek Machar, it was eventually agreed that the Convention be held in Chukudum, which was under Pieng's command. The Convention was attended by delegates from all over the South and the New Sudan Northern areas of the Nuba Mountains and Blue Nile. That also required challenging security and logistical arrangements. The Chikudum Convention proved a great success and became a landmark in the history of the liberation struggle.

As Pieng writes, "That Convention created a new spirit in the SPLM. That first Convention should be remembered in the history of the struggle, because it was there that we decided to put ourselves into the new set up, a shift from when we were supported by the Eastern Block, especially Ethiopia under Mengistu, Libya and even the Soviet Union. Cuba was supporting us materially and diplomatically, even with medical doctors. Also we were being trained in Cuba. But now the Cold War was ending and there was a new world order being set up with the presumption that the Eastern Block had been defeated. So, in that Convention, people started to rethink how we should adjust ourselves to this new world setup."

After the conference, Chiefs from Bahr el Ghazal asked to see John Garang. At the meeting they said to him, "You cannot keep this good son of ours away from us. The way we have seen him, the way he treated us, the way he behaves, and with all his successes that we hear about, why not send him to us in Bahr el Ghazal?" But Dr. John said to them, "I still need him here: I will send him to you later."

And indeed, he needed Pieng whom he asked to facilitate the return of the delegates to their areas all over the country. He also asked him to organize a meeting of all the military officers, numbering some 700, whose security and logistical arrangements were as challenging as those of the Convention.

Dual Mission in Bahr el Ghazal and Equatoria

With the Chukudum Convention and the Conference of Officers successfully concluded, Dr. John was now ready to send Pieng to Bahr el Ghazal. "After we captured Kit, we saw that it was a good position from which to defend the areas we had gained. Dr. John left Oyai and we went back with him to Ikotos area. From there he said, 'Pieng, elders from Bahr el Ghazal have been asking me to send you there. Now is the time for you to go back. You are going to be commanding all over Bahr el Ghazal. Go and reassemble all the forces there and organize them into the first division of the SPLA.' I said, 'But I want to take my forces, the 400 of whom more than 300 are already fully capable and need no training.' He said, 'Talk to Oyai because they are a reliable force at Kit.'

"Oyai accepted. But unfortunately, while I was planning to shift them from that place, one of my comrades, also a senior officer, took this force to attack an enemy position – the same officer who attacked the enemy without reconnaissance – and again many of them were wounded and killed. I was really mad when I heard that and I talked to Oyai who was also unhappy. I said to him, 'Your officers are misusing soldiers. Get them back and bring them to stay in a different area of your command.' We sent the remainder of that force to Chukudum and I took care of them. I got some uniforms and guns. And Oyai gave me some cars and weapons. Those soldiers regained their morale. Even the wounded refused to remain behind. There were some Nuer officers and soldiers in that force. I asked them to remain with Oyai, explaining to them, 'Where we are going is unlike other areas of our command where there have been no inter-ethnic killings. In Bahr el Ghazal, there have been mutual killings among the communities. So, you better remain here where people don't see these things in a tribal manner.' But they said, 'If we are killed under you it is good; we will be happy. But we cannot leave our force.'"

Pieng's initial work in Bahr el Ghazal focused on winning the civilian population. His reputation preceded him wherever he went. On a number of occasions, people would ask where Pieng was, sometimes asking Pieng himself. His behavior and that of his soldiers differed profoundly from the way Anya-Nya had treated the civilians. Then suddenly, Pieng received word that Dr. John Garang wanted to talk to him. When they connected, Garang said to him, "The enemy discovered that we have moved our forces. So, they're moving out of Juba and planning to take Western Equatoria. Gather your forces from Bahr el Ghazal and go back to protect those areas. Oyai, Jadalla, Cirillo, and Gier are training near Kajo Keji. When they finish, they will come and take their positions. In the meantime, you will hold the ground and keep gathering more forces.' We rushed and mobilized the forces. I sent the cars and got more forces. Then I moved. The enemy reached a place called Lui and I attacked them there to bog them down. We set a defensive position. The enemy tried to push us away but could not. We managed to maintain our position."

Surprisingly, Pieng was mandated to both, command the forces in Bahr el Ghazal and continue fighting in Equatoria. "Dr. John told me that I had to command my forces in Bahr el Ghazal and also take command of Western Equatoria. From October, we resisted the enemy and foiled their plan until our people came out of the training center and joined us. There, we planned a major operation code named, "OTB – Operation Thunderbolt." This was the second biggest operation for the SPLA after Bright Star Campaign One, which took Eastern Equatoria, Bor, Waat, Akobo, and Canal Mouth. Bright Star Campaign Two had failed under Riek Machar. It was launched in Upper Nile and was supposed to take areas from Renk and Meluth to Malakal. The Third Bright Star Campaign was in Western Equatoria under James Wani Igga to capture Yei. Operation Thunderbolt was now the biggest operation after the setback of 1991. It planned to capture from Yei to Juba and the rest of the surrounding areas, including Terekeka.

"From resisting the enemy from taking Western Equatoria, our forces pivoted and started to attack Yei. The overall commander was Dr. John. Salva Kiir was the head of operations moving with the forces. My force was to continue pinning down the enemy from Western Equatoria. Comrade Jadalla was moving with Salva to capture Yei. Gier Chuang was to block the enemy from the Ugandan border not to reinforce Yei. Thomas Cirillo was to move towards Juba to also block the enemy's advance in other directions, while I protected from the direction of Western Equatoria.

"We captured Yei under the direct command of Jadalla and supervised by Salva Kiir but Gier was overwhelmed by the heavy presence of troops on the Ugandan border. They succeeded to capture some tanks while our forces that had captured Yei moved to help Gier. They captured 1,000 enemy soldiers, which was a crisis to the Khartoum regime. They abandoned their equipment because of the swiftness of our movements and were confused because they could not understand how we were able to reinforce so quickly once they had overrun Gier's forces. The terrain was against them because the forest was overgrown, and they had no idea where to go because they were people brought from Khartoum and moved to the south without knowing the area."

That was a good example of how politicians and generals in Khartoum were deploying young men, sometimes recruited from schools, virtually children, and send them ill-prepared to fight, in the name of *Jihad* holy war. The result was sometimes disastrous. "We destroyed a significant part of Khartoum's fighting capacity with more than 5000 soldiers killed and captured. We took all their equipment, tanks and artillery. Our morale was high, and they were demoralized. Thomas Cirillo was moving to Juba capturing all their positions up to a place called 40 Mile where some of our tanks were destroyed. But Thomas still managed to resist and stop there. Oyai with Jadalla came through Lanya towards Jambo to meet me and asked me to come to where they were so as to attack Juba together from the western side. Comrade Jadalla commanded the attack on Jambo after our forces were unified. We dislodged the enemy and went onto Lanya and Lui capturing locations by dislodging the enemy without resistance.

"There was a place near Mundri called Amadi and we thought they were going to run away like the rest of the forces. We made sure that we checked Amadi, but the Sudanese army was strange. They were withholding information from being shared among the forces. This particular force was the presidential guard. They didn't know what was happening around them because they had not been told."

Pieng eventually returned to Bahr el Ghazal, where he confronted the Murahleen and had a mixed record of victories and defeat. Much of the defeat had to do with the superstitious belief of the soldiers that the Murahleen on horsebacks were invincible and could not be killed by the gun. However, some of the populations in the area of Abyei, who were South of the Kiir River under Ajing Path, the Commissioner and Alternative Commander, were able to attack the Murahleen and capture large herds of cattle, which averted famine in the areas of Twich and Gogrial.

One thing Pieng highlights is the ethnic mix of his forces and the bravery of the Equatorians within his force. "This display of bravery by Equatorians should not be surprising, but still it is important to mention because the stereotype is that they are cowards that do not fight. Now, because of these battles in Bahr el Ghazal, many people saw with their own eyes that these forces even fought more courageously than Dinkas who are known as warriors. Those Equatorian forces defended areas in Bahr el Ghazal from militias that were coming from Bentiu. And there too they proved their courage and bravery. These experiences during the war changed the stereotypical concepts people, especially Dinkas, had developed. Now, those who participated in the SPLA were able to see that all people can fight. A question began to circulate: what has Pieng given to these people to make them so courageous? But the truth is that the suspicion that I had some secret medicine to make my soldiers brave was simply based on the fact that people had been ignorant of one another and perceived each other through stereotypes."

The fact that Pieng always commanded ethnically mixed forces was also unusual. "For our Dinkas from Bahr el Ghazal, it was strange to see my mixed force from all over New Sudan – Nubas, Equatorians, Nuer, and others. They all moved with me and were courageous in battle. They made me proud of my comrades, soldiers and officers. But it affected me psychologically that many of them had lost their lives, especially since so many from other areas lost their lives defending Bahr el Ghazal."

But Pieng recalls the battles in Bahr el Ghazal with sadness, because of the human losses they incurred. "Those battles in 1998 were among my worst moments, that stressed me, and disappointed me, and caused me to become very sad, particularly for losing those courageous comrades. For example, a young officer called Aguek in my headquarters was killed in Abiem Dau in battle with Murahaleen. He was among those really committed to me as a person. There were many others and I wish I could mention all of them. I have only been mentioning the junior officers moving with me, but there were many other senior officers. I really loved them. They were among the most committed cadres of the Movement who fought for their people and their land. I ask Almighty God to still keep them in eternal peace."

Interestingly enough, since joining the liberation struggle, although motivated by the horrific situation in Abyei, and what he had witnessed in the terror and brutality inflicted on his people, Abyei has not featured in his heroic service for the cause of the South. But now in Bahr el Ghazal, Abyei comes into light. "Commander Salva Mathok and Colonel Ajing Path were under my command in Bahr el Ghazal. Ajing Path was in charge of Abyei County and commanded the soldiers in Abyei Area. He was the one who managed to facilitate the capture of all those cattle taken by our forces along with other officers whom I will mention later." Another important connection with Abyei was that Deng Alor, a member of the Leadership, was the Governor of Bahr el Ghazal at the time.

Pieng became engaged in operations against the enemy over Gogrial. For a variety of reasons, they lost a crucial battle whose consequences still haunt him to this day: "This defeat was among my sad moments as we lost Gogrial and most of the officers there. It was reported to us that most of the officers were captured alive, but someone called Tor Mayuen, who was with the Government, instructed that he didn't want to see any officer alive. Tor gave the order to kill all of them. He later became an influential advisor to our President. It is really painful that such a betrayer who killed our heroes would become an important person in South Sudan after our liberation. And he is not alone in this respect. There have been others. It is painful that our President hoisted such people who should have been punished for killing innocent liberators."

It was ironic that the Sudan government which was a party to international humanitarian law relating to the treatment of prisoners of war did not keep their war captives – they killed them. According to Pieng, "The SPLA on the other hand kept many enemy soldiers as prisoners of war, but the enemy could not save the lives of our fighters. Among those killed, there was a pilot, Caesar Madut Ring, who was a commander by then and Anyar Mayor, who was a commander, and Malual Minyiel. There were many other officers killed after the enemy captured Gogrial. That battle was a failure from our side as a command, and I have to accept that fact. It was one of the battles in which our defense failed and we allowed our officers to be killed."

Mission to Raja on the North-Western Border

Pieng was now given an assignment to go to Raja at the border of Darfur as part of Dr. John Garang's strategy of taking the war to the North. "John agreed with Salva that we have to move to Raja. I was called to Yei and we set the plan for the Raja Operation. In Dr. John's plan, which was based on a surprise attack, we were to move through Western Equatoria up to Raja Area, then capture Raja and bog the enemy down in Wau, while continuing northward across the border into Darfur. By recruiting forces across the border, Dr. John was taking the war into Northern Sudan. Our operations in Eastern and Western Sudan were a good idea by Dr. John, but Comrade Salva had a different opinion. He did not agree with the premise of the Raja operation as a steppingstone into Darfur. It was not clear to us at that time, but this disagreement was in the mind of Comrade Salva, although he could not reject the plan of Dr. John."

Extending the war beyond the Southern border into the North was controversial within the Movement. Indeed, when John Garang first mentioned the idea to me, I was myself quite skeptical, although I did not voice my skepticism. Salva Kiir was also opposed to it. But then John explained his policy by giving what to me were convincing reasons. Obviously, Northerners, especially in the marginalized areas, had already joined the struggle. So, it was only natural that war should extend to their area as among the territories to be liberated. But it was also important that Northerners generally, and the leadership specifically, be made to know that war was a threat to the whole country. They had to be made to share the pain. Sadig al-Mahdi, the Prime Minister in a democratically elected government, was reputed to have said that the war in the South was like amputating a finger; it pains but does not kill. Garang wanted the establishment to know that the war in the South could kill in the North. His strategy became increasingly understood and supported.

Pieng elaborates on the Raja mission. "Dr. John assigned me that mission to Raja and gave me part of his Headquarters forces and part of Jongo's forces from the Eastern Front in Eastern Sudan with forces mobilized from Bahr el Ghazal. I decided to move the NCOs who were in training in Tonj to join other forces in Maridi, which was my assembly area for all the forces to converge. So, I now had three forces, one from Bahr el Ghazal, one from Eastern Sudan, which included elements from Darfur, and the other from the HQs of Dr. John."

The mission to Raja was in many ways reminiscent of the hardships of Pieng's original journey to join the movement. It was an adventure about which one of his colleagues had a dream that warned against it: "One of our comrades who is now a medical doctor in the military hospital, named Jacob Malith, apparently had a dream about me. He went six miles west of Yei to Comrade Gier in Kagulu and told him the dream. He said, 'Pieng's movement to Raja is certain to succeed. But he will not make it back. Pieng will capture Raja, but then the enemy will recapture it and kill Pieng in Raja.' So Malith advised Comrade Gier to convince Comrade Salva and Dr. John to not send me. Gier came and spoke to me. I said, 'I don't believe in this and there is no need to convey the message to the HQ because I know nothing will happen to me.' Gier, concerned for Pieng's life, called on all the Church leaders in

Maridi to pray for Pieng. All the Church leaders in Maridi gathered and prayed for Pieng and his life. "With that act, Gier then agreed with me that there was no need to talk to Dr. John and that we would rather trust that God would protect us and make victory possible."

Pieng continues his account of the mission: "I continued preparing for our journey through no-man's land from Tambura along the Western border of South Sudan towards Raja. I was given guns and trucks. Although our weapons and other logistical support equipments were on trucks, I tried to push my forces on foot to Yambio, which took time. From the beginning, I wanted them to move on foot. From Yambio I pushed them by foot again to Tambura and completed the preparations. Finally, we had enough ammunition and shells for the mission. Dr. John was not in the country at that time; it was Comrade Salva with whom I was communicating. I told him I was ready to move."

The comparison with the March from Abyei to join the Movement really began when the road transport ended and the troops continued on foot. The difference here was that they were going through thick jungles rather in swamps. "I moved with the forces by car to Zangbara, which is where the road ends. We made the final Operational Order. I told our forces, 'We are going to Raja, but along our course there is no road and no trace of any human being. But there is a water divide between Central Africa and Sudan. All the rivers are small, smaller than even the Jur River, Tonj River and other rivers in the South that become large somewhere along the flow. So, we will be able to cross them.'

"While there were no traces of people, SPLA forces, led by Comrade Abdel Aziz, had used this route to go to Darfur in the past, and before him, Comrade Gier had been sent to explore that area. Whereas Comrade Abdel Aziz had moved towards Wau, we decided to go through Central Africa. I had GPS and good maps that Dr. John had given me. I always sent a platoon of 30 officers, equipped with GPS and Thurayas. In each place they arrived, they'd give me coordinates and we'd graft it on the map so that I would know where all the forces were. Whenever they crossed into Central Africa, I would tell them to come back to the border. This way, we were able to follow their footpaths. We would go through the forest cutting a path and then using fallen trees as bridges to cross the rivers. We found that no one had ever stepped foot in that place. When we tried to fish in the small rivers, we found certain kinds of fish that had never been caught. There was a blackfish in a stagnant pool that you could not cut; it could only be skinned because they had become old to the point that their skin had hardened like that of an animal. Our people started to fear that this was a magical place full of spiritual things. As for the fish with animal skin, I tried to convince them that the fish had lived for too long, that nobody had killed them, and they had become very old."

Pieng and his force were truly in a world of their own: "We moved and moved and moved. After three weeks we discovered an area where people from Western Sudan went to hunt animals, like elephants. We found traces of hunters but did not meet anyone. After four weeks of moving without any human trace, we discovered that some hunters were around. But they would not reveal themselves. Rather, we intercepted communication of hunters reporting to our enemy a movement of forces with many tanks and trucks. In that communication, Khartoum responded that no one could move in that forest with cars. And they were right. No one could believe that someone would pass through such thick forests. So, the enemy didn't believe the hunters and that was good for us. That intercepted communication convinced us that the enemy had not uncovered our Movement."

After 32 days, they arrived at Deim Zubeir, an area between Wau and Raja. The name of the area, which is Arabic for Zubeir's town, is named after Zubeir Rahma, a notorious slave-hunter and trader who had established an empire based in that area, from which he traded slaves to the Middle East. "We captured hunters from the area and detained them with us. We didn't harm them, but kept them with us and through them, we realized that human inhabitants were nearby. So, we decided to move quickly so that the enemy could not discover and preempt us with an attack in the forest."

At Deim Zubeir they reconnected with the world of roads and mechanical transport. Remote as the area was, the effect of the war extended in the form of remnants of mines. "As we moved, we learned that our forces, which went to Darfur in 1990 and 1991, had laid some mines around the area and that the enemies had also done the same. Now, we were about 17 kilometers from Deim Zubeir." And then there were hunters who signaled the potential of being reported to the enemy. "We encountered more hunters. They ran and we feared that they would likely tell the enemy and we'd be attacked. Besides, there was no water where we had reached, and I thought the soldiers would become thirsty." They, therefore, faced multiple sources of dangers: "There were mines and we had no one to clear the route. So, we could lose forces from thirst, mines, and the attack from the enemy. Unless we moved, regardless of the fact that it was already evening, we'd be stuck. I called senior officers together for an emergency meeting. I said, 'This is the situation – the enemy is near and civilians have run in their direction. They may tell the enemy, who could use horses to attack us. But now there is no water and the soldiers will have a problem because they will not cook.' Together, we decided to move with our cars and whatever happens we would not stop; if a truck hit a mine, we would move because that would preempt the enemy, who would need time to move to Deim Zubeir."

In addition to clashes with the enemy, Pieng became deeply involved in the controversial question of whether or not to extend the war into the North. That was the objective of John Garang, with which Salva Kiir did not agree. Dr. John's objective in sending Pieng to Raja was to launch operations in Darfur. He brought some forces from Eastern Sudan composed of Darfurians and other Northern Sudanese elements, including some Missiriya. As Pieng recalls, "Comrade Salva had a different opinion. He remembered that in 1991 most of the SPLA forces we had sent with Abdel Aziz had died or fled to Central Africa. So, when I finished controlling the area, Comrade Salva was in charge because Dr. John had traveled. So, when I asked about the next move, Comrade Salva said, 'Don't move anywhere; just maintain and consolidate your presence in the area, and don't move to Darfur or any direction.' I had to listen to the instructions of my commander."

But Pieng also had to follow John Garang's orders: "Dr. John still had an idea to send part of the forces to Darfur. So, we sent some of our forces to the border to do political work with the people. Alternate Commander Adam Bazooka, from the Masalit tribe in Darfur, moved with me. My plan was to send him to Darfur. I assessed the situation and said to him, 'There is no way you can move to Darfur now without the necessary support. But if we are given an OK, then we can move with the rest of our forces to the border and carry out a political mobilization. Then you can go once the ground has been laid.'"

Sudan's crisis of identity between Arabs and Africans was reflected in the area: "There was a problem on the ground. Most of the ethnic groups at the border call themselves Arabs. Other tribes who identify as African, like the Masalit, are far from the border of South Sudan, which is why Comrade Abdel Aziz found it difficult to reach Jebel Marra, because these tribes resisted fiercely. The Falata were occupying the areas with the only routes to Hofrat el Nehas. So, I kept Commander Bazooka with the rest of the forces and we sent officers to the area. They entered deeply into Darfur to make contact and mobilize people there to avoid repeating the mistake of 1991, where they tried to agree with Comrade Salva that there was no need for big forces to move. The same elements we sent were later used in 2002. Forces under Abdel Wahad, Abdalla Bola, and Mini Minawi went back to Eastern Sudan. That was how Dr. John could maintain communication with Darfur. Through those channels we mobilized the people of Darfur to make their own movement and fight the Government in Khartoum. We mobilized our people, and many forces came to fully support the Movement and even all the militias in the area became part of our forces. They were really convinced about joining the Movement and in turn, they convinced their population."

As always, Pieng was also concerned about the plight of the people and tried not only to ensure their physical safety, but also providing for their humanitarian needs. He eventually connected with international humanitarian organizations that began delivering humanitarian assistance to the area. "My officers approached me, saying, 'Commander, without you and your relationships with the international agencies, nobody will follow the coordination of humanitarian relief. So rather than go to Wau and leave us unable to care for these people; you should go to Rumbek. It may be possible for you to get a flight. From there, you can coordinate with the humanitarian organizations based there.'"

Indeed, Commander Gier Chuang, who remembered Jacob Malith's dream that Pieng would be killed in Raja, arranged to send a plane to pick him up to a place from where he could arrange humanitarian relief. Pieng used that plane to evacuate the wounded who could not move long distances. "Gier was so worried that he tried to influence the headquarters to tell me to move immediately. He also influenced our officers on the ground. They told him, 'Send the plane again to take him to Tambura and we will force Commander Pieng onto the plane.' But I said, 'I cannot go to Tambura because I will coordinate nothing there but if you want me to go to Rumbek, I'll go there and coordinate.'"

"And that is what happened, the plane picked me up and took me to Rumbek, which proved to be very helpful. I appreciated Comrade Gier and others because I was able to make contact with the World Food Program (WFP), through a lady who really sympathized with the situation that we were facing as we moved with thousands of civilians. She decided to go herself to where the population was because she could not approve the distribution of food without confirming the condition and movement of the population. I sent Comrade Elijah Biar to make a small airstrip along their route so that she could come in a plane. Comrade Elijah immediately started clearing the airstrip and within five days they confirmed that the airstrip was ready. So, the WFP sent a small plane to test the landing ground and they managed to land. Immediately, the representative of WFP went there, and stayed there in the forest, in no -man's-land, with the population and coordinated with the head-quarters. She cleared the dropping zone and sent food and medicines. The WFP staff also decided to move with the population so that they could inform their HQ about the movement."

The humanitarian needs of his people were fully provided for: "Wherever they went, they would always make an airstrip quickly and then the humanitarians would continue supporting them. It was a miracle for that population to move in no man's land and the humanitarians moved with them, their staff sacrificing their lives, and moving with the civilians all the way up until Tambura where they established a big displacement camp. That was one of the best things we accomplished through cooperation, for which I was really happy. Although we left the area of Raja, we managed to take the civilians safely to controlled areas of the SPLA."

Back to the Center of the War

Pieng was now back at the center of military operations in the South, based in Bahr el Ghazal, but still connected to Equatoria. "After the enemy recaptured Gogrial around May 2002, we continued defending the areas around Gogrial and Kuajok, which meant that the enemy could not reach Mapel. We controlled the whole situation in Bahr el Ghazal while mobilizing forces to send to Comrade Oyai. The importance of the planned Operation in Equatoria was to support the ongoing negotiation with the Sudanese Government. From June, our delegation went to Machakos where the Declaration of Peace was signed with Comrade Salva as the head of that Delegation. Comrade Deng Alor was also involved in that negotiation while he was the Governor of Bahr el Ghazal. It was always Dr. John's belief that progress on the political front required demonstrated military strength on the field of battle.

"In July (2002), Dr. John called the Governors and the Commanders of Fronts to New Site where he was doing most of his work. It was like a strategic headquarters for the Movement, but Yei was the overall Headquarters where Comrade Salva was. Most of Dr. John's meetings, seminars and conferences were held at New Site and New Kush. The objective of the meeting was to brief us about Machakos and the progress in the peace negotiation. Dr. John opened the meeting with appreciation to the Team, Comrade Salva and others, for what they had achieved. After he finished, he allowed us to comment. I raised my hand. It was not really good for a subordinate like me to just stand and talk his mind. But I did it anyway.

"I started by saying: 'Comrade, you have expressed your appreciation for the work of the team, but for me, as one of the Freedom Fighters and senior members of the Movement, I am personally not happy with the team. I believe that the team has betrayed the cause of our people, and especially our people of Abyei. Maybe they have betrayed all the people of the Three Areas and their causes, including Abyei, but I am talking specifically about Abyei. Abyei has been attached to the cause of South Sudan since Anya-Nya One, and I see no reason why the issue should at this strategic time be left behind. This also goes for the other two areas. Since the team left the issue of the Three Areas, I think it is a betrayal to one of the causes of the struggle of our people. And I think things will not go well now for these areas, even if there is an intention to negotiate them later. But as far as I am concerned this issue should not have been left behind in the Declaration of Principles since this is the base of our negotiation and will affect the future negotiation."

Other colleagues supported Pieng's position: "Although we did not coordinate our position with our Comrades, Comrade Oyai, Comrade

James Hoth, and other Comrades got up and talked in the same line, that they were unhappy. Comrade Salva raised his hand and said, 'Dr. John, since this is my constituency, the army, and I am the Chief of General Staff, and since these are my subordinate senior officers, I am asking you to accept my resignation from the peace talks. I cannot be happy if my subordinates are not happy.'"

But Pieng and his supporters were reprimanded by his colleagues for the manner in which they criticized their senior commander. "Other people got up and said, 'Pieng and you these other officers you are wrong to attack your leader.' Comrade John said, 'Comrade Pieng, you need to apologize for what you have said. I know it is an issue and we will not leave it out of the negotiations, but for now, you must apologize.' Then he appealed to Comrade Salva to drop his request for resignation, that he was still appreciated, and had done a wonderful job.

Pieng conceded, but with a reaffirmation of their principled position on the cause of Abyei. "I stood up and said, 'Even if I believe I have a legitimate issue, as a matter of procedure and discipline, I apologize. But this is a cause of the people. When I first rebelled, it was for Abyei, and this was even before the SPLM/A was formed. If I see that this issue is not being considered by my leadership, I cannot keep silent. And if anything happens like this in the future, whether by Comrade Salva or any other comrade, I will speak up. And I don't blame Comrade Salva too much, because it is Deng Alor who is a son of the area, who should have taken the issue seriously. Anyway, with this apology, you should also know that this is an issue that can cause me to differ with any one at any time.'"

That incident reflected more serious differences on Abyei that would linger on with lasting effect: "I think this was where things began to fall apart and even now, I believe that it is because we left Abyei out at that critical time that the issue remains unresolved. And this was one of the things that Omer el Beshir and the Government of Sudan used later, when they said that Abyei had nothing to do with the implementation of the Comprehensive Peace Agreement (CPA). Later on, Dr. John stood his ground to include the Abyei Protocol in the CPA and it is one of the things we can appreciate in the leadership of the SPLM/A. This was where differences over the status of Abyei emerged for the first time in the conflict.

Pieng was again called upon by Dr. John to organize the second meeting of the SPLA officers: "Following this narrower briefing in New Site, Dr. John then called all the senior officers of the SPLA to Rumbek to be briefed on the continuing negotiations. One of the best things our leadership used to do was to always brief us and keep all the leaders aware of what was going on. With Dr. John's belief that there is no way you can gain in the negotiations if you don't have gains in the field, we all went into mobilization to send forces to Comrade Oyai to capture Kapoeta and Torit. This Operation was to pressure the enemy to accept our negotiating positions.

"It was my responsibility as Commander of the Third Front to organize the meeting for the senior officers. I was privileged because this was the second meeting of all senior officers, and it so happened that the first one in Chikudum was also under my command. So, resources were mobilized by Bahr el Ghazal region and the General Headquarters, and I was made responsible for the security of that conference, which happened around August or September 2002."

It is interesting that while my brother was sacrificing his life for the cause of the South, and although I was not formally a member of the SPLM, I was dedicating my intellectual and diplomatic energies at the Brookings Institution to promoting the cause of the South and eliciting political and material support in Washington. In 1987, having declined in 1983 the appointment as Ambassador to Addis Ababa and resigned from Sudan's Foreign Service, I organized an all meeting of the Sudanese parties at the Woodrow Wilson International Center for Scholars, where I was a Research Associate. General Olusegun Obasanjo was invited to the meeting, initiating a close partnership between him and me through which we became actively engaged in mediating between the warring Sudanese parties. The Woodrow Wilson conference resulted in a book, *The Search for Peace and Unity in the Sudan (1987),* which we used as the basis for our initiative. Our shuttle diplomacy began with Sadig al-Mahdi as Prime Minister and extended to the Omer Hassan El-Bashir era.

Then as one of the first Jennings Randolph Distinguished Fellows of the newly established US Institute of Peace, I got the Institute actively engaged with the situation in South Sudan and I co-chaired with Chester Crocker, former Assistant Secretary of African Affairs, who chaired the Board of the Institute, a periodic forum on the Sudan. When the IGAD countries started their peace initiative to resolve the Sudan conflict in 1994, I was one of a small resource group which the Ethiopia-based Inter-Africa Group founded and directed by Abdul Mohamed of Ethiopia, put together to assist the peace process. The group included Bethual Kipligat of Kenya, Bona Malual, the other South Sudanese, and later Abdel Wahab El-Affendi of the Sudan, with occasional participation of such other eminent personalities as General Obasanjo of Nigeria and Chester Crocker, former Assistant Secretary of State for African Affairs, and Professor William Zartman, all of whom I had earlier mobilized for the cause of South Sudan. We developed a close working relationship with the Foreign Ministers and the Presidents of the IGAD Mediating Countries and also with the Carter Center in Atlanta, Georgia. Abdul Mohamed informed me that the Declaration of Principles, which the mediators presented to the parties was based on a concept paper which I had prepared for a USIP discussion group and later at a Carter Center meeting of the parties.

There was also an initiative taken by the Swiss Government to discreetly promote talks between the Movement and the Omer El-Bashir regime, which became known as the quartet meetings because they involved four people, two on each side. Garang asked Bona Malual and me to represent the SPLM as non-card-carrying members and told us quite candidly that if he liked what we did, he would claim us, but if he disapproved of what we did, he would disclaim us. The government representation alternated at different times and involved Ali Osman, Nafie Ali Nafie, Mutrif Sadig and Ahmed Abdel Rahman. The process went on for a while and because it was intended to be discreet, I do not know what became of the records of our discussions.

Most importantly perhaps, I put together a dedicated group of individuals who became known as 'The Council' and which an eminent journalist legal scholar later described as 'The Wongs.' The man whom we named 'The Chairman' was Ted Dagne, an Ethiopian American, whose first name Theodore (Ted) sounded imperial to me so that I gave him the joking title of Emperor. Others included Roger Winter, Brian D'Silva, John Prendergast, and Eric Reaves. Other influential personalities, among them Susan Rice, became associated with the Council and enormously facilitated our work in policy circles. And of course, through all of them we penetrated the institutions of government, legislative and executive to influence the shaping of U.S.-Sudan policy. And we worked very closely with Dr. John Garang.

Rebecca Hamilton, the academic lawyer journalist, wrote a Special Report for Reuters, July 11, 2012, under the title 'The Wonks who sold Washington on South Sudan', in which she gave a detailed account of our work. Hamilton wrote, "Nationhood has many midwives. South Sudan is primarily the creation of its own people. It was Southern Sudanese leaders who fought for autonomy, and more than two million Southern Sudanese who paid for that freedom with their lives. U.S. President George W. Bush, who set out to end Africa's longest-running civil war, also played a big role, as did modern-day abolitionists, religious groups, human rights organizations and members of the U.S. Congress. But the most persistent outside force in the creation of the world's newest state was the Council, a tightly knit group never numbering more than seven people, which in the era before email, began gathering regularly at Otello, a restaurant near Washington's DuPont Circle."

Rebecca Hamilton then proceeded to offer details of our method of operation: "After ordering beers, they would get down to business: how to win independence for Southern Sudan … They called themselves the Council …The Council is little known in Washington or in Africa itself. But its quiet cajoling over nearly three decades helped South Sudan win its independence one year ago this week across successive U.S. administrations, they smoothed the path of Southern Sudanese rebels in Washington, influenced legislation in Congress, and used their positions to shape foreign policy in favor of Sudan's southern rebels, often with scant regard for U.S. government protocol."

The story of the Council began with a surprise visit to me by Roger Winter, then the Executive Director of the US Committee for Refugees who was involved in humanitarian causes. Rebecca Hamilton wrote about my rather colorful encounter with Roger who would become a very dear friend and partner: "A man with a ponytail came to see me," recalled Deng, who is now the U.N. Special Adviser on the Prevention of Genocide. Deng hails from Abyei, a fertile area straddling north and South Sudan. He thought Winter must be some 'wealthy hippie-type' who wanted to give money to the rebels. When Winter explained that the best he could do was disseminate information, Deng suggested that the American public needed first-hand accounts of people affected by the war. He called a cousin in the rebel movement to ensure that on future visits, Winter would have access to all the so-called liberated areas – the parts of Sudan held by the rebels – where he could gather direct testimony on the impact of the war." The cousin was Deng Alor, then the Director of the office of the Chairman, Dr. John Garang.

We were of course navigating against a strong current of opposition to the SPLM/A which was misperceived as 'communist' because of its ideological alignment with Mengistu, the leader of Ethiopia, a staunch ally of the Soviet Union and Cuba, and a strong supporter of the Movement. Many in Washington, therefore, associated the Sudanese rebels with the Soviet bloc which left the SPLM on the wrong side of the Cold War. Hamilton quotes me as saying, "It took a lot of hard work to remove the prejudice against John Garang." She also quotes Roger Winter saying, "We never controlled anything, but we always did try to influence things in the way we thought most benefited the people of South Sudan," said Roger Winter, "I actually think it was a miracle we got something."

When I first spotted our Council's future Emperor, I initially tried to have him join me in establishing the African studies program at the Brookings Institution, where I was conducting research and organizing discussions on African and Sudanese issues, but I was glad that I failed because he soon proved to be much more valuable to our cause as a very effective member of the Congressional Staff. Ted Dagne was a true American success story. He got through college by working two menial jobs and by 1989 earned a masters degree, acquired U.S. citizenship and began working on African affairs at the Congressional Research Service, the non-partisan policy-analysis arm of the U.S. legislature. He soon became the right-hand man of successive Chairpersons of the House African Sub-Committee of the Foreign Affairs Committee, specifically Harry Johnston and Donald Payne who became our strongest supporters in Congress. Many wondered how this young migrant could be so influential in the US Government.

As Hamilton observed, "Winter took two members of Congress to meet Garang on one of his visits to rebel-held areas of Sudan. The trip had a big impact. After that, D'Silva, Deng, and Winter finally managed to get a delegation led by Garang on an official visit to Washington. It was on that visit to Washington that Dagne met Garang for the first time.

More than any other member of the Council, Dagne formed an intense friendship with the rebel leader. There were periods in the years ahead in which they spoke by phone every day, Dagne says. By the early 1990s, the group's work was starting to pay off. Dagne was seconded from the Congressional Research Service to the House of Representatives Subcommittee on Africa, where he began to build allies for the Southern Sudanese cause.

Congressional staffers are supposed to be neutral, but it was an open secret that Dagne's allegiance lay with the Southerners. "Ted was very suspicious of the Sudan government, and so I became very suspicious," said former Democratic Senator Harry Johnston, who headed the sub-committee. Dagne himself acknowledged to Hamilton, "I pushed the envelope quite a lot."

Hamilton wrote, "In 1993, for instance, Dagne drafted a congressional resolution stating that Southern Sudanese had the right to self-determination. He passed his draft to Johnston, who reviewed it and then presented it to his colleagues in Congress. The resolution was not binding, but it passed unanimously. It was the first time any part of the U.S. government had recognized the right of the Southerners to determine their own relationship to the Sudanese government."

A group of us senior South Sudanese formed themselves into 'Concerned Citizens' to try to influence the Movement to focus on self-determination as an objective of the struggle rather than convolute it with the vision of New Sudan. The group first met in Limerick in Ireland. Among those who attended that meeting, including myself, were Gordon Muortat, Bona Malual, Clement Janda, Abdon Agau, Peter Nyot Kok, Dunstan Wai, Lual Achuek Deng, and David De Chand. The group later reformed into the Morge Group that began meetings in the resort area of Morge, Switzerland, with Swiss funding. I began shuttling between the Group and the SPLM leadership, including flying to New Site, to try to forge a common ground on the objectives of the struggle. For a while, my efforts seemed promising until John revealed to me one day in New Site that elements in our group were working with Northern political parties to undermine the Movement and that he would come out openly against our initiative. That was when I said that my sole objective was to promote the unity of the Southern struggle and that if our initiative was becoming a source of disunity, I did not want to continue to be part of it. I resigned and the Swiss Foreign Ministry told me that they had 'exploited' my name and could not continue the funding if I was no longer part of the initiative. That created a rift between me and my colleagues that took considerable time to mend.

My position on the issues involved remained unchanged. I strongly defended both self-determination and unity in the Task Force that was organized by the Center for Strategic and International Studies, CSIS, in July 2000 to develop a coherent US policy to end Sudan's war. Our report was to guide the incoming administration of either George W. Bush or Al Gore. At the behest of USIP, the funding institution, I was asked to co-chair the Task Force with Stephen Morrison, the Director of the Africa division of CSIS. Our friends on 'The Council', specifically Ted and Roger, opposed the Task Force because they suspected that it was a pro-Khartoum initiative by some American friends of the Sudan. They even advised me not to participate in it. I resisted because I felt that it was an opportunity to advocate our cause. Besides, if I did not co-chair the Task Force, someone else would and we had no way of knowing what that would mean for our cause. Under the influence of our friends, Garang initially also opposed the Task Force initiative, but he agreed that my involvement would at least minimize the harm.

The Task Force was comprised of fifty individuals who were knowledgeable on the Sudan. Virtually all of them were against self-determination for the South and the division of the country. They did not even see the US playing a leading role for peace in the Sudan. For them, the Sudan had no strategic importance for the US. The only importance of the Sudan was its support for international terrorism, its destabilization of friendly neighbors in the East African region, and the humanitarian situation caused by the war. In their opinion, which was of course proven wrong, if George W. Bush became President, he would have no interest in world affairs, far less in the Sudan. They thought that efforts to end the war in the Sudan should be left to Europe, with the US supporting from a distance.

Playing my cards carefully to avoid being seen as abusing my position as Co-Chairman, I made a contrasting case for US leadership in the search for peace in the Sudan. I reversed the three priority areas identified by the participants. Sudan's involvement in international terrorism was based on the fact that the government viewed the Christian West as supporting the cause of the South. They therefore saw the Islamic terrorist organizations in the Middle East as allies on the principle that the enemies of my enemies are my friends. It is for the same reasons that Sudan was destabilizing the countries of the region, which they viewed as sympathetic to the cause of the South. The humanitarian crisis in the country was also caused by the war. My conclusion was that by ending the war, we would stop Sudan's involvement in terrorism, its destabilization of the region, and the humanitarian crisis.

As for the strategic importance of the Sudan, I made the point that Sudan was the meeting ground of the great religions of the world, Christianity and Islam, and of the two regions, Africa and the Middle East. It could be a point of either reconciliation or confrontation, with far-reaching implications. As the sole superpower, the United States could not afford to be indifferent to an area of such global strategic importance. It must instead take the lead in ending the war.

I argued that the best way of promoting unity was to use self-determination as a threat to pressure the regime to create a conducive climate for unity. To ensure unity in some form, we needed to reconcile two seemingly irreconcilable realities, the Arab Islamic Vision of the North and the African Secular Vision of the South. That was the root of the 'One Country, Two Systems' formula which the Task Force recommended for the interim period. Although Garang, under the influence of our friends on the Council, initially reacted rather negatively against the formula, he was eventually persuaded that the formula was the same as the one he proposed in his Model Two of his Five Models, which proposed a dualistic system for the country.

It must be reiterated that Garang was not a categorical unionist. His five alternative models included: New Sudan as the ideal, which I personally supported (1); coexistence in a framework of 'one country two systems'(2), a formula which our Task Force stipulated as an interim and perhaps even a permanent alternative, (which he initially opposed but eventually embraced as consistent with his own mode two; an Arab-Islamic model, which had failed to ensure the unity of the country (3); an African model which he considered to be only theoretical (4); and an outright partition of the country (5), which was the preferred option of the overwhelming majority of the people of South Sudan, as the 2011 independence referendum eventually affirmed.

The Task Force also strongly recommended that the US play a leadership role in the mediation to end the war. And indeed, the US took the lead in the peace process and adopted the One Country, Two System formula, which was eventually widely accepted and became very influential in the negotiations. Mutrif Siddig, a leading member of the government's negotiating team, told me that he read our report at least four times during the negotiations. Surprisingly, Northerners generally took it as a clever separatist ploy. I met with former President Jaafar Nimeiri while he was visiting Washington and our report was very much in the news. He said to me in a matter-of-fact manner, "I hear that you have become a separatist." I asked him what I had done to become a separatist? He mentioned my advocating One Country, Two Systems formula. I asked him whether the arrangement he had established under the Addis Ababa Agreement was not 'One Country, Two Systems.' He suddenly changed, "*Wallahi*, 'By God' what you are saying is correct." That ended the matter. But I was to keep hearing from the Sudanese later that our One Country, Two Systems formula became a basis for separation. What was intended to be a promotion of unity in a way reinforced separatism.

Furthermore, in retrospect, the formula implied uniformity or consensus within each of the two systems. The fact is that the country was being governed by an Islamic system to which not all Sudanese adhered. Even among Muslims, there are different sects or visions of Islam. The South too is not monolithic, as the post-independence crisis of tribalism, in part a self-fulfilling prophesy of the North, tragically demonstrated.

I remember giving a lecture at Khartoum University on the Task Force and its recommendations. Professor Alamein Hammoda, from the Nuba Mountains, who had been a colleague at Khor Taggat Secondary School and at the University of Khartoum, asked me where we would place the Nuba in our One Country, Two Systems formula. That was when I thought of changing the equation to One Country, Multiple Systems that would give all the five regions of the Sudan, South, North, West, East and Center, the right of self-rule within the framework of national unity. But it was too late; we had already succeeded in selling the formula of One Country, Two Systems.

As is well known, George W. Bush won the elections and became surprisingly active on the global scene and in ending the Sudanese war. Our Task Force Report and its One Country, Two Systems formula became the cornerstone of US policy to end the war in the Sudan.

The message of Dr. John to his officers was that negotiations with the Khartoum regime had started in earnest, that the mediators wanted him to get personally involved in the talks, and that they needed to strengthen their military position in the field to support the talks to reinforce their negotiation position. As Pieng recalled, "Dr. John insisted, 'It is very important that we continue fighting, not because we love war, but because it is the only way for us to continuously exert pressure so that the conditions we table will be accepted.' Dr. John continued to brief us after every negotiation session. In the process, we learned about his strategy and tactics. When he first went to Naivasha, he built a personal relationship with Ali Osman, the First Vice President of Sudan. Often, he asked the mediators to give a chance to him and Ali Osman to discuss directly. This built friendship between them. I remember one time he brought their families to Naivasha and they spent time together as individuals for some time. I believe that gave a push to the negotiations and the personal relations they built helped. I think Dr. John as a person demonstrated a lot from which we can benefit."

Power Struggle in the Leadership

Pieng became actively involved in the negotiation process in a security and military role. Dr. John's strategy continued to maintain a three-prong approach. He remained intensively engaged in the negotiations with Ali Osman. But he also stressed the critical role of military strength for which he intensified recruitment all over the South. He also continued to reach out to the rebel groups in the marginalized areas of the North, primarily in the Southern Kordofan (Nuba Mountains), Blue Nile and Darfur, as well as Northern opposition parties with which he formed the National Democratic Alliance."

Pieng was the key coordinator with the opposition groups in both the East and Darfur. He writes that while they were unwaveringly committed to supporting these forces, Dr. John advised caution with the Darfurians because of the Islamic orientation of the region that Khartoum might exploit by alleging that they had joined a movement of infidels against Islam. There was also the intertribal dimension to the complexity. Pieng observed: "While Dr. John's vision of taking the war to the North was a strategic move for both the ultimate goal of a New Sudan and our success in liberating the South by extending the theatre of combat, the tribal nature of Africa cannot be underestimated. Bonding within groups based on a shared ethnic identity tends to be strong, as in the cases of the Fur and the other Darfurian tribes, but bridging between them is often fragile. In a military context, this can have devastating consequences, as it did in Darfur and across the South more generally."

Indeed, tribal competition and conflicts continued to plague the South in the struggle. Even as the negotiations were moving constructively and the Movement was gaining ground, rivalry and suspicions were threatening the unity of the struggle, specifically pitting Salva Kiir against John Garang. I give Pieng's detailed account of this incident because it was a conflict that risked destroying the Movement and all that had been gained: "In 2004, when all the Protocols had been initially signed, we were called to discuss the Implementation Modality and Permanent Ceasefire Arrangement. So, we went to Naivasha. At the same time, Dr. John was visiting Ramchiel, a place at the crossroads of the three historic regions of Bahr el Ghazal, Upper Nile and Equatoria. We planned to establish the transitional headquarters of the SPLM there during the six months pre-interim period that would commence the formal implementation of the agreement. In Naivasha, we finished the implementation modality and waited for 9th January 2005, when the agreement was to be signed.

But Pieng was suddenly confronted with a situation of grave magnitude that would absorb him in an intense mediation for peace. "I decided to pass through Kampala where my children were, but before I left Nairobi, my brother Monydhang, who was a Commander at that time, called me one evening. Monydhang's voice was filled with emotion as he asked, 'Pieng why are you doing this?' 'What am I doing?' I asked in return. 'You want to go to Bahr el Ghazal to mobilize forces and arrest Comrade Salva,' he said, as if it were a well-known fact. 'Nonsense, that is not true. I'm now going to see my children in Kampala.' We finished talking.

"In the morning, I boarded a bus going to Kampala. When I arrived and went to the house, I found that Monydhang had called my wife. She began to quarrel with me immediately, posing the same question

Monydhang had posed to me: 'Pieng, why are you doing this? I heard that you have been sent to Kampala to receive a Ugandan force from the President to go back to South Sudan and arrest Comrade Salva.' I asked her, 'Who told you that?' She said, 'Your brother, Monydhang'. I called Monydhang and said, 'I see you are convinced that I intend to arrest Comrade Salva, despite what I told you. Who could have told you that and you trust their word over mine?' Monydhang said, 'I have been informed that you are getting a force from Museveni to go to fight Salva.' I said, 'That is not true. I am here with my children. I don't even have any contact with Ugandans here. I will go back to Rumbek after seeing my children. Someone must be up to no good.' I learned from Monydhang how serious the issue had become."

Having now realized that the allegation was more than a rumor, Pieng began to act in earnest to correct the situation. "The story was that Salva was about to be attacked or killed, and my name was front and center in the plot. I decided to go to Yei directly instead of Rumbek. I boarded a small plane, Eagle Airline, and called my cousin and Comrade, Kuol Deng Abot, who was in Arua, Uganda, visiting his children. I said, 'Kuol I am coming to Arua and I want you to accompany me to Yei, using your pick up and I don't want us to be accompanied by any of your security officers at all.' He met me at the airport and went to change his clothes. We moved, just the two of us, with him driving, and I in the front passenger's seat. We left at 8 pm from Arua and drove the whole night and reached the bridge of Yei at 5am. We crossed the bridge and entered Yei. We were planning to go to Kuol's house in Yei to brush our teeth, take tea and then go to where Salva was. But I changed my mind, 'No, if Salva hears that we are somewhere in Yei and not seeing him, he will think we are planning something. Let us go directly to his house.'"

What followed is a remarkable combination of Pieng's desire to resolve the misunderstanding and the depth of mistrust and animosity on the part of Kiir that was not easy to dispel: "We drove to Kiir's house, just the two of us, and were stopped at the gate by the soldiers. I said, 'It is me, Commander Pieng.' All of the officers were awake, in full uniform, with all their guns. Comrade Akok Nyuon went to Comrade Salva, who was also awake, in his office, with full uniform and his guns. He called us into his office. We saluted him, 'Hi comrade, how are you?' He asked me, "How many soldiers came with you?' I said, 'Only my brother Kuol.'

"He said, 'I've learned that you've come to arrest me'. I said, 'Ok, now is your chance to check the truth of those rumors'. He looked at me intensely but did not respond. So, I said, 'Why are you afraid now when that has never been your character?' He said, 'Comrade Pieng, you too like all men can be brave until you become a coward.'

"Kuol left us, and Salva continued with me, his gun on the table, and said, 'Comrade John, with your help, now wants to kill me.' I said, 'That cannot happen. If Dr. John tries to arrest you or kill you at this time, I'm sure the signature of the CPA will not take place. And if that happens, Dr. John will not achieve what he has been striving for. I believe there are people who are trying to convince you so that this agreement will not be signed. I am sure those people are connected with the enemy.' He said, 'Then why is Comrade John not calling me? That means that what people are saying is true.' I said, 'I am sure that Comrade John is not thinking of anything like that, especially at this particular time.'"

The complicating role of third parties in the dangerous misunderstanding becomes increasingly obvious. "There were two senior officers staying with Comrade Salva, Dominic Dim and Salva Mathok. I said to Kiir, 'One of those two officers can go with me to Yirol and we shall see for ourselves. I don't think Dr. John is the type of person who would want to spoil all his efforts at the last minute. It's better you send one of those officers whom you trust, and I will ask our friends to send a plane.' Comrade Salva accepted my suggestion, 'Ok, you go with Comrade Dim and see for yourself.' I talked to our American friend, Brian De Silva, and he managed to send me a small plane. When I was going to the airport, I passed by Comrade Dim, and told him that the plane was ready. Dim told me, 'I'm not going.' I said, 'Ok there is no problem; I will go alone.'

"Comrade Salva was at the airport to receive his wife before I got there. But I found that he had left by the time I got to the airport. So, I boarded the plane myself and went to Yirol. When I arrived, I found that Dr. John had gone to Ramchiel. So, I waited. I was sitting in the compound. When I learned that he had arrived, I told his security, 'I need to see Dr. John.' They responded, 'He is tired and taking a rest. You cannot see him tonight, but you can see him tomorrow.' I went to my sleeping place. Early in the morning I heard that Dr. John wanted to go to Nairobi to meet members of the Security Council, who were coming for the final meeting before the signing of the Agreement. So, I went at 6am and waited for him. But instead of seeing Dr. John, I saw his luggage going to the airport. Meanwhile, those soldiers kept telling me to wait. I saw them all going to the airport to leave.

"Then I saw Comrade John standing, also about to leave. So, I approached him directly. 'What are you doing here?' he asked. Then, in a rush, he added, 'If you have any problem, see me when I get back.' I told him, 'This is an urgent matter and it cannot be discussed while we are standing; it is a serious issue.' He asked, 'What is that serious issue?' I said, 'Can we sit, as it will not be appropriate for us to talk standing?' 'Ok,' he said. 'Let us sit.' The soldiers saw us going to sit and they went to Rebecca and said, 'Pieng is delaying the plane.' She came and said, 'Brother-in-law, let us go.' I said, 'Mom, leave us a bit. There is a serious issue I have come to convey to the Chairman.' I sat with Dr. John, and said, 'Comrade, I think I will say what Osama said to America – 'While I was attacking you, your president was playing with children.' While SPLA is under attack, there are issues you are addressing, but Comrade Chairman, if you don't address this one, even the meeting you are going to attend will not succeed. If nothing is done today, then Comrade Salva will declare tomorrow that he is the head of the Movement.'

"Dr. John was stunned: 'What?' I said, 'This is what I understand, but before I say more let me call Comrade Salva and you hear it from the horse's mouth.' I took the Thuraya and called Salva, 'Comrade John is here, please talk to him.' They spoke and after they finished, Dr. John came back to me and said, 'Nobody has told me all this, but I see the issue is serious.' I said, 'Yes, and it is important for you to know this and this is why I went to Yei.' Dr. John asked, 'Then what do we do?' I said, 'Since you have heard Salva and his mood is not settled, let us do two things: First you write a message to all units disputing all the rumors about the arrest and dismissal of Salva; tell them that the information is false. Second, talk to Comrade Salva and tell him that you must meet as soon as you come back from Nairobi. You write these things and after you leave, I will use the radio here to transmit it to all units and to Salva. Then I'll go to Rumbek so that we try all efforts to resolve this situation. I don't think it will be easy; but if we want to meet the signature date of 9th January, then we must engage with comrades immediately, such that when you meet the Security Council, there is no objection from Comrade Salva.'

"Dr. John agreed. Then he called for his briefcase and wrote those two messages. I went to the airport and saw them off. Then, I called the radio operators to transmit those messages and called all officers around Yirol, including those in charge of the county, to brief them. I told them, 'This issue is extremely serious. We must all go to Rumbek and discuss it and address it by all means. Those officers supported what I said, and we all travelled to Rumbek. When I arrived at Rumbek, I called everyone together. It was good that I had a good relationship with the administration of NPA and USAID. They helped with all the support I needed, including picking people up from other directions so that we could all come and meet in Rumbek.

Pieng mobilized some of the chiefs and elders of Bahr el Ghazal to assist in the mediation process. "Many leaders from Bahr el Ghazal met with us. While we were meeting, Comrade Salva called me and told me, 'I had not known you were my enemy.' I said, 'What happened?' He said, 'I have information that you are getting all Bahr el Ghazal leaders and mobilizing them against me.' I said, 'Time will tell who is your enemy and who are your people. I want you to know though that I am not mobilizing against you. Instead, I want you to talk to them, so that you can try to convince them about whatever you want to do.'"

More names of individuals involved in the conspiracy were revealed. Pieng's account continued: "I left Yei to Yirol where I met Comrade Marial Chenuong who informed me that he was called by Dominic Dim, who said, 'Pieng is coming to you; he is mad, don't listen to him.' I discovered that it was Comrade Aleu Ayeny who was conspiring against me. He was close to Dr. John as he was his security officer responsible for collecting all his intelligence in Nairobi. He had a de-mining company and was at the same time in charge of the de-mining authority of the Movement. Comrade Nhial, who was senior to him and in charge, eventually had him removed and replaced him with Comrade Jurkuc Barac. This made Aleu bitter. He told Salva, 'I was close to Dr. John, so I know his secrets. He is now planning to replace you with Nhial.'

"Salva thought that Aleu was correct, and he accordingly convinced Dominic Dim and Salva Mathok. Together, they were determined to see that I did not succeed in stopping their rebellious move from happening. So, they had to tell Salva that I was working against him. But many Bahr el Ghazal leaders agreed they should not undermine the war when the peace agreement was about to be signed. They questioned the motives of those senior officers by asking why we would spoil what we had long been fighting for and after having lost so many lives. The chiefs and elders said they must all go to Salva and convince him. More than 40 chiefs and elders were ready to go. I managed to get a plane from NPA for the delegation to go to Yei, under Honorable Ayen Maguot, an elderly lady and committed member of the Movement, and Chiefs like Nyal Chan, and some officers; they all went."

But Salva had been persuaded to be suspicious of the elders' motive. He refused to meet them. "Comrade Salva called me and said, 'I am not going to meet these people of yours.' I said, 'Please meet them. As a leader, you have to meet your people. If they are wrong in what they say, you can try to convince them otherwise.' Comrade Salva eventually met them. But the situation remained tough. Some officers began to mobilize in Yei. People were now standing behind whatever Salva was going to do, including declaring his usurpation of power. After the elders returned from meeting him, they said they did not think Salva would act rashly. Still, things were tense."

Fortunately, Dr. John was fully cooperative with Pieng. "When Dr. John came back from meeting the Security Council, he said he wanted to go to Yei. I told him, 'No; since Salva is not ready to go to Nairobi or New Site, we better find any other neutral place – perhaps Rumbek or Mapel or Malual Kon.' I had discovered that Salva had almost lost confidence in me. So, whatever I told him then, he would probably not listen. But I also got information that he was in direct communication with my Deputy, Comrade Malong, and I knew that unless he had someone to trust, nothing would work. So, I thought that person could be Malong."

What followed was an intriguing zigzag of progress and reversal due to the interplay of vested individual interests and influence. "So, I tried to convince Malong to come to Rumbek so that we could think of where the two leaders could meet. He agreed. So, I sent him a small plane. But the same elements, especially Comrade Aleu, learned that I wanted to bring Malong and they intervened, trying to convince him that I was a dangerous person. They said I was working with Dr. John to arrest and execute Kiir. The plane went and waited for four hours. Then Malong sent it back to me. He called me and said, 'I am not going; you want me to be like one of our commanders who was accused of plotting with Makuei and was subjected to fire squad by SPLA. You want them to execute me while they leave you.' After Malong's refusal, the plane came back to Rumbek. I called Malong and asked him, 'Why are you doing this?' I recalled to him how we had been together and the trust we used to have. I asked, 'How could I betray you?' Then, I got to the point, 'This is a matter of national interest. If we don't do something, all will be spoiled, and the Agreement will not be signed and all we have done will be for nothing.'"

Malong became a pivotal partner in the mediation. "I convinced Malong, and he accepted my suggestion, but with reservations. He said, 'Tomorrow you send me the plane and I will come, whether you kill me or not.' I sent a plane and Comrade Malong came and we discussed everything together. I said, 'Let us go to Yei so that we convince Comrade Salva to come to Rumbek. Dr. John will have no problem.' Malong said, 'I don't believe that Comrade John has no bad intentions towards Salva. So, I don't agree that we go first to Yei. Let us first go to Dr. John, look into his eyes, and see if he has a bad intention or not.' I said OK. I called Brian De Silva, who was influential within USAID, and said, 'If possible, please get us a plane for the whole day tomorrow for us to go to New Site and then proceed to Yei.'"

As noted earlier, Brian D'Silva was one of the members of our 'Council' in Washington. He had been a colleague of John Garang in college and was his close friend and strongly committed to the cause of the South and the Movement. It is therefore not surprising that he was cooperating with Pieng. "The plane came and we decided not to take anyone with us, but only the two of us; we flew to New Site. A small car took us to Dr. John and we spent from 11am to around 4pm. Dr. John assured us that he had no intention to remove or arrest Salva or to do anything against him. He said that he was ready to meet Salva anywhere, including Yei. We advised him against going to Yei. 'You should not go to Yei; rather we ourselves will go to meet Salva. Our plan is for you to meet him in Rumbek, where the leadership of SPLM/A will convene for a meeting.'"

While John was cooperating, the attitude of Salva was less amicable, precisely because of the spoilers around him. "We left to meet Salva in Yei and went directly to greet him. Comrade Oyai was there, and we stayed in his house. We started to discuss with Salva the first day, and he insisted that he didn't want to go to Rumbek. 'The people of Rumbek support Dr. John,' he said. 'They will not help the solution. If you want, let us go to Northern Bahr el Ghazal or Mapel.' We said, 'No, Rumbek is the headquarters, and where all the meetings have been taking place, and it has facilities, a good landing strip and hotels to accommodate people.'

"The second day we almost convinced Comrade Salva and were to leave Yei to Rumbek, but when we came back to Salva the next day, we learned that Comrade Dominic Dim and Comrade Salva Mathok had changed everything. This happened each time we left Salva's house. This created confusion for Comrade Salva. We would always go and stay with them for the whole day, eating lunch together, and staying with him up to the evening. Then, we'd come back to Comrade Oyai's house. The three of us would sit and discuss the situation. But when we left, the others would influence him to change his mind."

Malong then proposed a plan to break the circle of spoilers. "Comrade Malong came up with an idea. He said, 'Tomorrow morning, we should have separate meetings – everyone of us will meet each one of them separately – Comrade Salva, Dominic Dim, and Salva Mathok. Comrade Oyai, you'll meet Dominic Dim, Comrade Pieng will meet Salva Mathok, and I will meet Salva Kiir. And we must discuss with this reconciliation meeting with each separately.' We agreed and the next day we all went to our respective meetings, in their homes, and we discussed separately and seriously with each of them. Then, after some time, we were called in after Comrade Malong had finished with Comrade Salva. All of us convened, six of us – Salva Kiir, Salva Mathok, Dominic Dim, Paul Malong, Oyai Deng and me. We were surprised when Salva said, 'I have accepted to go to Rumbek and I am ready any time to leave. But I don't want my security to go with me because they are very agitated and they will clash with the security of Garang.'"

Salva Kiir had made an about-turn and wisely advised against his going with his bodyguards as that might trigger a confrontation. Pieng had a different security plan. "I said, 'The security guards will be our responsibility. We will instruct some of them to go with us, myself and Comrade Malong. They can come with us and we will ensure everything is secure. Then you and Comrades Salva Mathok and Dominic Dim can come after. At the same time, we'll bring Dr. John.' So, we went with forty of his soldiers back to Rumbek to prepare for the meeting.

Malong and I were in charge, and it was good that both Dr. John and Salva accepted. But when the information went out that part of Salva Kiir's security had gone to Rumbek, Comrade Malual Majok, who was in charge of Dr. John's security, sent a company from Yirol to Rumbek. When I heard that, I called him and said, 'I don't want more soldiers in Rumbek – I will handle this from the Third Front. You cannot have more than two companies and Salva will have two platoons. We quarreled and I said, 'There is no reason why you shouldn't trust our arrangements. It is your security that cannot be trusted and will cause problems.'

"We knew we had to make this succeed by all means. Comrade Salva came with Deng Alor and we heard that Comrade Riek and Kuol Manyang came to Rumbek through Yei after attending a meeting of the leadership Council and High Command. Dr. John came. And in the evening, Oyai, Malong and I went to greet him. Salva did not go to John. Dr. John said, 'I want to go to greet Salva.' We said, 'No, it will be Salva to come and greet you.' We went to him and said, 'It is for you to meet Dr. John.' He said, 'I want to go and greet him, but if I go with my security, there will be problems. You call Deng Alor, and he will be my driver. Only he and I will go.' The two of them went alone as Salva had suggested and broke the ice. While the mood was still not as friendly as before, it was a good step in the right direction and a sign that things might succeed after all.

"When Comrade Salva and Comrade Deng Alor went back to their places, we organized the meeting to include the Leadership Council and Political Bureau, plus the SPLA Command and the regional administration, governors and their deputies. The meeting started with Dr. John briefing on the progress of the peace and the possible signing of the CPA. After that, Comrade Salva and others, such as Comrade Elijah Malok, talked. The talk was not straightforward, and we could tell that Comrade Salva was not convinced by the briefing and looked uncomfortable.

"I was among the first persons who raised their hands to speak after the briefing and was selected to talk. I said, 'Let us be frank. You two comrades need to accept that there is a problem between you, and you need to be open so that you solve that problem.' I tried to talk in a way that first blamed Dr. John because he was the leader; problems are always blamed on the leaders. I tried to stress the need for Dr. John to change the way he was running the Movement. I said that Comrade Salva was

feeling that he was not being involved in most of the decisions and activities of the Leadership. I talked in a way that opened up the discussion.

"Other comrades, especially my colleagues in the SPLA, followed me.
The officers admitted that they were mostly critical of Dr. John, but they
were also thankful to God that he understood that their intention was to
solve the problems. They stressed that no position had been precooked
against Dr. John's leadership. The talk was rough, but it was good that Dr.
John understood us.

"After my talk, he gave the floor to Comrades Gier, Mamur, Oyai,
Hoth, and many others, indicating that he was interested to listen to
what we were thinking. Although our message was tough, and sounded
as though we were siding with Salva, most of it never went beyond the
need for them to come together. Dr. John thanked all of us for how we
had talked, and for really laying the issues on the table. Then he asked
Salva to talk.

"Comrade Salva said, 'I don't have any problem, but I wanted to
correct the things that are wrong in the Movement.' Then he added
something that wasn't healthy, but was good for him to say it, 'I will not
say anything more, but will be like a dog that barks at night, as he sees
something that others are not seeing.' He said it seemed that people did
not see what he saw, 'But I will continue like a dog barking at night.'
In his talk, he tried to explain why he thought that Dr. John was not
involving him, for example going to places without telling him, despite
the fact that he was in charge of security. This meant that Dr. John was
taking all the authority in his briefcase when he traveled, leaving the
liberated areas without any delegated authority. Dr. John, he alleged,
was working directly with officers without involving him, despite his
being the Chief of General Staff. For example, Comrade Bior Ajang as
Military Intelligence just stayed with Dr. John. He asked how such an
important officer could be far from the Chief of General Staff. In the
end, he said, 'I am ready to continue working with Dr. John and I hope
things will change.'

"The reconciliation in general ended well, but I was personally in
trouble because my sister-in-law, Dr. John Garang's wife, whom I called
my mother-in-law, Mama Rebecca, came out of the meeting, obviously
angry. When I went to greet her, she refused to greet me in return. And
I initially understood that it was because she was not in the meeting

from the beginning but came later. Someone might have conveyed to her how I had talked and that I had attacked her husband. But I took it lightly. And she didn't take well how all of us senior officers had talked. She held the view that we had sided with Salva against her husband. This especially applied to me."

I became tangentially involved in the crisis at its peak. I was called by someone who was close to both John and Salva and knew my relationship to both. They told me that Salva Kiir had regard for me and would listen to my advice to avert the crisis. I had indeed established a cordial relationship with Salva. Whenever I was in Nairobi, with Bona Malual, Salva's close friend and political associate, Salva would call on us and we would discuss issues. Even when I was alone in Nairobi, he would also visit me. One of the most touching experiences with Salva was when I visited New Site to meet with John Garang. As I discussed with Garang, he asked me whether I had met with Salva. When I told him that I had not yet met with him, he advised me to make a courtesy call on Salva. As I was about to go to Salva, he came to see me. I learned later that Salva gave me his Cabin to sleep in while he moved to a more modest one. So, there was indeed a mutual regard between us.

In response to the request that I intercede in the conflict between Kiir and Garang, I chose to call my brother, Dr. Kwol, who was in Yei to facilitate contact with Salva. Kwol surprised me by saying that Dominic Dim, who was his contact person with Kiir, told him that Kiir did not want to talk. I went to Nairobi and met with John Garang and asked him what was going on between him and Kiir. Garang explained to me that what was being alleged by the rumors was not true and that he had no plan to replace Kiir with Nhial. Deng Alor was there. John said that Salva had changed and that he was not 'our Salva we have known for all these years.'

Eventually, Salva called me. I do not remember what prompted his call. When I told him that I had tried to call him earlier, and that I was told that he did not want to talk with me, he strongly denied and told me that he could not possibly refuse to talk to me. "My respect for you is known only to God," he said in words which deeply moved me. When I told him what John Garang had said, he argued that the so-called rumors were true. He said, "I know the man well. When he wants to make a decision, he throws it out as a rumor to see how it will be received.

And if he concludes that it will not provoke a negative reaction, he would then take that decision."

Salva went into details in which he listed the grievances he had against Garang. He told me that he had told Garang that even if he wanted to be a dictator, he should establish institutions through which he could then lead. When I later received the records of what had been said against Garang in the Rumbek meeting, including people who accused John Garang of 'lying,' I was most impressed by the magnanimity with which he had received the criticism.

I now return to Pieng's account. "After the meeting, we were called again to Naivasha to finalize all the CPA processes and prepare for the signature. We, the senior officers who had spoken at the reconciliation talks, decided to ask for a meeting with Dr. John. Since his wife had not taken well what we had said, we thought that he might also have the same feelings against us. So, we resolved to speak to him to find out how he was feeling, and make sure we were not solving one problem by creating another. He accepted our request for a meeting, and we went and tried to explain our position. Oyai spoke first, 'Comrade, we'd be happy for you to tell us how you feel about the last meeting with Salva.'

"Dr. John said, 'If it weren't for you, the issue would not have been resolved as it was. This is how resolutions take place, especially in our Dinka culture. We Dinka and other Nilotics always try to make it easy for the complainer, or someone feeling aggrieved. We all knew that Salva was the aggrieved person; and so your standing with him was a good tactic. I have no bad feelings about how you handled the situation. I still see you as my cadres and the leaders who will really help this Movement and lead it to the next generation.'

"Although it was a good meeting, my sister-in-law still refused to greet me. I continued to take it easy for the next two months. Then I decided to meet with her and talk to her personally. We spoke and resolved the misunderstanding. She apologized to me, saying 'I took it seriously with you because you were the first who started the type of talk that attacked my husband, and I couldn't believe that you could be the one to do that.' But I told her, 'There was no other way, because if it wasn't me to start, no one would have done so. Now we are going to sign the Agreement, and it will be Dr. John who will be credited with that Agreement. And I will be proud to be part of delivering that Agreement.

This is why I went to Yirol and made sure this meeting would happen.'

"I managed to help resolve a dangerous and explosive issue for all of us, especially Dr. John. I achieved what I thought was right and I congratulated myself on successfully serving the national interest by keeping the SPLA from splitting at a time when all South Sudanese and friends were upholding the CPA. I am also thankful to Comrade Malong who joined me in Rumbek and Comrade Oyai who had been trying in Yei. Although some people in Yei, who were with Comrade Salva, were ready to fight, Comrade Oyai stood firm and tried to convince Comrade Salva not to follow that path. And so, when we joined him, we all convinced Salva together. I don't want to underestimate the efforts of others, like Riek Machar, Deng Alor, and Kuol Manyang, who also worked hard to persuade Comrade Salva to avert the conflict."

Pieng reports on an important development which would later feature in my discussions with both John Garang and Salva Kiir. "After the signing of all the Protocols and while we were awaiting the final signature in Nairobi, Dr. John organized three clusters: military/security cluster led by Comrade Salva, Administrative cluster led by Riek Machar, and political cluster led by James Wani. Each cluster was given a task to fulfill. I was one of those officers assigned to the security cluster, and we were supposed to propose how all the security institutions should be organized/reorganized. The administrative cluster was to organize political administration for the coming period. The political cluster was to prepare the Party for governance in a peace environment. I can't talk about the other clusters, but I will address the security cluster in relation to the CPA."

Peace at Last But

The Comprehensive Peace Agreement, CPA, was signed in Nairobi on January 9th 2005 in the large Nyaya Stadium. The ceremony was well attended by regional and international leaders, not to mention large crowds of euphoric South Sudanese who stood in the blazing sun chanting joyous slogans. The SPLA marched at the tune of their war songs, whose fiery lyrics were not explicitly sung, but were well known and easily discernible from the music. Pieng, who attended this spectacular event, presents this description: "It was a good day when we finally signed the CPA on January 9, 2005. Dr. John invited the representatives of chiefs and heads of command and those in the negotiations to attend; all of us were there. Our military band was also there to represent the SPLA soldiers. And when the Sudanese national anthem was performed by our military band, the reaction showed that most people present, especially from the Kenyan government, were standing with the SPLM/A. The Sudanese, on the other hand, didn't bring any music, except some singers from Khartoum. Many traditional dancers came from different liberated areas of the SPLM/A. It is something that I can't forget. The speech of Dr. John was long, but useful and people enjoyed it. For the whole period of his speech, people were happy and excited."

As I sat, keenly observing the ceremony, I was struck by how conciliatory Omer El Bashir's message was, and how still adversarial John Garang's speech was, as he elaborated with absolute candor the injustices that had necessitated the war and his plans for the New Sudan of justice and equality. His message was echoed by Museveni who stated that people do not go to war for nothing and highlighted Sudan's distorted national identity as Arab, which was the core of the injustice against non-Arab Black Africans. The scene remarkably reflected the identity symbols in conflict. The loud chanting of Allahu Akbar, by an overzealous South Sudanese Muslim, was met with an even louder chorus of Alleluia by the Southern crowd. I watched the Northerners sitting next to me, looking clearly distraught and not at all joining in the applause by the audience surrounding them. It was for me a glorious event, but with obviously mixed feelings from significant elements in the crowd.

At a luncheon that was held after the signing, I sat at the same table with Dr. Lam Akol who surprised me by asking me to persuade John Garang, whom he described as 'your friend', to go to Khartoum immediately as a gesture of good will. Dr. Riek also spoke to me in the same vein. I asked them why they needed me to speak to Garang when they were comrades in the Liberation Struggle and colleagues in the Leadership. After that, Garang gave a reception which was attended by our international friends for whom he had words of appreciation. Hilde Johnson, the Norwegian Minister for International Cooperation, spoke, describing the Agreement as 'very good' for South Sudan. I thought that was rather unfortunate as I was sure there were friends, allies, or spies of Khartoum at the reception, and if the Agreement was 'very good' for the South, they would most likely consider it 'very bad' for the North.

That evening, John Garang gave a dinner party for the leaders of South Sudan. The festivities included music by Abyei Band which energized the crowds and Abel Alier pulled me for us to join in hailing the Band, clearly spotlighting the cause of Abyei which featured in the songs. John Garang's speech was typical in reflecting his creative ambiguity as he, the leading champion of the New Sudan of equitable unity, now highlighted the option for independence from the North. He said that the Movement had delivered the right for the people of the South to choose whether to remain second class citizens of the Sudan or be first class citizens of their own independent country. James Wani spoke very colorfully in Biblical metaphor, declaring, "We have reached the Mountain top and now see the Promised Land." The vote for secession would obviously be the next step to the Promised Land.

After the signing of the CPA, Pieng continued to be at the center of the implementation process, especially those elements that related to security and the military. He was in the team that went to Khartoum to prepare for the arrival of John Garang. Negotiating the size of the SPLA that was to proceed to Khartoum to ensure security proved to be very difficult and was resolved only by reducing the size substantially. The momentous arrival of Garang to be sworn in was both a source of great joy for the people of the Sudan, who flowed into the Capital from all parts of the country, and for the same reason a source of great concern for his safety. The numbers who gathered at the Green Belt, which Pieng calls "too much", was unprecedented in the history of the country. And when the sound system for his addressing the crowd failed, there was suspicion of foul play. But John was relaxed and seemingly unconcerned. He was duly sworn in and immediately assumed his responsibility as First Vice President.

I had gone to Khartoum with the advanced team the day before and was struck by what I saw displayed high up above the entrance wall of the Hilton Hotel, where John and his entourage were to be accommodated. There were huge photos of John Garang and Ali Abdel Latif, the 1924 Dinka-Nuba rebel leader, who, along with other Black Officers in the Egyptian Army in the Sudan, led the rebellion against colonial rule and called for self-determination. When their rebellion failed, the sectarian religious Muslim leaders of the North published racist statements

decrying the denigration of the country to be led by Blacks with no social standing. I feared that the photos would send the signal that Garang
represented the revival of Black African consciousness reflected in the
leadership of Ali Abdel Latif and now John Garang, which might provoke Arab backlash. Dr. Mansour Khalid, a prominent liberal Northern
Sudanese, later disputed my concern, arguing that the photos represented a historical fact that was well known.

At the swearing-in ceremony, which was very well organized, the
speeches were a replay of the signing ceremony in Nairobi. Omer al
Bashir was very upbeat in his conciliatory theme, while John Garang
sounded still confrontational, restating with great details the cause that
had led to the war and how the Agreement represented triumph for
freedom. "You are now free," he told the people of the Sudan. "Put on
your wings and fly to greater freedom." He also announced that the
SPLM would establish offices in all the States of the Sudan. I felt somewhat apprehensive that the Peace Agreement might dramatically unfold
in the face of the sharply conflicting visions reflected at the ceremony.

The evening of the swearing-in ceremony, John Garang called me
to his hotel room. He had no real agenda, just an opportunity to reflect
on the situation generally. I congratulated him, but also shared with
him my concerns. I questioned the confrontational way he had spoken,
pointing out specifically his declaration that the people were now free
and should put on their wings to fly higher. "Free from whom?" I asked.
"Not from the people who were sitting next to you and with whom
you have just concluded a peace agreement? When you also said that
you would establish SPLM offices in all the States, were you not declaring competition with them?" As usual, John listened to me very calmly
and then responded by explaining that while armed struggle had ended,
the conflict still existed and that the cause was too important to be underestimated by nice talk. "Besides, I softened what I said by adding that
what I outlined was the best way to consolidate national unity."

I also elaborated to Garang what I had hinted to him on one of
his visits to Washington. I told him that even his close friends were
concerned that he was carrying the very heavy burden of leadership
by himself. Now that he was assuming the responsibilities of First Vice
President of the Republic and President of Southern Sudan, he should
establish institutions through which to exercise power and delegate

powers to colleagues. His response was that he had distributed the responsibilities on the basis of a new organization, the one Pieng outlined. He said he had assigned responsibility for the Party to James Wani, the Army to Salva Kiir, and the Administration to Riek Machar, but that they had not delivered the reports he had asked them to prepare on the mandates assigned to them. Salva would later dispute this and affirm that he had indeed delivered his report to Dr. John Garang.

That was also the day the Abyei Boundary Committee submitted its Report, which seemed quite favorable to the Ngok Dinka. A group of Ngok Community members came to the hotel in a euphoric mood. I met with them. Monylam, Ali, one of our brothers, said exuberantly, "We have been given Meirem and Nyama." They said they were organizing a public demonstration to celebrate the Report. I advised them against the idea. I told them that their celebrating would send the signal that they were the winners and the Missiriya the losers. The Missiriya would most likely hold a counter demonstration against the Report. That would be certain to escalate the conflict.

I sat with them to discuss the situation. There were several of our brothers, including Kuol Adol, the Paramount Chief, among some twenty persons. All of them, except three, among whom was a police officer, strongly disagreed with me. One lady was almost offensive in her attitude, basically asking who I was trying to block the will of the people wanting to express their happiness. In the end, I told them that fortunately, the leadership of the Movement that had made that gain possible, were in the hotel and that we should seek their advice.

Fortunately, at that point I saw Pagan Amom and sought his advice. Then I met with the South African member, and he too agreed with me and advised our people to celebrate privately in their homes. Then I looked for Deng Alor who sealed the decision against public celebration. Although I knew the US ambassador who was the Chairman of the five men Committee and two additional members, I made it a point not to be in contact with them to avoid being seen as unduly trying to influence them. I only met with the Chairman at his request when he was appointed, but we did not discuss substantive merits of the case.

In my meeting with John Garang, he briefed me on how members of the Presidency had responded to the ABC Report. Beshir's reaction was, "We will have another rebellion in our hands," implying that the

Missiriya would violently oppose the Report. John Garang's response was, "That will be a rebellion we will face together." He then told me that he would like to meet with representatives of the Missiriya, but that I should make the request come from them. That was what I did quite effectively. In my meeting with them, they asked me to arrange for them to meet Dr. John Garang. The planned meeting was unfortunately leaked to the press the day after I left Khartoum and they denied it, claiming that I had met with them to discuss private family matters between us. Garang therefore did not meet with them. Sadly, the Report became highly contested and its fate a well-known example of the Northern Sudanese record of dishonoring agreements.

Pieng was also in Khartoum at the time, and he had this observation in his recollections. "After Dr. John assumed his tasks in office, we happened to be there as senior generals and officials. One time we went to his office in the Sudanese presidential palace. Most of the senior officers were there, and the one who was serving in his office was a Northern Sudanese who brought juice. But one of us, Comrade Mamur, would not take the juice. Dr. John, who was watching, got up from his chair, with a pen in his hand, which he moved over the glass. Then he told Mamur, 'You now take it.' Mamur laughed and asked, 'Can this pen remove poison?' Comrade John said, 'You drink it because I have checked it.' Mamur said, 'It's good if you have power to check it because we've been afraid that you'll be poisoned. So in this case, I'll drink'. That was the degree of our suspicion." That pen would later play a crucial role in identifying the body of Dr. John Garang at the scene of his tragic plane crash.

After assuming his central government position as First Vice President, Dr. John instructed the leadership of the SPLM/A to return to the South and followed shortly after. What follows is of immense historical importance. So, I again reproduce Pieng's account of the events in details: "While we were in Rumbek, Dr. John told Comrade Oyai, who was now the new Chief of General Staff of the SPLA, that he should be preparing the command of the SPLA to go to Bentiu. Dr. John himself would also go to Bentiu, but I cannot tell what exactly was the objective for us to go to Bentiu and for him to visit Bentiu as the first of the areas under our control that he would visit. He instructed us to send forces for that purpose, and we started to send forces. The first flight was denied to land in Bentiu with our forces. So, the plane had to go to Heglig and land with our forces there. We continued to discuss, and they eventually accepted, and our forces went to Bentiu. I think it was Paulino Matip, head of the Sudanese militias, who first refused for our forces to land in Bentiu. Comrade Bior and I, who were responsible for operations, were handling the arrangements. While we were preparing for his visit to Bentiu, Dr. John told us that he would first visit Uganda and Kenya and then come back to Rumbek to fly to Bentiu from there. He wanted us to go to Bentiu before him.

"After the signing of the CPA he also instructed us to mobilize forces, and we mobilized four thousand, with each front contributing forces, and we sent them to New Kush, where they were being trained. That force was meant to come to Juba, to the seat where he was coming as President of South Sudan. That four thousand was under training. He told us that his visit was to look for equipment and armament from Uganda for that four thousand, and that he also wanted to explain the situation to the leadership of Kenya. After that, he would go to Bentiu. Later on, we speculated that Dr. John was seeing Bentiu as the only area where we could get challenged by Matip; and so, he wanted to start with Matip and bring him under control by any means. If there were elements of Sudanese army that would continue supporting Matip, he would start addressing that issue too.

"He left Rumbek to New Site as we continued sending forces to Bentiu and getting ready to go ourselves to await his arrival there. On the 29th of July, we got a plane which was supposed to take us to Bentiu, thinking Dr. John would join us at the beginning of August. In the evening of 30th, I did not know what had happened. I think Comrade Oyai had gotten a hint of the disappearance of Dr. John's plane. But he didn't tell us, as we prepared to go to Bentiu the next day.

Tragic Death of the Founding Leader

The unbelievable tragedy occurred the following day and Pieng was to play a key role in the developments, as he recounts: "Early in the morning I got up and heard Comrade Oyai talking over Thuraya. I went to him thinking there must be a serious problem, 'Comrade Oyai, what happened?' First he evaded my question and tried to avoid talking to me;

but then he said, 'Yesterday evening, Comrade John left Kampala, but has failed to reach New Site.' 'With what?' I asked. 'With a helicopter.' I said, 'Comrade Oyai, he is dead; let us not waste our time talking. Let us go to New Site and look around because he has crashed in the mountains. Dr. John cannot spend an hour without talking to people. If he were alive, he would have communicated. So Dr. John is dead in the helicopter crash. The question now is how we control the situation.'"

Pieng virtually assumed the management of an extremely shocking situation for the Movement and the entire people of South Sudan and beyond. "We agreed to go to tell Pagan Amum the situation and then go to New Site and coordinate with the UN to take us to the scene. We instructed our forces to search around New Kush and towards the hills which I suspected should be the crash area. 'You Comrade Oyai, as the one commanding the Second Front, you must talk to the most senior officer there to control the situation. I will talk to Malong Awan to control the situation in Bahr el Ghazal. You talk to James Hoth to control the situation in Upper Nile. Let you and me go to the scene where we can address the situation.' We went to Pagan Amum and told him what had happened and that there was no reason to think that Dr. John was alive. How to control the situation and our people was now the most important concern. I said, 'When we leave here to the airport, you call the senior officers and tell them what has happened and what they should be doing.'

"We went to Rumbek airport and tried to check who was near-by. We learned that Comrade Daniel Awet Akot and Deng Alor were in Juba. We decided to pick them up and went to New Site. Mama Rebecca was not convinced that anything had happened to her husband. So, she was in a good mood." Whether her attitude was denial, or as it turned out later, encouragement of the people to bravely respond to her husband's death, her attitude was to prove very constructive in the situation. It minimized the suspicion that her husband had been assassinated, which would have fueled an explosive situation even more. Pieng's account continues: "Comrades Atem Aguong, Chol Biar, and Peter Garwich were commanding officers in New Kush. They told us that the night before, they had seen something flickering on top of the hills. We told them to follow that flicker. Although there was rain, the fire was still being seen burning on the top of the hill."

The leadership qualities with which Pieng and his colleagues managed that devastating situation were remarkably heroic. "When we reached New Site, close to 3 o'clock, we were informed that our forces under Peter Garwich had reached the site and had found that everything was destroyed and that there were no survivors. We went to Comrades Daniel Awet and Deng Alor and told them that the accident had been confirmed, and that Dr. John was dead. We went to the site to see for ourselves. I had made friendship with a UN force that was in Juba – Vladimir, from Russia, who was the officer in charge of UNMISS – and told him, 'We have a serious situation; can you help us with a helicopter.' Immediately, he came to New Site with a helicopter and came to us where we were staying. I told him, 'We need to go to New Kush after we instruct the officers to clear a landing strip.' We had already told them to carry all the remnants – even flesh – that they collected from different directions by the evening."

The magnitude of the horror then revealed itself at the site of the crash: "When we went there, we were in dilemma of what to do. Now, there were almost four thousand soldiers who were there and being prepared to go to Juba with Dr. John. So, we decided that Comrade Oyai and Bior Aswat and other Comrades should go and talk to those forces. Comrade Taban Deng Gai and I went to where the remnants, including pieces of the bodies, were collected. I decided to be the one directly involved in the identification. One cannot really describe what I saw. It was horrible. Bodies were burnt into unrecognizable pieces. So it became a problem: How do we verify the remnants of our leader, Dr. John?"

The scene, which Pieng describes in graphic details, is both one of the most gruesome in his war memories and also a remarkable instance of his leadership under most dreadful circumstances. "I took the courage – without wearing anything over my mouth or hands – and began checking the flesh of the human beings. But it became a problem: How do we identify the pieces? There was a body that I assumed to be that of our leader; it did not have a head, but the rest of the body was there, including legs. There was a ring on one of the fingers. I decided to ask. We had left Deng Alor and Daniel Awet Akot to inform Madam Rebecca. I did not want to talk to her directly. I called Comrade Deng Dau to ask him some questions. I asked about the ring, Deng Dau went to Madam

Rebecca who said that John was not wearing a ring. That made me drop that body. I went to a leg that was lying somewhere, with white Shilluk beads. I remembered once seeing such beads on Dr. John's legs. There were two legs, one with one round bead and the other with many round beads. Madam Rebecca confirmed that there was one round bead on his leg. So I put aside the leg. Peter Garwich brought me a pen, the same pen which Dr. John used in his office when Comrade Mamur did not want to drink juice in Khartoum. When I saw that pen, I knew that it was his pen. I asked, 'Near which part of the body did you find it?' He said, 'The pen was near this body.' It was one of the bodies without a head. I tried to see under the arms where there was a part of the shirt that was not burned because of the fat between the arms and the body. When I pulled it out, it showed the same shirt Dr. John was wearing, an African shirt which was seen on the TV when he was leaving Museveni."

What they took back was not the full body of their dead leader, but pieces of bones and reconstructed into his body. "We managed to put together all the parts of Dr. John. Vladimir – the UN officer, went back and said he would return to pick us up. He told us that he could not pick up all the bodies; he would only pick up Dr. John's body, if we found it. So, my first interest was to collect all the parts of the body and put them in one place. Vladimir brought black bags. We put the body of Dr. John in one bag. We also put other bodies in bags, trying to put each together as best as we could. The helicopter came to pick us up with the remains of Dr. John. Meanwhile, we talked to officers and told them that they should stay with those other remains until the next day when a flight would come to pick them up."

Then came the precise moment when Pieng shed his precious tears. "When we entered into the helicopter with the body, those four thousand soldiers were in a parade in the same ground where the helicopter took off. It is unfortunate that no one took a photo, because the four thousand were moving after the helicopter crying. That was when I started to drop tears from my eyes. I was not anticipating that scene. When the helicopter turned, they all ran after it as it started going straight up. All the soldiers were standing underneath it watching as we rose and went to New Site."

The reality of Garang's death began to sink in, but Pieng's exemplary courage remained solid: "I couldn't even imagine Dr. John was gone.

But I was thinking of how we could manage the situation. We made the decision to focus on moving forward. So, we sat as a senior command and said, 'What do we do now?' The only thing that came to mind was for Oyai to ask all the senior officers to come to New Site. Commander Salva was in Nairobi about to go on a mission to Japan. Riek Machar was in Yambio. James Wani was in Malakal. All senior officers were in different states where they were assigned. So, first we called Nairobi and Comrade Oyai told Comrade Salva, 'You need to come to New Site because we got the body.' Comrade Arop Moyak was with Salva in Nairobi and they came together; so did Riek, James Wani, and Lam Akol and others, including the two from the Leadership Council – Awet Akot and Deng Alor."

One of the unsolved mysteries of the situation was the attitude of Salva Kiir. "After some time, Arop Moyak said that Salva was not coming to New Site, but that he would go directly to Rumbek. We thought that that was not the right decision because Comrade Salva had to come to New Site as we could not meet in an area far from where the body was. We would be deciding the new leadership and where to bury Dr. John. We sent word to Comrade Arop Moyak to call those of Yasser and Comrade Majak Agot to go to Salva and convince him to come to New Site. We were serious that Comrade Salva had to come to New Site. I thank those Comrades because they managed to convince him and confirmed to us after some hours that Comrade Salva was coming. The Kenyans provided an army plane. That was important. Before I left Rumbek, I talked to Comrade Malong Awan to come back to Pariak to control our forces."

Pieng's account of how the people of Rumbek had initially thought the leadership was going to the airport to receive their leader only to find out that he was dead reminded me of the way the Ngok Dinka thought that the expected plane was returning their leader after treatment abroad only to learn that what was being flown back was his coffin. In both cases, joy turned into pandemonium. "I should say that before we left Rumbek, when the news of the loss of their helicopter was still uncertain, on the 31st as we were going to the airport, it was rumored that the senior officers were going to the airport to receive Dr. John, that he had been found and was already on his way to Rumbek. All the citizens of Rumbek were moving after our cars, thinking that we were going to receive Dr. John. From the center of Rumbek to the airport the way was full of the people. And when they learned the truth, that we were going to look for him, all those people were crying. That scene came back to me when I saw the four thousand soldiers at New Kush, when we were taking the body. That was the way it was when we left the people in Rumbek. I imagined that in other areas where I was not present, most of them had similar displays. In the morning, before I had heard about the loss of the helicopter, very early, even before going to Oyai, my brother Kuol Deng Abot, who was one of the advance team that went to Abyei, called me and was crying like a child. He told me, 'Dr. John is dead. The helicopter is not found; it is lost.'"

Salva was persuaded to go to New Site and his response to seeing Garang dead was another unexpected incident: "After we asked all the members of leadership to come to New Site, where we collected the remains of late Dr, John, as I mentioned, Comrade Salva was the only person who said he was not coming. We did not know why, but after those comrades convinced him, the next day he flew to New Site. He arrived from Nairobi around the second of August. We went to the airport to meet him and took him to the place where Dr, John's remains were. He collapsed at the door. We pulled him up, and told him, 'It is not the time for you to cry now; you should be strong and encourage the people. You must now think of how you will lead the nation and continue the mission.' He got up."

From that time on, Salva's succession was formalized and he firmly assumed leadership. "On the third of August, or maybe the second, the day after Comrade Salva came, we went into the meeting – all the High Command members and the leadership council – all of them were there. We went with the senior officers, the command of the SPLA; and Comrade Malongdit were there. People started to discuss the issue of who was going to replace Dr. John. First there was the issue of the legal procedure. Just before Dr. John died, he dissolved the Leadership Council. He was going to form another body, but he died before that happened. So, Salva, as Deputy Chairman, reconstituted and revived the Leadership Council, as it was the only legal body to take the decisions around the leadership. Now, our meeting was turned into a Leadership Council meeting, according to the SPLM Constitution, to appoint the Chairman of the Movement, who would also be nominated to be the

First Vice President of Sudan, as the Agreement stipulated. The unanimous decision that no one really opposed was to have Comrade Salva the next Leader of the SPLM."

The atmosphere was still tense with suspicions that Khartoum had a hand in the death of Garang. And yet the previously warring parties had made peace and reconciled. That left a rather ambivalent situation in Khartoum's response to the death of John Garang. Pieng recalls, "The same day, a delegation from Khartoum was said to be coming and we said that there was no problem. Nafi Ali Nafi and others from the party came. Judging from their faces, it was obvious that they were not expecting that they would not face problems. They came and found the atmosphere peaceful. South Sudanese fought in Khartoum and other parts of Sudan when they heard of the death of Dr. John. But on our side, they found that we were peaceful. They spent the day with us, and then returned to Khartoum."

One of the anomalies of the situation was the absorbing preoccupation with Garang's death and the need to honor those who were dedicated to protecting and serving him and died with him and also needed to be treated as heroes. "The day after we collected the bodies, my friend Vladimir of UNMISS, who was an operational officer, managed to get us two more helicopters to collect the remains of the others. They were taken to New Site. I am really thankful to him because he helped us in those very difficult days."

It is interesting that where Garang was to be buried was somewhat controversial and the paradox was that this great leader, whom the whole nation was mourning, was still viewed in the context of ethnic and local identity politics. "When Comrade Salva was elected as the next leader, we discussed where to bury Dr. John. It was a debate. Some said he had to be buried in Rumbek. They feared that if he were buried in Juba, and the Equatorians, who always resort to the divisiveness of Kokora, again went back to raising Kokora, and decided to chase people away from Juba, it would be difficult to leave the grave of Dr. John.

At that time, Clement Wani, who was then governor of Bahr el Jebel, which is now Central Equatoria, came to New Site and was with us. There were other Equatorians, such as Comrades Jadalla, Samson Kwaje, and Theophoslis. It was a serious discussion. Comrade Taban Deng Gai raised his hand and said he wanted to pose the question to our brothers and comrades from Equatoria; after they answered his question, he would then offer his opinion. 'Are you sure this idea of Kokora will not come back again?' Clement Wani said, 'We don't think it will because the leaders of Equatoria today are not the same as the leaders of the past'. Taban then said, 'I am asking you because definitely, if we bury Dr. John in Juba, we will not go away from Juba; if we are asked to leave Juba, we will fight and no one will tell us to leave Juba. So, all of you should understand that and commit yourselves against the return of Kokora.' And they all committed themselves. This was our second agreement after the selection of Comrade Salva."

One of the wise decisions taken by the leadership was to reaffirm the unity of the liberated areas by taking Garang's body around those areas and making the people share in the mourning. "We agreed to take the body to all the liberated areas, including Nuba Mountains and Blue Nile in the North and all the liberated areas in the South. We decided that after four days we would then take the body to Juba for the burial. Comrade Salva and Comrade Oyai were to accompany the body to all those liberated areas. And I and others were asked to go to Juba to ensure security and prepare the grave before the body was brought to Juba. So we divided ourselves. We came to Juba and Comrade Salva and Oyai moved with the body. Dr. John's body was received by mourners in large numbers in all the areas to which it was taken."

Juba as the resting place for Garang became the converging point which reaffirmed its status as the National capital of South Sudan. "We coordinated with the Sudanese government and its army to receive the body at the airport and take it to the Episcopal Church. Most, if not the whole of Juba population, came out to receive the body. They were all wearing black – all of them. And they cried, and prayed at the Church, and at the Mausoleum. People were following the procession in big numbers and crying. We buried Dr. John on the seventh of August; it was a very sad moment for us; really sad; but anyhow, we buried him to his last destination in Juba."

I was personally associated with those tragic developments. From the time I first heard the rumors of John's helicopter missing, I remained in close contact with those following the situation and kept hoping against hope that it was after all just a rumor. Once the crash and John's death were confirmed, several members of our 'Council,' among them Ted

Dagne and Roger Winter, and I, planned our immediate travel to South Sudan. We arrived at the New Site to find a gravely mournful situation. We could only look at the coffin without seeing the body which was said to be too mutilated for viewing. Then I accompanied the body around the liberated areas: Kauda in the Nuba Mountains, Rumbek, Bor, Yei, and Juba, the final destination. The plan to go to the Blue Nile had to be abandoned because of the rains.

What I found most moving was the culturally diverse way people expressed their grief. In the Dinka areas of Rumbek and Bor, the huge crowds that assembled were deadly silent – not a sound – as Dinka culture of mourning a Chief or a hero dictates that people must not cry. Occasionally, a woman was heard wailing and was immediately silenced or whisked away. In sharp contrast, in the non-Dinka areas of the Nuba Mountains and Equatoria, where almost everyone came out to meet and follow the body, the air was filled with wailing, people with hands over their heads, and women falling on the ground, some fainting and others willfully. Whether it was through silence or wailing, it was a scene that was unbelievable, and I could not help feeling that I wished John Garang could see how loved and sorely missed he was.

At Yei, President Museveni came, having driven from Uganda and made an impassioned speech in which he openly alleged that John had been assassinated. He said that his helicopter which had taken John was a top of the art aircraft that was well equipped to avoid weather or physical dangers and that the pilot was highly qualified. He absolutely ruled out any possibility of an accident and pointed fingers at Khartoum for his allegation of assassination. Southern leadership, including Madam Rebecca Nyandeeng herself, wisely accepted the version of an accident, which averted a crisis, elements of which were revealed where violence erupted with South Sudanese to what they assumed was the assassination of their beloved leader.

In Rumbek, I was approached by Dr. Lual Achuek Deng, one of the organizers of the funeral program, who informed me that I would be called upon to speak in Juba as a friend of Dr. John. I accordingly prepared my talking points and throughout the ceremony, which was attended by regional and international leaders, I anxiously waited to be called upon. But there were many speakers and time did not allow for me to speak. But back in the United States, I would attend numerous events commemorating Garang's death on which I was called upon and used the talking points I had planned for the Juba funeral.

A few days after the burial of John Garang, I met with Salva Kiir. I told him that the death of John Garang was God's act, but that it was public knowledge that he and Garang had serious differences over the running of the Movement. I said that it was now for him to correct what he thought was wrong with Garang's leadership and to do what he believed was the right way. I said that Garang was a strong leader, but that the South had also been divided under his leadership. He on the other hand was known as a man with the qualities that would favor unity and reconciliation. It was now for him to unify the different factions that were dividing the country. Kiir listened very attentively and then responded in agreement, "I will reach out even to those who stood with Garang against me." He specifically mentioned Nhial Deng, whom Garang was said to want to replace Kiir as his deputy.

I also recalled to Kiir what I had told John Garang about sharing the responsibilities of leadership and how he had told me of the assignments to the three clusters led by the three colleagues and how they had not delivered on the assignments. That was when Kiir disputed what John had said and told me that he had indeed delivered his report to John.

After the death of John Garang, Pieng remained actively engaged in the implementation of the CPA in its various aspects and phases. His specific area was security and the military, with a focus on the formation and management of the Joint Integrated Units – JIUs: "After we deployed all the Joint Integrated Units into all the towns, including Abyei – which had a battalion, it was a plan that we must make sure that all the JIUs entered into their deployment so that we urge the SAF to go out from all the areas. So we were very serious, and prepared JIUs all over, before even the signing of the agreement, because the agreement on security arrangements was signed earlier and we were prepared. It was not very difficult for us because we had the metrics of the days and months, including our schedule of withdrawal from Eastern Sudan, Blue Nile and Abyei; it was something fixed in the security arrangements and ceasefire.

"The good thing was that I was a member of the SPLA in the Joint Defense Board and Ceasefire Political Commission, and one of those who were effectively participating in the design of all security arrangements. It was very easy for me. This is why I was supported to represent the SPLA in those bodies, because most of those who were in the Joint Defense Board were the deputies and chiefs of general staff and intelligence of both armies, but we made the point that the operations officers also be members."

The agreed Referendum itself became a subject of intense controversy at both the regional and international levels. Khartoum continued its campaign against it and, in particular, the risks of potential Southern independence. They argued that once the uniting opposition to the North was removed, South Sudan would be torn apart by tribal conflicts. It would become a failed state and a source of instability in the region. I remember intense discussions with the leadership of the African Union, including the Secretary General and the Panel of the Wise, and with IGAD leaders, all of whom argued that the independence of South Sudan would set a bad example for the African Continent and the Horn Region. Even the Secretary General of the United Nations was apprehensive about the Referendum and the potential of South Sudanese independence. After a long discussion, he asked me to write him a note on the issue, outlining my arguments in favor of the referendum and respecting the will of the people of South Sudan. I wrote a piece which I later included in my short book, *Sudan at the Brink,* on the challenges of unity and self-determination in the Sudan.

Although African leaders were generally adverse to the prospects of Southern Sudanese secession, the late President Julius Nyerere, with whom I developed a warm relationship, used to say that the case of Southern Sudan should be an exception to preserving colonial borders. When the IGAD leaders first undertook their mediation initiative, I had a long meeting with President Isaias Afwerki who asked me why Garang was for the unity of the Sudan. He said that as refugees in the Sudan, they had closely observed the racial discrimination in the Sudan. He said that the Arabs of central Sudan were the first-class citizens, followed by the non-Arab Sudanese of Western Sudan. They, the refugees from Eritrea and Ethiopia, came as third-class, while South Sudanese came last as fourth-class citizens. Why would they want to be in such a discriminating unity? I gave him a detailed explanation of the position of the SPLM/A and that Garang was not as committed to unity as he might appear and that secession remained the option Southerners generally wanted. He understood. The late Prime Minister Meles Zenawi of Ethiopia, with whom I also developed a close relationship, also supported the cause of the South. When I once heard him speak in public in Washington against the risks of Southern independence, I approached Afwerki and asked what that contradiction meant. He told me not to worry and that Meles was fully supportive of the South.

My main arguments for holding the referendum on time and respecting the outcome was to invoke the theme of the famous sub-title of Abel Alier's book, *Southern Sudan: Too Many Agreements Dishonored*, and make the point that if that latest Agreement was dishonored, no other agreement would be possible between the North and the South in the Sudan. Besides, I asked what reasons would lead to the collapse or failure of an independent South: Would they be internal or external, and could they be prevented?

As the date of the referendum was approaching, the United Nations organized a symposium in Khartoum about the prospects of giving national unity a chance and asked me to give an opening statement. I argued that it was too late to give unity a chance. But I was urged to address the meeting, if only to make that point. I did address the symposium and made my arguments for why it was too late to make unity attractive, but stipulated what could be done, even at that late hour, to improve the grim prospects of unity. This meant expanding the principle of 'One country, two systems' into 'One country, multiple systems' to cater for the demands of all the regions of the Sudan. When I made that point to the Secretary General of the U.N. his response was that providing for two systems within one country was bad enough, which for him ruled out the wisdom of multiple systems within one country.

Ironically, while I was in Khartoum for the symposium, I had an intense discussion with people who argued for the postponement of the referendum in order to give unity a chance. A prominent South Sudanese who had been one of the leading proponents of Referendum with the prospects of Southern independence, also now opposed holding it at the scheduled time because of the fear that the country would be torn apart by ethnic conflicts. His reason was that he could not recommend Southern independence if it would mean continuing the conflict with the North or risk tearing the South apart through tribal warfare. I asked him whether he was implying that the South should remain under

Northern domination to avoid the risks associated with independence. His answer was that he did not mean that. But the alternative was never clear. I dismissed all that as part of Northern strategy, but in retrospect, in view of what the South has suffered since independence, his fears were prophetic. I did convey my concerns to the leadership of the South, and I was consistently assured that, "We will not be a failed state." I argued, "Let us not be complacent; let us prove the skeptics wrong every day." While my concerns and views were politely received, they obviously had no impact.

I subsequently published the book, *Sudan at the Brink,* in which I included my keynote address to the UN pre-referendum symposium in Khartoum. In that statement, I saw independence to be unavoidable, and began to advocate post separation cooperation between the two independent neighboring countries. Until the end, the option of independence was still controversial and indeed undesired by the international community. Even as close a friend as Meles Zenawi, with whom I had developed a close relationship and shared the same views on the situation in our region, surprised me when he said that holding the referendum was a decision that had serious ramifications and had to be very carefully considered, implying some reservation on the prospects of Southern secession.

What our people do not seem to fully realize is that it was the United States, and specifically President Barack Obama, that eventually turned the international tide. Prime Minister Zenawi was speaking at a side event in the United Nations General Assembly in October 2010, which he jointly hosted with the U.N. Secretary General Ban Ki-moon, attended by world leaders, including the Heads of State of our subregion. With some arm twisting, it was decided that the referendum should be held on time and the will of the people of South Sudan should be fully respected. But Prime Minister Zenawi's caution was shared by most African leaders.

The Dilemmas of Flawed Elections

Despite the obvious indicators that South Sudanese would vote for independence, Khartoum still hoped that unity had a chance and worked hard to influence the referendum. The ruling Islamist National Congress

Party, NCP, was particularly active. In his Memoir, Pieng addresses the situation in the highly controversial elections of 2010 and the remarkably unanimous vote for independence in the referendum: "Up until 2010, when elections were about to take off, it was really very unfortunate that we discovered that the SPLM was not organized. We learned of the preliminary selection of SPLM candidates, and they formed electoral colleges to select the nominees. That was unfortunate and sad. Those who were in the electoral commission were not real members of SPLM. Our comrades who were tasked to organize SPLM had not done a good job. Many were unhappy with SPLM. And many who were knocked out by the electoral college decided to run as independents. Our intelligence informed us that SPLM was going to lose in most constituencies, including for governorships.

"We were concerned that NCP was coming with money to rig the elections. So, the SPLA command decided to tour the states so that we did not allow the NCP to succeed in rigging the elections and when the referendum for independence came. We divided ourselves as army command: Comrade James Hoth and other comrades went to Upper Nile; Comrade Mamur and myself went to Bahr el Ghazal and Bentiu; and Comrade Biar and Kuol Deim went to Jonglei and then Equatoria. We went to mobilize our people and make sure that they voted in the referendum. That was our idea. And it was true that without our going around, most of the SPLM candidates would have lost. And if others had been elected, we could not have been sure of the unanimous vote for independence.

"Our group started with Rumbek and found that the NCP was the one in charge, and someone called Maluil was going to be the Governor. And we found that one of our wounded heroes was his bodyguard. I won't go deeply into what we did, but just to say that we influenced the situation there. We also went to Western Bahr el Ghazal, Aweil, and Wau, and found that things were not good. The SPLM never worked on the ground there because they believed that the legacy of the SPLM/A was going to make people vote for them. They forgot that the work that had been done during the struggle was really associated with individuals whom people knew by name. So, if those who were famous during the war ran as independents, they would win. The electoral college could not select the real SPLM/A and the election proceeded in a way that was not easy.

"The elections were not as fair as people might have wished, but we did not rig them, although we did influence the result, by making sure that we advised people. We still suspected that the Sudanese Government and SAF military forces would try to interrupt the referendum, which is why some of us did not stay in Juba during the elections and the referendum. I was in Bentiu, where we thought the SAF would start fighting before the announcement of the result of the referendum. I remember that the day of the declaration of the results, and even the Independence Day, I was not in Juba; I had to be out where I thought SAF would start fighting.

"On the 9th of July, when independence of South Sudan was formally declared, I was with Taban Deng Gai in Bentiu and the soldiers started shooting in the air. They even included Comrade Taban's bodyguards. Disapproving of their conduct as a violation of discipline, Taban ordered them to be lashed. I remember one person, while he was being lashed, singing a song in which he said, 'If you kill me today I will be happy because it will be said that I was killed on independence day.' So I told Taban, 'You should allow them to be happy because there is no way we can control them.' Our people were very excited."

The Independence Declaration was a momentous event. I was then U.N. Secretary General's Advisor on the Prevention of Genocide and had been included in his delegation which went to Juba to attend the celebrations. The President of the U.N. General Assembly also attended, and it was said that it was the first time for both to be absent from New York and attending the same event together. The occasion was well attended by prominent figures from around the world. It was as though the whole of Juba was out in attendance. In a blazing heat, they filled the John Garang Mausoleum marching in different formations or performing their tribal dances. I recall feeling very ambivalent about the event. On the one hand, I shared the jubilation of the people of South Sudan that they had at long last achieved their dream for which they had struggled for half a decade and even longer. On the other hand, I felt that we had abandoned the people of Southern Kordofan and Blue Nile who had been staunch allies in the struggle and who were now left to languish under the Arab-Islamic domination from which they had fought jointly with the South to liberate themselves.

I recalled John Garang telling me that some Southerners wanted to disentangle the South from the cause of these areas that they still saw as part of the North that had dominated the South. He told me that he disagreed and emphasized that without the role of the people of those areas in the liberation struggle, the South could not have achieved what they got in the agreement. He also told me that some mediators and Southerners wanted the case of Abyei to be deferred to be addressed later, rather than be tied to Southern independence. He said he strongly disagreed and argued that if Abyei was left out of the Agreement, the South would lose the area forever.

The situation had been resolved through a Protocol that provided for a vague stipulation of popular consultation for the people of the two areas to determine the system of administration they wanted to run their own affairs within a United Sudan. The case of Abyei was also to be resolved through the Abyei Protocol that stipulated that the Ngok Dinka would be given the right to determine through a referendum whether they remain under the administration of the North to which they were annexed in 1905 for security reasons or revert to the South, the same right which had been granted to them by the 1972 Addis Ababa Agreement that was never implemented. Neither the Protocol of the two areas nor the Abyei Protocol has been implemented.

I had been to both the Nuba Mountains and Southern Kordofan before the referendum in the South. In my public meetings with the people, the view was strongly stated that they could not see the South choosing to separate and leave them under the domination of the North. They said that they saw South Sudan as their elder brother and wondered how an elder brother could abandon his younger brother in danger. But they said that if South Sudan became independent, they would continue their struggle and look to the South for support. But even then, I realized that if an independent South supported them, Sudan would not honor the independence of the South, but would indeed work to undermine Southern independence.

Despite my ambivalence at the independence celebrations, I was happy to hear President Salva Kiir say in his independence speech that South Sudan would not abandon those Northern allies and that they would support their cause through peaceful means. And that has indeed been what South Sudan, balancing between discreet support for the struggle of the people of the Nuba Mountains, Southern Blue Nile and

Darfur, with a more open support for a negotiated settlement with the central government within the framework of national unity. And on Abyei, although Khartoum has impeded the implementation of Abyei Protocol, Juba has been treating Abyei for all intents and purposes as an integral part of the South, despite the yet unresolved status of Abyei between the two Sudans.

Indeed, the leaders of Abyei in the SPLM/A remained active in the independent South Sudan as full citizens of the country. Pieng's role in the military and security sectors, and that of other Ngok personalities in South Sudan, as elaborated in his account, remained prominent: "After independence, we started to do many things. We worked on developing the National Anthem. It was we in the army who decided to do that. We organized a committee under General Kuol Deim Kuol, who was in charge of the Political Orientation of the Army. He exerted effort with his team and involved many sectors of our society, including universities. They eventually came out with the National Anthem.

"Also, during the transitional period, there was an issue of the flag. I thank the gallant forces of the SPLA who made it possible for the former flag of the SPLA to be the flag of South Sudan. But it was not easy. When the South Sudan Assembly was opened, it was the Sudanese flag that was on the Assembly building. We were all invited to the Assembly. Some officers decided to bring the flag of the SPLM. While Comrade Salva was still in another office, and Comrade Riek was the one who first came into the Assembly, those officers came with a big flag and put it behind in the background, behind the seats of Comrade Salva and Speaker James Wani. All the people stood up and started singing SPLA songs. They went and got a police officer and told him to salute that flag. They took down the Sudanese flag and put up the SPLM flag. Comrade Riek said, 'Those officers should be arrested.' Comrade Salva said, 'Leave them.'

"When those officers heard what Riek had said, they went at night and put the SPLM flag on the doors of all the offices, including Salva's and Riek's. Later on, we influenced the Assembly, and the flag was passed to become the flag of South Sudan. It was decided that SPLM could look for another flag or make a logo in the middle of that flag. This was an achievement of the SPLM/A cadres. Our argument was that it was the flag of most of our heroes who were shot fighting carrying that flag.

There was no other way we could honor them – that flag had to be up. "So, both the National Anthem and the Flag were our initiatives."

An Episode of Return to War

Pieng describes the developments that triggered a violent confrontation between the now two independent Sudans, including the infamous confrontation over the Heglig (Panthou) oil fields. "Everything was going well, but in 2012 some unexpected developments happened. It started in 2011 when the South separated from the North. SAF forces occupied many oil fields in Unity State. When that was reported to us, and immediately after the Declaration of Independence, SAF decided to redeploy their forces to our areas. Upon receiving the report, I went there to confirm and found that SAF was still controlling more than fourteen oil fields north of Unity State. We agreed that the matter could be discussed politically. But at the beginning of 2012, SAF deployed a small force that encroached into our areas. Although there was an agreement that our forces should pull out some distance from the border, instead of redeploying towards their own areas, they deployed towards our areas, close to our military position. That sparked the fight for Heglig and other areas.

"We discerned their plan to occupy the oil fields. We notified our forces, including Comrade Mamur, who is my friend, and who would sometimes come as head of moral orientation. And then there was Comrade James Gatduel and Santino Deng Wol, commander of Division Three, and Andrea Dominic Commander of Division Five. We thought that it was very important for us to make sure that SAF did not advance to the oil fields. It was not something decided by our political leadership. It was not even decided by the leadership of the Army. But it was between me and the commanders who agreed that we had to show SAF that it was not acceptable for them to occupy those areas. Our forces were at Pan Akuach on the axis of Heglig (Panthou), whose real name is Alich, but is mispronounced as Heglig. Some people believe that Panthou is connected to the tree Thou, but the real name is Alich. So our forces of Division Four attacked that outpost that came into our territory. They dislodged it to their area. Instead of SAF going back, they tried to get reinforced by nearby forces, which sparked the fight.

"Now, monitoring our soldiers became a problem and we thought that Division Four could be reinforced by Division Three and Five. But we also attacked areas near to those Divisions, and it became a wider fighting. So, Comrade Mamur went to the Heglig axis and I was in Division Three Areas, including Abyei, Aweil and Raja. We managed to capture all those areas up to Heglig and we were advancing. We wanted to preempt the enemy reinforcement, and we decided to send forces through Mayom, to Nhianyagany (which the Missiriya call Baloma) and on to Diffra (Kech for the Dinka). We would then fight from the side of Muglad. We captured the bridge along Kiir in Aweil area and headed towards Meirem. I moved from Raja, and we captured Kafi Kenji and those areas where SAF was south of River Kiir. We were going toward Sungu and Hofrat el Nahas and that scattered the efforts of Sudanese army. It was not easy, but we chopped them up. But then the commander of UNISFA called me saying, 'Your forces have entered and are now in Nhianyagany on the road from Abyei and Meirem going to Diffra. Can you ask your forces to go back because this is creating a problem for us.' So, international pressure ended that showdown.'

On the downside, differences within the SPLM/A began to emerge after Garang's death and especially after the independence of the South. And as always, Pieng was in the thick of that development too. "As soon as Comrade Salva took over, there were those elements of Yei 2004 (confrontation between him and Garang) that tried to come around him, but he tried to distance himself from them, especially in 2007. At those times, they always tried to create rumors that the army leadership always tried to make coups. We continued in that way but could not resolve or end that accusation until in 2012, when he relieved most of us and remained with only a few. He did not assign us, except for me, whom he assigned as Inspector General of Police."

Toward the end of Pieng's memoire, by no means the end of his life story, Pieng addresses the challenges he faced as Inspector General of Police, shifting the focus from his war experiences to what should be a peaceful preservation of law and order but is sometimes ambivalently feared as a source of insecurity. Pieng presents details of the controversies on such issues as the police law, car registration, plate numbers, professional training of the police, and the competition between the central government and the states over the control of the police. These issues are in many ways elements of a technical field that is less dramatic than the accounts of battles in war.

But the police are often the most consequential in the lives of the citizens and therefore paradoxically both less connected with political power and yet the most directly linked to the peace and security of the citizens in daily life. The police can either be the protector or the persecutor of the citizen. Pieng had a glowing reputation among international actors who interacted with him during their visits to Southern Sudan. Upon their return, many would report to me in my capacity as the Representative of South Sudan to the United Nations and without knowing my connections with Pieng, would speak about him in raving praise for what he was trying to do and to which they committed their support.

Even after he left the army, Pieng remained connected with what was going on at the level of the leadership. The tensions and rivalries among the leaders continued and became worse after independence. According to Pieng, "The same elements came around President Salva Kiir. Some even held positions in his office and other areas and became more active. Rumors always started to come against many of the cadres of the Movement. In earlier 2013, I remember that Comrade Taban Deng Gai went to America and was looking after possible investors for his state, Unity State. As soon as he came back it was rumored that Taban was agitating against the President and was meeting the Americans for regime change. He was relieved upon return. Some other governors were also relieved. All this was happening on the basis of rumors. And people were busy crafting those rumors.

There is a Dinka folktale which goes like this: 'Once upon a time, all the animals disappeared; only the Elephant and the Hyena remained in the forest. The Hyena could not kill the Elephant to eat. So, he thought of camouflaging himself with mud so that he looked the same color as the Elephant. The Hyena was moving with the Elephant, and he would always come near the baby of the Elephant. Each time the big Elephant turned away the Hyena would bite the baby Elephant. The baby Elephant would cry, and the big Elephant would come back to look. Upon seeing blood on the body, it would hit the baby and kill it. The Hyena would eat the baby and keep following the elephant. For some time, the Elephant realized that her babies were finishing. She decided to cross the river; but Hyena had forgotten that mud could be washed off and followed the Elephant. When they arrived at the other side of the river, the Hyena was exposed and was killed by the Elephant.'

"So, I thought that elements of the NCP had put on Hyena's skin and had come disguised as the SPLM/A and started to bite the children of the elephant, which are cadres of the Movement. They wounded them through rumors, alleging that they are thieves, among many other accusations. Whenever Comrade Salva would hear his cadres being accused of things, he would immediately sack that cadre as an enemy. That became the case in 2012 and 2013. This is when I started to see the disorganization of the SPLM. It is not the real decision maker and the ruling party that are responsible; most of the decisions and initiatives were taken on individual and personal bases. That was why the committees that were being established were not part of the SPLM Secretariat. So, decision making was taken away from the Secretariat. There was no consultation with the Secretariat of the Movement. I discovered that most of the cadres who were ministers and holding constitutional positions didn't even know where the Secretariat was."

Tearing the Country Apart

Pieng's account then focusses on the misunderstanding that led to the crisis in the Movement which triggered the 2013 fratricidal conflict from which the country is still suffering. "It was rumored that Riek Machar wanted to contest the leadership with the President. The same was alleged of Pagan, Wani, and Rebecca. All were rumors. When we learned about this, we knew there would be a problem. So, I met with my friend, James Hoth and Taban Deng Gai, who had been relieved. We had been advising him to be calm. We decided that we should talk to the President. So James Hoth and I approached the President, and requested that we all talk to Taban. The President accepted. So, all of us, myself, James Hoth, Taban and Salva met in his office. Taban explained himself. And Salva said there was no problem, 'I have no bad intention, and I want you to come into the center of the SPLM.'

"But when the rumors of the SPLM cadres who wanted to compete intensified, we also took another initiative. Comrade James Hoth talked to the President, Riek and others, and he coordinated a meeting with the President. Hoth was touring the forces, but when the time came, he called me and said, 'The meeting of the leadership is tomorrow, and you must attend it.' I was in Rejaf graduating some trainees who were in a course with my Minister, Allison Mogai. When I was called, I took permission from the Minister. I went running to J1. Most of the cadres of the Movement attended, except for James Wani who was on a mission. Comrade Rebecca was also not in the meeting. Everyone else was there – Salva, Pagan, Deng Alor, Mayom Akec, Nhial Deng, Oyai, Gier, James Kok, Kosti and many others. When the meeting started, the President, in his capacity as Chairman of the SPLM, said he could not chair the meeting, and it should be chaired by James Wani. But as he was not there, Deng Alor should chair. So, Deng chaired the meeting and introduced the topic. The President said he had nothing to say and suggested that we should hear those with complaints."

"Riek Machar started talking about his six points of the President's failure, that the chairman had failed, and so he had decided to contest the leadership. Then Pagan said, 'I don't have an intention to contest, but we heard rumors that you do not plan to contest in the next election. So, if James Wani or Riek Machar is the alternative to you, I will contest. But if you want to contest, I have no problem.' James Wani, who had joined the meeting, also concurred, 'If the rumor is true that you are not going to contest then I will run against Riek Machar, but if you want to contest, I will be your running mate.'

"I spoke, 'You should all be proud that you have succeeded and made South Sudan to be an independent country. I don't think that the things Riek Machar has mentioned should be put on one person. We should all talk among yourselves and address those issues. I don't think there is a big problem in terms of human rights, or the things mentioned by Riek. As leaders, any failure by anyone among you will affect all of our people. So, there is no reason for you to blame any failure or anything on others. So, I implore you to come together and leave this issue about who will contest. It is anyway still far away in 2015; it is not something to decide now.'

"After all this talk, there was no clear position because Comrade Salva did not really express himself. All he said was, 'It is your right to contest, and I will be ready to contest against you people.' But there was no clear message. Comrade Riek was also not having a clear position as he did not say, 'I have changed my position and am ready to work with Comrade Salva.' After that meeting, we learned that the President had relieved the whole Cabinet, including his Vice President. With all the rumors and that meeting, he took back all the powers that were delegated to Riek Machar. Even the Committee that Riek Machar was leading – the Peace and Reconciliation Committee – was taken away from him and given to Archbishop Daniel Deng Bul."

I came to Juba shortly after the dismissal of the Cabinet and met with the President. Even before coming to Juba, I was telling people that I believed the President was reacting to what he saw as the perception that he was weak and wanted to show them that he was not. To my surprise, that was precisely the reason he gave me, almost word by word. He even appeared to relish his showing them that he was not weak. With a sense of drama and humor, he referred to a military strategy of massively attacking the enemy, with demoralizing effect. He said they were now moaning helplessly in their houses unable to do anything.

I told him that what he told me was precisely what I had been telling people. I also said to him that I had been telling people, that if I were to advise you, I would say that while your reaction is understandable, you should not allow your enemies to change your character. I said that he was known as a calm, cool-headed person, and that he should not allow that characteristic to be changed by angry reaction. He nodded his head and said that he would reach out to them in time.

I also met with Riek Machar, who surprised me with his apparent calm and magnanimity, stating that it was the President's constitutional right to reshuffle his government. He, however, alleged that the President was becoming dictatorial. When I reiterated to him what I had told both Garang and Kiir, that our culture was an egalitarian one that would not allow dictatorship, Riek commented, "Could you please remind Salva Kiir again?" Pagan Amom also told me that he was convinced that President Kiir wanted to rule as a dictator. Several times, I found many of the ministers who had been dismissed congregating in Deng Alor's house, brooding over the situation and predicting a violent explosion in the country. Several times, I asked what would cause the explosion and whether it could be prevented. Deng Alor repeated my question a number of times, but no response came from any one of them. Developments would soon prove them right.

Pieng's account of the developments resumed: "It now became obvious that the cadres of the Movement had not been seeing the danger of neglecting the SPLM. Now, once relieved, they began to be a group of individuals who were not using the SPLM institutions. They were not paying attention to the mistakes of the elections. They were following what was happening when some elders tried to approach everything as community based. Communities became more effective than the SPLM itself. All of these individuals were in power as ministers, but they never talked about this problem because they all thought that their communities had brought them into their positions, not the SPLM. That was a mistake that began to affect not only the Movement, but also the whole country. All political cadres never thought of transforming the SPLM into a real political party. Their interest was each to get a position and that was the end.

"We should not single out for blame the Chairman, Comrade Salva, because since 2005, those who held constitutional positions were mainly cadres of the Movement. But because they were not organized or not serious to develop the Party, the SPLM, they now started to feel the failures of the Movement and placed them solely on the Chairman. They, therefore, decided that they had to challenge Salva. As Inspector General of Police I learned that the leaders of the Movement were going to have a press conference. It was rumored that the National Security would stop them. I said in our security meeting, 'If they do it outside the Party premises, then there is a need for us to inform them that they needed to ask for permission. But if they were meeting in the SPLM House, then that was an internal Party issue. Whoever would hold or attend a Press Conference would be up to them. But we had to make sure that there would be no chaos. We agreed with the National Security on that. And I contacted some of them, and they agreed that they had to hold the meeting within the SPLM House. That was a turning point, and I hoped that the matter would stop there and that they would challenge each other inside the Party.

"Although we were not following their political moves, we learned that there was a disagreement within the Party about the meeting in Juba. Some wanted it to be that of the Liberation Council. Others disagreed and wanted the Political Bureau to meet first. This is where they differed. There were documents, like the Constitution, that needed to be passed. Whatever their internal differences, our concern was security."

"Comrade James and I had been trying to go between the President and some of the cadres in the Party. We managed to coordinate a meeting. It happened that when the meeting was scheduled, Comrade James was not in Juba. The President called me and asked to take the comrades to him for a meeting. Those who had been dismissed were there. I brought Oyai, Chuang, Mijak Agot, Mayom Akec, and Taban. President Salva told me to also call Deng Athorbei. We started the discussion before dinner. People enjoyed themselves. We were happy. Comrade Salva said 'Although I have dismissed you, it is not the end of the world. I want some of you to help me reorganize the Party and for some of you to be in the leadership of the Party and others to serve in foreign missions. There are now no senior people in the Party.' Comrade Mayom Akec said, 'There is no problem with us to be dropped from the Government. It is as though you have dropped us from the car, and you are now riding with others. But never let them open the boot, because they might destroy the engine. When you are ready for us, come back and get us.'

"The meeting ended with good resolutions. The President charged the comrades to go and write up everything that was agreed he should do and take it back to him in three days. We then had a late dinner and started drinking until very late at night, almost three o'clock in the morning. We then departed and went to the house of Mayom Akec. I was told that in three days I should collect what the President had asked them to do. After three days, I tried to go to the President. But the meeting with him kept being delayed. The morning of the day the meeting was finally arranged, I learned that many people were curious and wanted to know what the meeting had been about. Then my minister, Aleu Ayeny, said to me, 'I heard that you took those people to the President?' I said, 'Yes.' He said, 'There is no need for reconciliation. You are making a mistake.' I said, "If there is any way to stop the situation erupting into fighting, we should do that." And I left. I went to collect the proposal from those people. I was called to the office of the President. He said, 'If you can convince your minister, why not ask him to come so that he can be present in our discussion.' I said, 'No problem.'

"But I knew then that my minister was the cause of the delay in my meeting the President. He and I went to Wau. So, while we were in Wau, I went to his room and told him about the meeting with the President.

He asked, 'When?' I said, 'The President said the day after tomorrow. So, we can go back to Juba tomorrow.' He said, 'It's ok.' So, I arranged the plane, thinking that we were going to Juba together. But in the morning, I saw all his vehicles were packed. When I asked him, he said, 'I want to go home and make a sacrifice; then I'll come.' I said, 'But there is an important meeting.' He said, 'I will come.'

'Upon arriving back in Juba, I realized that the President was not interested in meeting those comrades. So I spoke to Comrade Malong, and we conducted many meetings to try to avoid problems. We met with Oyai and Taban. James was engaging Riek Machar and the President. Comrade Malong organized dinner in his house, and he called us – me, Oyai and Taban – and the four of us discussed this issue thoroughly. It was not easy. There were sharp disagreements and tension was high. Comrade Malong even said to Taban and Oyai, 'You get out of my house.' Comrade Oyai said, 'You are Nilotic...how can you invite us for food and then chase us out of your house?'

"But we made some progress. There was going to be a rally at the Mausoleum, but we were concerned about security and were not going to allow it. But the organizers said, 'If you want us to call off the rally, then convince the President to have a Political Bureau meeting and not a meeting of the National Liberation Council.' We tried to persuade the President, but it was not possible. And we learned that the meeting of the Liberation Council was going to be held. I was told not to allow the Secretary-General of the SPLM to go to the meeting. I was not aware of the reason why he would not be allowed to attend the National Liberation Council Meeting. The Minister decided to send mounted vehicles of police to stop Comrade Pagan from going to the meeting. I went to him and said, 'There is no need for the police; I will go and convince him and make sure that he will not go. The police will draw unnecessary public attention.'

"When I went to talk to Comrade Pagan, his reaction was, 'Am I under arrest?' I said, 'There is no arrest warrant.' 'Then what about the police?' I said, 'I am just advising you not to go.' It was reported in the media that when Comrade Salva went into the hall, it was attended by those who had arranged the Press Conference. The environment was not good. The President did not greet Riek Machar. And in his opening remarks, he was very aggressive, not at all conciliatory. He was attacking

Riek directly. That was not healthy. We saw that the situation was not going to be easy. Rumors started going around Juba that the Dinka and the Nuer were going to fight. We did not see why it was being viewed in tribal terms, since those who held the Press Conference were mixed Dinka, Equatorian and other ethnic groups, with only three or four Nuers. I started to fear that if any gun shot was heard in a crowded place, people would kill each other. We became concerned and decided to prevent that from happening. Comrade James started going between Riek and Salva. They eventually agreed to meet and discuss, to calm the situation."

The situation was rapidly escalating and Pieng felt duty bound to take preventive action. "The day after the Liberation Council meeting, Comrade Malong and I went to Oyai to convince our people that they should not magnify the problem. When I came back home, I was called by Comrade Taban, asking me to talk to Marial Chinuong, who was the commander of Tiger Force, that there was a captain who had been arrested and that his arrest would create a problem. Marial assured me that there was no such arrest. I tried to convince Taban that there was no captain arrested. Then at around 10 pm I heard gunshots and the sounds of gunshots became many. The sound of gunshots came from the army barracks in Giyada, the headquarters of Tiger. I put on my uniform and went to my office and tried to find out what was happening. I discovered that there was fighting going on. We tried to coordinate to stop the fighting, but it was not possible. Fighting went on for the whole night."

Pieng's role as the General Inspector of Police and his lingering connection with the military, especially his colleagues and friends in the army, were converging. "In the morning, I moved with some of my police to Giyada (military headquarters) and found Comrade James and others. They confirmed that there was fighting. We saw the fighting going on. People were attacking where we were. I had two guns, 12.7, with me. It was good that those with those guns were former SPLA soldiers. They started fighting back. One of the bodyguards of Comrade Oyai, who was moving with James, was wounded there. He later died from that wound. It was difficult to know what was happening. We managed to stop that particular battle. But the fighting began to spread and became a general fighting, until the second day. I remained in Giyada, so that I could discuss with Comrade James. Malong joined us. We tried to address the insecurity situation. Information about the killings started to reach us, but it was very difficult for us to control the situation. It was such a serious situation that one could not have imagined that the problem could go to that extent."

The lingering problems between Aleu Ayeny, who had played a sharply divisive role in the 2004 confrontation between Kiir and Garang, and who was now the Minister of Interior and therefore Pieng's boss, emerged and came into focus. "One of my officers, Major General Marial Abur, called and told me that the Minister had ordered him to arrest some politicians. I asked him, 'Has he written a warrant of arrest?' He said, 'No'. I said, 'Then we cannot be involved. Let him go to the National Security. We cannot be involved. But I am coming.' I found the Minister there. I said, 'Minister, you have to give us a written warrant of arrest where you detail the charges.' He went and called an officer called Major General Sayid Abdel Latif, and gave him instructions. The police went to Gier Chuang and others. Gier called me and said, 'Some police have come to me and are asking me to go with them.' I said, 'You go, Sayid is a good officer and he cannot hurt you or anyone with you.'"

Despite Pieng's resistance, the Minister held a number of senior SPLM/SPLA leaders who had been central in the struggle. "They rounded up politicians who later became the Former Detainees or the G-10. I saw that only Pagan was not there. I called him and told him to stay at home or come to Buluk police. I called Taban and asked where he was. He said he was at Tongpiny. I asked him to come to the police headquarters. He said he was not sure of his life. He told me his whereabouts and I said, 'Stay there; I am coming for you.' But when I got there, he was gone. Later he called me to say that he had left town. He told me that the cars were somewhere, and that the keys would be delivered. The situation became very confused. It was the most difficult moment anyone could experience."

That night, the conflict was rapidly developing into a full scale civil war. "On 15th December, around 10 pm, the shooting started. And round 11 pm, Comrade James called me and said that his cousin, Rieth Director General in Ministry of Finance, left the house and had not returned. I called some of my officers and asked them to go around Leu junction in Gudele where he left the house. His driver was coming back from town and returning to Gudele when he was stopped by some people. His phone then went off. So, he left the house to find him. That was how the killing started. The officers could not trace the cousin of Comrade James. They reported that the situation was very confused in that area. They said, 'There are wild people who are stopping people, taking cars, and killing people.' This is why I could not deny that there was pre-arrangement. When all those things were happening, with the President dismissing the Cabinet and his Deputy, there were people saying, 'Let us see what will happen.' And from Riek's side some people were saying, 'We will show them.' Others from the other side, were saying, 'Riek will never repeat what he did in 1991.' So, that is why we were trying hard to stop the violence.

"So, the fact that the fighting started at 10 pm around the same time the cousin of James Hoth disappeared means that there were some people who were prepared. I am not in a position to share now how that happened, but there was a pre-arrangement that people were ready to do what they did. It was really very unfortunate. The next day, December 16th, the fighting continued. We were meeting with our colleagues in the army. It was unfortunate that the forces inside the town were not in a position to take decisive action to stop the fighting. In our meeting in the army base, I suggested to James, 'Your forces in town will not act; you should check other nearby forces who may be more organized than those in town.'

"Magri force was the nearest force which could do that. Comrade James asked Comrade Boutrous Bol Bol to send two companies from Magri. It is they who came and rescued the situation. That was the time when everything in the evening became somehow calm. That force was organized. That helped. But the situation remained unclear. Those fighting around New Site and Bilpam were also dislodged. Inside the town, no one was fighting in a conventional way; there were those who were killing people inside their houses."

Pieng's concern for the safety of the civilians was paramount and transcended jurisdictional barriers among the security forces and even narrow indication of sovereignty against UN protection. "There was an arrangement I made before this fighting for unified security forces in Juba, and for which I gave the commander of Tiger, Marial Chenwang, and two senior officers from the police, General Sayed Cholom and another senior officer of police, Didor, the assignment to coordinate with Tiger so that they could help control any situation that might arise. Some civilians were calling us, and especially me, to provide protection and I would direct those officers to rescue them. This is where the idea of going to the UN for protection came. Our capacities were overwhelmed. We, therefore, directed that if there were people near the UN compounds, who felt threatened, they should run to the UN. Those officers always directed people to the UN."

Pieng was also keen to ensure the safety of all those needing protection with no regard to ethnicity or political affiliation. But he willingly admits failures and shares responsibility for those failures. "What was important was that all the police officers and NCOs and men, especially from Nuer ethnic group, were brought to us at Buluk with their families. And we tried our level best to protect them. But unfortunately, we could not protect the rest. It was also unfortunate that one of the police stations in Gudele was used for the detention and slaughter of many people. This was a mark on the police and on me. In the UN report, the police would later be accused. We tried to manage the situation, although we did not succeed 100%. But it was unfortunate for us as the law enforcement agencies that we were unable to fully protect the civilians and their properties. It was shameful for the command, including me. I saw that as one of the first failures of my command that I could not fulfill what I was supposed to have done. More than 700-800 people were massacred in Juba, most of them during the first and second evenings."

Pieng elaborates with impressive candor the massacres that were committed as a result of the failure of the police to provide protection. "We tried to assess the situation in Giyada (the barracks), together with our army comrades, and arranged for Comrade Mac Paul as Military Intelligence Chief to send a force to Gudele 1, so that we could verify what was happening there. We got the report that there was a massacre in the police post there. The force got those mad people who did the massacre. That force fought with them and killed two from among those criminals. They got to the scene and found that it was horrible. They reported to us that many people had been killed. So, we decided that those bodies and all those killed should be taken from there to the hospital, where they would be verified. Two days later the bodies were rotting and could not be identified. That scene was terrible."

While the conflict was dividing the country on ethnic lines, Pieng's professional and personal relationships cut across those lines. His relationship with James Hoth, a Nuer, was and has continued to be, special. "I really appreciated the efforts of James Hoth, who was the Chief of General Staff by then. He was the first to lose a relative in those events. Most of those people killed were from Nuer, where he comes from. But he was still very strong and was trying to command the situation. We supported him to control the situation. But as much as we tried, the situation kept getting out of hand. Officers were acting out of command, but they behaved as if they were under command. They moved around claiming that they had met the President. Even relatives of the Leadership were assuming command. This was something that could not be understood. Comrade James was acting as a true nationalist. He did not allow himself to be negatively influenced by others. Some individuals, both Nuer and also Dinka, with certain tribal marks, were killed, and those trying to save their friends were also all killed." Once again, Pieng admits to sharing the guilt and the failure to prevent the massacres. "It really hurts me to say that I was one of the leaders charged with protecting civilians and their properties. Even now, I feel ashamed that we did not manage to defend those who died."

But objectively, Pieng and some of his colleagues did the best they could under extremely challenging circumstances. "We were always getting together as security organs. We discussed and decided to form an investigation committee and a court to punish those responsible for those serious crimes. As the police, we investigated all who were in the police who had been accused. We found that out of the 23 cases in which the police were accused, four happened in the areas controlled by the government and the rest happened in the areas controlled by the rebels.

"Before the crisis fully exploded, it was reported that Riek and Taban had left the town and were moving towards Mangalla. We would meet every day and explore the course of what we should do. We tried to talk to the people in Magri where there was a division." Ethnic loyalties undermined the command of senior officers. "We talked to Comrade Boutrous Bol Bol, who was the commanding officer, to maintain harmony among his forces. And we talked to another officer, Tito, in Mangala, to intercept the movement of hostile forces. Those officers were not telling us the truth. Boutrous said, 'Nuer forces under my command have already rebelled.' Then Tito Biel said, 'I am very firmly in control and still able to arrest Comrade Riek.' Later we found that Riek was received in Mangala by Tito and taken to Bor. Peter Gadet did the same thing, saying he was ready to arrest Riek. But other officers told us that Peter Gadet had already rebelled. We would tell those officers to hold firm, control the situation, and arrest Riek. All the reports were untrue and Riek reached Bor and senior officers were massacred in Pariak where Gadet had been. We have to accept that we can also be blamed for the death of those officers, because we were telling them to hold their ground and did not listen to them that Peter Gadet was a rebel. He killed them, then took over Bor, and massacred people in Bor. They were mobilizing the White Army from Lou area to join them in Bor. That was what happened."

The complexities and complications of ethnic loyalties were also rendered formidable by the fact that they were not clear cut as individuals of differing ethnicities also cooperated in defiance of those divisions. Pieng's cooperation with Hoth continued to rise above ethnic divides. "We were staying with James Hoth and tried to monitor the situation in Bentiu, where we were in touch with James Kong. He told us that he had a plan to evacuate all the non-Nuers in Division Four to Abiemnhom. He managed to take all those to Michael Dut Alier at Abiemnhom. But later, James Kong shifted to Riek. According to his testimony later, he said he shifted because as he tried to save the lives of those who were non-Nuer, there were orders coming from Juba to counter what he was trying to do. The tank operators who were Dinka were told by Juba, 'Don't leave the tanks unless you fight and are defeated.' He said that when he was returning to his headquarters, he was shot at. So, he ran from inside his HQ to inside Bentiu and that he was pursued, and those soldiers ran to Pariang with tanks."

Correlative to the divided and shifting ethnic loyalties was also the unreliability of information. "The situation all over Upper Nile had become confused as messages went out that Nuers were massacred in Juba and so all over the Nuer were revenging. In Division Three, commander Deng Wol, told us that the Nuer in his area were calm. We tried also to prevent other forces from getting involved in the crisis that was happening. But the situation was generally grave. When Riek reached Bor, they started to mobilize armed civilians. We were getting reports of attacks on Malakal and Bentiu. There were also the movement of the armed civilians to Bor so that they would advance to Juba."

The situation was getting out of hand for the government forces. "The rebels managed to dislodge our forces around Bor and were advancing. Comrade James tried to pull out forces from different areas to fight them in Bor, but we were not sure what was happening. Perhaps the morale was low among our forces. So those rebels were able to dislodge our forces with all the tanks. We were getting those reports. Riek's so-called White Army with forces that joined them, mainly from the Nuer ethnic groups, were moving toward Jameza. Our forces under General Malual Ayom were fighting. But it was not going well. In Juba, people were very worried."

As is now obvious, although Pieng was retired from the army and was now the General Inspector of Police, he continued to be actively engaged in the affairs of the army through his colleagues, and specially his friend, James Hoth, the Chief of General Staff. But there was a popular demand for him to get actively involved in the fighting. "Many people, including our citizens in Bahr el Ghazal, were asking, 'Where is Pieng?' And when they were told, 'He's around,' they would talk to me asking why I was not engaged. I would tell them that I was a police officer without an army to command."

But pressure on Pieng continued: "While I was in the office of James Hoth, an old man from Yirol called me. He just told me, 'Pieng, we hear that you are in Juba, and the enemy is going to Juba. What are you doing in Juba when the enemy is approaching Juba? Pieng, God always gives blessings to certain people. I am sure, if you now go, the enemy will not go to Juba. We beg you, we the civilians; we see that it is you who can do that.' I said to him, 'Why do you people always think that I can do miracles? I don't have forces. And I am not even in the Army. I am only helping the Command of the Army.' But I told him that I would think about it.

"About forty minutes to an hour later, the old man called again and said, 'Pieng, I am coming to Juba so that I talk to you. I am very serious.' He said that there was a spiritual message which God had revealed to him. He said that God had said to him, 'Pieng must go to the Front.' I said to him, 'That's okay; there is no problem; I will go.'"

Pieng eventually succumbed to the pressure. In a meeting with his colleagues in the command, he said that the problem facing the army was morale: "The morale of our forces has dropped, not because the enemy is strong, but maybe because the command is not harmonious and there is confusion. I see that somebody like me can help. I can be behind the commanders and help them by talking with the forces. This is the only way we can encourage our forces to continue fighting. If this enemy comes and they are armed civilians, however bad the situation is now, it will be much worse. Civilians will murder at random. They will go murdering people all over the city. They will destroy everything. They will even kill foreigners. That will be very serious for the image of the country called South Sudan. It will be the end of the state of South Sudan." Malong volunteered to join Pieng, "I will go with Comrade Pieng. We will go and help with mobilization from behind." James agreed. "We moved the same evening. And it was really going to be a disaster if we didn't move." Together with the field commanders, they contributed effectively to the efforts that eventually saved the situation.

Ambiguities of Superstition

The case of the elder who urged Pieng to join the defense against the forces of Riek in 2013 and claimed that God had instructed him to pass that message on to Pieng illustrates some of the ambiguities Pieng faced in his command that relate to the ambiguities of his soldiers' spiritual beliefs and related mental stresses in war. Pieng's account covers specific instances of such ambiguities of the belief system among his soldiers. One involved a dream: "Before the operation to take Western Equatoria, our soldiers had an unfortunate tendency to desert to their home areas. I arrested some of them and formed a court martial that decided to fire squad the soldier who was determined to be the ringleader. The situation began when one officer under me, Chol Tong, who commanded one of my task forces, reported to me that one soldier had complained to him of a dream that his own mother was going to die. In the dream, his mother said, 'If I die before you come, then you too will die.' The soldier went on to say that the same had happened to his father and other relatives before. So he took it seriously.

"Captain Chol asked me, 'Can we allow him to go?' I said, 'No, this is an example of people creating excuses to go home. Bring him to me.'

The soldier came and reported the same story to me. I said, 'You are lying'. I told Chol to put him under arrest. The soldier insisted, 'My mother is going to die within days and if I stay away for a month, I too will die.' After one month, I called him to me and said, 'Look, you have not died'. He said, 'I was not intending to go, but I was just telling you the truth.' I released him. And when we moved to ambush the enemy during our defense of Juba – Yei Road, he went as a machine gun operator. His task force, which was under Chol Thon was the first to ambush the enemy, as Chol was the most senior commander. I went with them and had my tactical headquarters behind them. The fight started. The first casualty was that soldier who had foretold his own death. A bullet passed through his head, and he was almost unconscious when his dying body was brought to me. I was shocked and felt guilty. If he was going to die, I felt that it was me who killed him. If I had allowed him to go, he would not have been killed."

Another incident involved a man who offered Pieng his daughter for a wife and although Pieng turned the offer down the old man blessed him and his soldiers before going for a fight, with puzzling consequences. "While I was moving towards Twich before the two battles, an old man in Apuk, who was thought to be a magician, was moving around the area with a young girl. I saw him for two days in the camp, where we were stationed, and I asked, 'What does this old man want, and why have you not brought him to me?' They said, 'Leave him to us. He has a problem that we will resolve.' I said, 'No, you are obviously not handling his problem. That is why he is still around.' They said, 'This old man has come with his daughter and he said he is bringing his daughter to you as a wife. And we are telling him that Commander Pieng is not interested.' I said, 'You bring him to me so that I convince him.' I then spoke to him and he told me why he had come. I tried to convince him and finally succeeded. Then he said, 'I know you will now fight. Let me bless you.' He had spears and other traditional spiritual objects. He said, 'You pass between my legs and spears; this is a blessing.' An officer from Yambio called Patrick asked, 'How can we do this when we are Christian believers?' I said, 'Let us just treat him psychologically and do as he asks.' I asked them to follow me, passing between his legs. One officer named Manute Ajang decided not to pass between his legs. The rest followed me. After that, we went for the first battle and I lost most of those officers, but not Manute, who was only wounded. The soldiers were angry and came back to the old man to try to kill him. I told them that there was nothing the old man had done. I told them that I did not believe in those traditional ideas, and that he had nothing to do with the deaths of our comrades. But I was really surprised why only Manute of all those officers survived. It is something I still remember, but I still believe that their deaths were not connected with what the old man had done."

Then there was the case of a beautiful woman whom a witch doctor warned against, and the soldiers wanted her killed. Pieng writes this about her: "I was near Raja supervising the operation when a certain woman came running from the town. She was apparently scared. But rather than try to assist her, the soldiers who were with me cocked their guns. One among them said, 'We must kill this woman!' I ordered, 'Do not kill her, she is a civilian.' Another person among them said to me, "Commander, this is a witch about whom our witch doctor warned us.' I was confused by this talk. I didn't know that while in Deimzuber our soldiers had gone to a witch doctor. He had told them, 'When attacking, there will be a beautiful woman who will come out of Raja; if you do not kill her, she will curse you, and the enemy will dislodge you.' That is why they wanted to kill her. But I stopped them. I told them, 'Keep her safe'. I protected her in the same way I would protect all civilians. She was taken to a secure place with our wounded. Although she was released, it was reported that she kept reappearing under mysterious circumstances, and the suspicions against her lingered on."

Finally, there was a cat which seemed to be a spiritual messenger. Pieng recalls, "We had intercepted an enemy message stating that there might be a chemical weapon attack. That idea scared some soldiers who spread it among the rank and file. That night a cat came to my room and remained there up until morning. Early in the morning, I discovered the cat had never left my room. So that reminded me of something that had happened to me twice before, once in Torit and again in Yei. In both cases a cat came in the evening and stayed in the room all night. And in both cases an Antonov came, destroyed my room, and killed the cat. It was now happening to me again in Raja. Even though I did not believe in those things, I told the soldiers to remain in their shelters with no movement. I too stayed away from my room. In the afternoon, the

Antonov came straight to us and started bombing our places. There were few casualties. And where I was, two of my soldiers were almost buried by shells. Although they lost their hearing, and were psychologically affected, we all survived, and they later recovered. Thank God, while the Antonov did come and bomb us, as both the intercepted message and the cat had predicted, there was no indication that there were chemicals."

Another instance had more to do with trauma and mental stresses in war rather than spiritual belief. Pieng received reports of one soldier whose behavior indicated mental disturbance. "Deng Kilai came to me and said, 'I have received a report that there is a soldier who has cocked his gun and has been moving with it for three days. People fear that his mental condition is not good.'" Pieng said, "Let his comrades watch him and disarm him when it is possible, so that he doesn't harm people." Captain Kilai tried to disarm him. "And just as I was about to rest, I heard heavy shooting and I realized it might be that same man. I moved from my place, but my guards tried to stop me, saying, 'There is someone shooting people!' They warned me. I said, 'How can we allow him to shoot people?' So, I moved in his direction and found that he was the only one firing bullets and no one wanted to shoot him because there were no orders.

"As I reached the scene, I was surprised to see a young lady tying two people together with a rope. One was the disturbed man. He had already killed four of his colleagues who had tried to disarm him. Then he moved on Deng Kilai to kill him. His plan, it seemed, was then to advance on to me. When Kilai saw him coming, he hid behind a tree and jumped on him and wrestled him to the ground. When he called for help, this young Nuer woman, who had been brought from the village as a wife to one of my officers, Peter Garwich, tried to tie the two of them with a rope. She managed to tie them and their guns as they wrestled. I took out the magazines of the guns, untied them, and tied again the man's hands, so that only he was captive."

Pieng called his officers and gave orders, "This man must face the fire squad." But Captain Deng Kilai, his task force commander, who had thought the man wanted to kill him, said, "Commander Pieng, if you kill this man now, you will lose the evidence." According to Pieng's account, "He was thinking there might have been more to the man's odd behavior than what we saw. He might have been part of a bigger conspiracy. If that were true, then killing him by firing squad would allow for the conspiracy to brew on further. So, we put him underground in a detention cell so that he would not run away." The man demanded to see Pieng, "I want to talk to Commander Pieng." When Pieng was informed, he agreed to meet him, but his soldiers objected, "For what? Leave him." Pieng said, "I want to know his problem."

So, Pieng went to him. "I knew that all those he killed were from his own area. I asked, 'Why did you kill your brothers?' He said, 'I had to kill them because you had sent them to kill me.' I said, "Why do you say that?" He said, "In the parade, you told us, 'You have to hunt those lions who used to attack your cows.' As you spoke, I saw Captain Kilai pointing his tongue towards me saying, 'I am the lion.' So, I knew that when you came back from the fight, you were coming to kill me. And this is why, when I heard the sound of the motorboat, and knew you would soon be crossing the river, I went and waited for you. But you were lucky you did not come first, otherwise I would have killed you just as you planned to kill me."

Pieng writes, "That was when I realized that the man was not of sound mind. But I also knew that he was among those people who had tried to desert together with the man who had been fire-squadded. So, that was the source of his paranoia. This is another thing I regret. It showed me how the consequences of our decisions can linger and grow, in ways that may be totally unexpected. Therefore, I learned the seriousness of decisions in command and not to take any decision lightly."

Other stories of mystical experiences related to dreams or spiritual revelations continued to haunt Pieng's operations. One dream by a colleague foresaw that Pieng would be killed in his Raja operations. Another related to an elder who claimed that God had told him that Pieng had to go to save the situation from the threat of Nuer assault on Juba during the 2013 internal war. Pieng never dismissed these superstitions lightly, although he did not believe in them either.

A Diplomatic Self Defense

In the wake of the 2013 conflict which the government determined to be an attempted coup, but which the international community saw differently, a meeting of all the ambassadors was convened, the objective being to brief our representatives abroad on what was officially labeled an attempted coup. The so-called Group of Ten who would later become known as The Former Detainees were in detention for their alleged role in the coup attempt for which they were to be formally charged. We were told by the Minister of Justice that the case against them was very serious and that nobody was allowed to visit them. Anyone wanting to visit them had to submit a written request giving reasons for wanting to see them. The application would then be considered on its merit and a decision made accordingly. The instruction was that we were to carry the message alleging attempted coup to the international community.

As the most senior ambassador, I became the virtual leader of the group. In my statement, I reiterated my familiar theme that foreign policy was an extension of domestic policy and that the effectiveness of an ambassador lay not in being well-spoken, but in being credible with a positive message on the basis of which to win external support for national policy. We visited the injured in the hospital with food supplies and two bulls to be slaughtered. I prayed in the Dinka fashion for the bulls to accept the sacrifice as they were going to die for a good cause, obviously a ritual of self-justification.

I requested a meeting with the President and it was granted. I found the President in a positive mood. We talked about the Detainees and I said to the President that since they were not being heard, there was no way of telling whether or not they they were with Riek. The President surprised me by saying that he did not think they were with Riek. I said that we had been told that no one was allowed to visit them, but that if I were allowed to meet with them, I would be interested to know where they stood and report back to him. He told me that I could visit them. "How?" I asked. He called his Security Minister, Mamur, to arrange it. While I was waiting to see the President, I met Deng Alor and Gier Chuong emerging from a meeting with the President. They were going to the airport to fly to Nairobi. The President of Kenya had offered to keep some of them under his protection, while four of them, whose offense was considered more serious, remained under detention in Juba. I went with Mamur to the airport to bid them goodbye and then proceeded to the detainees in Juba. Later, on my way back to the United States, I stopped in Nairobi and also met with those detained there. In both sets of meetings, I found that as the President had correctly observed, they did not support Riek Machar's resort to violence, even though they had serious concerns about the state of the Party and the country. I wrote a report to the President which I later included as a chapter in my book, *Bound by Conflict: The Dilemmas of the Two Sudans*.

The African Union intervened and mediated to end the conflict. Pieng was a member of the South Sudan delegation in the peace talks. After the agreement was signed, the issue of the increase in the number of states became one of the stumbling blocks that would continue to threaten the effectiveness and viability of the agreement. "When this idea of states arose, those who created the idea of more states – 28 and then 33 states – elders from the Jieng Council of Elders (3 of them) came to my office and talked to me about the recruitment of the police in those states. I told them that I was not in favor of creating many states and that the idea posed some legal problems. I said that there were no legal clear borders and that increasing the number of states would create problems between our people.

"They said, 'Although you don't want the additional states, it is now a reality. We can organize a meeting for you with all the members of the Jieng Council of Elders to explain the situation to you.' They set up a meeting at a hotel. Almost the whole Jieng Council showed up. I told them that I would never support such an idea. They wrote a strategy paper after that. In that paper, they called for my removal on the ground that I was against the policy. The President might have been aligned with their position. Before long, I was relieved, and I knew that they were behind that decision.

"In 2015, when the agreement was signed and the security arrangement workshop was called, I became a member of the government delegation to Addis to finalize the security arrangement. The person heading our delegation was Comrade Michael Makuei Lueth. Other members were Peter Beshir and me from the police and Comrade Malek Ruben from the army. On the other side were Taban Deng Gai and Simon Garwich. We were to sign all that had been agreed, including the implementation modality. We were supposed to sign the next day. In the evening, when I knew everything was okay, I tried to visit friends in Addis. Later, I was called by Sumbeiywa and Mesfin. They said I should go back to the hotel. I went and was informed that the delegation of Southern Sudan would not sign the next day as planned. I asked Comrade Makuei, and he said we were to send the agreement to the President and wait for him to tell us what to do.

"I said, 'Can you call the delegation for a meeting so that we discuss.' He did it in his room. I said that it was better for us to say that we did not want the agreement and that it was not good for us to say that we had to wait for our president to tell us what to do. We are technical experts; we should be the ones to advise the president, not the president to advise us. There is no reason why we should embarrass our country, our people and our leadership. Those from the army supported my position, and the other members of the delegation also agreed. We decided that we would surprise the mediators by signing. That was what happened the next day. Makuei declared our readiness to sign. Comrade Taban also declared that he was going to sign. Makuei Lueth declared that he would sign. We all signed. The whole hall stood up applauding. The mediators, Sumbeiywa specifically, came to me and said, 'What did you do?' I told them that we had discussed and agreed to sign.

"We went to Juba and briefed the President. The signing of the principals was to take place in Juba. The advance team was to come within seven days. The heads of state were to come a day later. But Makuei got up and said to the President that although we had agreed and signed, the advance team should not come yet because we needed to finalize the issue of the states. He said, 'If we don't resolve that issue now, they will come and confuse us and the signing will not take place.' I said, 'What Comrade Makuei has said is incorrect because we signed. So all must come and we take hold of the agreement.' Immediately the President shouted at me saying, 'No one will get us to do what we do not want to do.' Comrade Jadalla, my acting minister, said 'Just sit down.' Shortly thereafter it was announced that we would have twenty eight states and shortly after I was relieved."

Warring, Mediating and Learning

As might be expected of a movement embracing a wide variety of people of different backgrounds, ethnicities, political persuasions, ambitions, and rivalries of different kinds, tensions and conflicts are unavoidable. Here too, Pieng provided remarkable leadership as a wise mediator, sometimes between and among his superiors. He combined objectivity, frankness, and courtesy, with the ability to explore a convincing common ground for consensus and reconciliation. He always kept his eyes on the prize, the overriding goal of the struggle, the cause of the South. Ironically, although what motivated him was the cause of Abyei, throughout the struggle, his stated goal was nearly always the liberation of the South, of which Abyei was an integral part and parcel that did not need specific mention. Only once, when the Machakos agreed principles excluded Abyei from the self-determination for the South within the 1956 borders with the North did Pieng and other Ngok Dinka leaders in the movement come out in open criticism of their Southern Sudanese superiors in the movement. Even then, he made a calculated apology that did not compromise the cause for which he had taken up arms in the first place.

Although Pieng often mediated for a common ground, the role of a mediator in acutely divisive situations is never easy. The mediator is always confronted with the question, often not explicitly stated, as to which side he or she is on. Pieng struggled to avert the 2004 showdown between John Garang and Salva Kiir which might have fatally derailed the march to self-determination and Southern independence. Although he succeeded remarkably well, that mediation caused suspicions on both sides that lingered on and may have left permanent scars in the relationships. There are instances where Pieng introduces an anecdote but refrains from telling the story. And there are a couple of instances where he clearly saw his leader angry with him for reasons he did not know and does not speculate about. The tragedy is that personal differences that do not relate to the cause might seriously damage relations in a manner that might seriously damage the overriding common cause.

One evening in Rumbek, after the 2005 Comprehensive Peace Agreement was signed, I was invited to attend a meeting of the SPLM/SPLA leadership which was a preparation of the post-war responsibilities of governance. Pieng organized for me an informal get-together with his colleagues over drinks in the evening. As we sat in a large circle, one of them said, "Dr. Francis," – the South Sudanese way of combining formal titles with first names – "the people you see here are the core of the SPLA." He stressed the point by moving his hands around the circle to highlight every one of the seven or eight individuals who were assembled. Most of their names feature prominently in Pieng's story, which reaffirms the point I was told. Today, most of them have been dismissed or side-lined from positions of responsibility. Why? That is the question that seriously calls for an answer, as it points to the underlying cause for the crises affecting the nation, a cause for which these people had dedicated their lives and for which so many people died.

One of the moments when Pieng's anger and bitterness come across most powerfully was that incident in Gogrial when they lost a fight and many of their officers were captured by the enemy. The Governor of Warrap representing the Khartoum Arab-Islamic Government, against which they were fighting, was a Southerner. There was nothing surprising about that because the central government in the South was represented by Southerners loyal to the regime, although they often played a most challenging conflicting role between officially serving the interest of the enemy while privately safeguarding the interests of their people. What outraged Pieng about this particular incident was that the Governor gave instructions that he did not want to see any of the captives, a not so coded way of saying that he wanted them all dead. All those brave soldiers, who were sacrificing their lives for their people and country, were summarily executed. What still pains Pieng to this day is that the man who did that now holds a senior position in the post-war Government of independent South Sudan.

Pieng's book is a straightforward account of his war experience, told in a matter-of-fact manner, without theorizing or editorializing, only from time to time drawing some conclusions and lessons learned from specific events. It is the story of a man who is determined to fight, kill or risk being killed, and yet compassionately values the life of every one of his soldiers, treats the civilian population with great respect, and ensures the safety of captured enemy soldiers who no longer pose a threat. It is the story of courage combined with intelligence and respect for life and humanity. A battle for Pieng is more than a fight; it is planning which involves a great deal of intelligence, administration, and human resource management.

I once had an insightful conversation with John Garang about the complexity of warfare. I told him that my wife tells me that I became restless when I finished a book and before I started another one. John Garang told me that he felt the same with his battles. He then explained to me what was involved in fighting battles. The process, he explained, involves careful planning, meticulous execution of the plan, and a diligent follow up analysis that deals with the consequences, lessons learned, and implications for the next round.

One of the remarkable things about Pieng was that as he was fighting, he continued to learn from the battles he fought. "I learned something else during those battles. While we had no means of supply and transport, we did have proper organization. I had taken time to consult with all my senior officers and effectively planned. Before we went to battle, we selected two task forces for logistics. They were coming from far, so we faced the question of how to ensure that our food and ammunition did not run out as we waited for them. I realized then that those officers providing logistics were actually more important to the battle than those who were fighting. This is where I realized that the most important thing in war is how you organize your forces. After organization, the second most important thing is administrative preparation. Continuous logistics supply leads to success.

"Another lesson was that command is more important than personnel. For example, Lumumba, the second force after Nyachigak 1, was composed of many ethnic groups, such as Bari, Bor, Latuka, and many others, under Captain Deng Kilai. They did well under strong command with good fighters. Those commanders had gone with me to Cuba and were well trained. They managed to control their forces.

"The other thing I learned from these early experiences in battle is the importance of cooperation and understanding among the forces. I, with those officers, had achieved a common understanding, partly because we were from the same training group – Shield One. Although I was senior, we cooperated as colleagues. Whatever the case, they respected me, and I respected them, and we were friends. That was the secret of our success and it is an important learned lesson. In our ambush of the enemy, the enemy forces reported that we had tanks and mounted vehicles. This was not true, but the enemy could not imagine how we had put into position anti-tank artillery and other big guns without transport. The truth is that we had carried all that on foot because of pure determination. So, they believed that we had much more equipment than we actually had. This affected them psychologically, weakening their morale and giving us an advantage."

One of the qualities I find most remarkable about Pieng is that he seems to seamlessly reconcile contradictory characteristics. He was a warrior who was also committed to peace and reconciliation. He was a ferocious fighter who was also a peacemaker. He was an angry man who was also composed, calm, gentle and considerate. He looked for virtues even in his enemies. He was confident and proud, yet modest with glowing humility. He was a young man who respected his elders, even when he was their leader.

The Paradox of War and Peace

Pieng's memoir is one of two works I have recently read which provide insight into this paradox. Pieng's story illustrates the general understanding that there are causes that are worth fighting and dying for. The other book, *When Political Transitions Work: Reconciliation as Interdependence,* by Dr. Fanie du Toit, a white South African, argues that even the causes that are worth fighting and dying for can be pursued peacefully by agreeing to reconcile before the resolution on the basis of a credible commitment to negotiate a mutually agreeable solution. In other words, atrocious violence and devastating destruction can be avoided through credible understanding that a mutually agreeable solution can be found through peaceful and cooperative search.

This is a theme I will explore more fully in my conclusion to this collection of war experiences. The question that the history of war in the Sudan poses is whether such horrific destruction to life and property over prolonged periods is necessary when the just cause of the freedom fighters is so glaringly obvious? Again, the history of war in the Sudan shows that in the end a solution that addresses the problem must not only be found but was indeed predictable from the beginning. Is it lack of foresight and wisdom that accounts for such failure to address just causes in a timely way or is war itself a necessary eye-opener and a prerequisite to the pivotal value of justice?

The experiences documented in this volume indicate that going to war is not a necessary show of force by overzealous warriors, but a pursuit of justice and dignity that has no gender qualifications. While the story of Pieng reflects the standard view of war as a function of men who provoke it and suffer their consequences, women have always been partners in war, whether through morale boosting or by taking care of the victims of war. Although this may be indicative of the gender distribution of roles in which women are generally considered subordinate to men, modern wars, especially those that are fought with very destructive weapons fired from afar, shatter the old order and the stratification associated with it. Traditional roles that are based on physical strength and valor become relatively outmoded and a major restructuring becomes imperative. Women join men in war and perform functions that are in part a continuation of their traditional roles and in part stand at par with men as warriors. The following parts of this volume narrate the role of women in modern warfare alongside their male comrades in arms.

Awuor Deng Kuol

Awuor Deng Kuol

PART TWO
FIGHTING FOR RESPECT

The Rebellious Rage of Awuor and Awuor Deng

Introduction

PIENG DENG WAS PROVOKED into joining the rebellion that escalated
to an armed struggle against the Sudanese Government by the Sudan
People's Liberation Movement and its Army, SPLM/A, by the brutalities and atrocities he witnessed inflicted on his people by the security
agents of the oppressive Northern-dominated Arab-Islamic regime in
Khartoum. His half-sister Awuor Deng, who was later joined by her
sister, also called Awuor, was outraged into joining the rebellion by a
racist mistreatment by a Northern Sudanese teacher in Junior Secondary
School in Khartoum. Pieng saw what was happening to his people as
a personal assault that challenged him personally. Awuor saw what was
happening to her as part of what was being done to her people of the
South. Ultimately, Pieng's warring for justice and Awuor's fighting for
respect united in the collective war against denigration and humiliation
and the demand for human dignity with full recognition and equality.
How they would pursue the struggle would largely be one of comple-
mentarity based on their gender differences.

What is remarkable about Awuor's story is that it sounds like the
straw that broke the camel's back. It is not clear what the teacher meant
when Awuor asked her whether the word *ghuzlan* was a plural for either

word *ghazala* (gazelle) or the word *ghazal*, (romantic flirtation) and the teacher responded negatively by saying, "No" and then added "But that is the *mustawa,*" meaning 'level.' Awuor took that as a put-down, a demeaning insult. She explained that they were living in Khartoum and understood the meaning behind certain expressions. She was certain that the reference to *mustawa* was a way of telling her that not knowing the meaning of that word reflected her real level, in contrast to her belief that she was very intelligent. This is clearly paradoxical.

The teacher was allegedly surprised that Awuor, who was a bright student, did not know the word, which means that her expectations about Awuor were high, and yet her saying, "But that is the level" is interpreted to imply that her not knowing the word is a reflection of her low level of knowledge with the racist insinuation of her Southern Sudanese identity. Awuor understood her to mean, "What else would you expect of a Southerner!?" But even if that was the case, is it possible to interpret her comment as an innocuous reference to the fact that Southerners were not expected to know Arabic well rather than a racist insinuation of lower intelligence?

I suspect that the case of Awuor reflects an even deeper damage which humiliation and denigration can do to the ego of otherwise proud people. A strong sense of dignity and self-confidence becomes threatened and undermined, and incrementally replaced by insecurity and exaggerated sensitivity to perceived insult. In a way, that sensitivity is symptomatic of diminishing self-confidence. This makes emotive reaction to insult a paradoxically complex symptom of fractured pride.

If the attitude of her female teacher left some room for ambiguity, the uninvited involvement of Ustaz Hatem, the male teacher, who shared the office with three of his female colleagues, left no doubt about the institutional racism Awuor was detecting. As Awuor was explaining to her female teacher her quest for understanding the meaning of words, Hatem got up holding a whip and intruded by reprimanding Awuor about the way she talked to her teacher and ordered her to get out of the office. Awuor responded with a courageous combatant mannerism that was totally unexpected of a student. She said to Hatem that he was intruding in a matter that was not his concern and told him to get back to his seat and sit down. The teacher was understandably enraged, but his response was obnoxiously racist: "*You,* a Southern girl telling *me* to go back and sit down !?" Awuor continued her combatant mood, stating that she was indeed a proud Southerner, "Father and Mother," and challenged Hatem's identity as a Northerner or by implication Arab.

Awuor described Hatem as blacker than most South Sudanese and questioned his claim to be a Northerner, implying Arab. Of course, Awuor was not implying that he would have been justified to discriminate against blacks if he were genuinely an Arab. What she was obviously implying was that while it was wrong to discriminate anyway, to discriminate on the false ground that you are different and superior to the person discriminated against compounds the wrong. The exchange was mutually acrimonious. Awuor told the teacher that she had lost all respect for him and compared him to a man in the street. With the intercession of her guardian cousin, Mustafa, Awuor was made to apologize the following day, which she did by uttering the word 'sorry' in a scornful way that left no doubt in Hatem's mind that it was not sincerely intended. Awuor also received a lashing in the hand, which she received with an air of defiance, signaling its futility. She felt that Hatem should have been the guilty party because of his racism. A point of no return had been crossed.

As Awuor elaborates, that blatant demonstration of injustice was the trigger which prompted her to join the rebellion. But outrageous as the behavior of Hatem was, seen in isolation of the structural racism and discrimination that was the lot of the Southerners in Khartoum and the overall system in the country, it would be difficult to read the words "But that's the level" as a racist insult. It would be equally surprising to take the racism of Hatem as sufficient ground for embarking on the existential threats and imminent dangers of rebellion. Pieng witnessed a gruesome slaughter of innocent members of his family and community and internalized it as a justification for rebellion. Awuor experienced a discriminatory treatment that was personally very painful and externalized it into a collective racial humiliation that her people were fighting against in the liberation struggle, which she felt propelled to join.

The link between the individual insult and the general cause of the people of the South was reflected in the racist statements, including by the President, that were being broadcast by the radio and television, which compounded Awuor's determination to rebel. Even those who were not planning to rebel shared the aspirations for rebellion. This exchange between Awuor and her brothers is telling: "President Nimeiri at that time described the leaders of the Sudan People's Liberation Movement (SPLM) as 'dogs of the world' and we would laugh upon hearing this statement. We were with our brothers Mijak Mou, Noon Deng, Kuol Fog and Arop Chol. We used to laugh when we heard President Nimeiri describing the SPLM leaders as 'dogs of the world' but we used to say: 'We will be with those people whom they call the dogs of the world soon.'"

One of Awuor's half-brothers, Mijak Amou, while sharing the indignation of the people of the South about the racist policies and statements of the Government, stressed the impracticalities of rebellion for most people and challenged what he saw as the unrealistic dream of his sisters. He said to them: "What nonsense! How are you going to be with them (the rebels)? Do you think that the men and youth in Khartoum do not wish to revolt? And you girls think you will be the ones who will find the path that leads to rebellion here in Khartoum?"

His sisters responded with confidence: "Mijak, you will definitely see this happening." We told them that the young men in Khartoum were of two minds; they did not really want to join the rebellion because they were wavering in their opinions and therefore would not join the rebellion. 'But if you want to rebel, you will rebel, even if it means passing through the den of an ant, as our Dinka people say, you will pass through it. These people have not decided to revolt, but you will see us soon. We will do what we tell you here in Khartoum. We will go out and join the rebellion, but they didn't take our words seriously.'

And indeed, the level of determination which these young women demonstrated was extraordinary. Their guiding principle can be summed up as "the goal justifies the means." The goal was of course joining the rebellion; the means included lying with no hesitation whatsoever. The first lie was that they had a brother who was a military officer who had been posted to the South and had not been heard from; they were therefore going to look for him.

The first occasion was interaction with a Ngok Dinka man in Renk who recognized them as the daughters of Deng Majok and asked where they were going. This was their response: "We played the game of Bulabek Angui, God have mercy on him, as our cover up story. If you will recall Mading, Bulabek Angui organized a party in your house in

Riyadh after his graduation from military college. (I could not recall as I was in the United States and never heard about it until the conversation with Awuor.) He organized a party in your house for the whole family in Riyadh after graduating from the Officers College. We had the party in your house. The entire family gathered together there in your house. After the party, he joined the rebellion. By organizing that party, he meant it as a farewell party. We thought it was a party for his graduation ceremony at the Officers College. He intended to join the rebellion. So, he was bidding farewell to the family. A week later, Bulabek disappeared. People searched for him. It became clear later that he had joined the rebellion.

"We took advantage of the story of Bulabek to deceive that Ngok man. We told him that we had a brother who had graduated from the Officers College in Khartoum. After his graduation ceremony, he was sent to Malakal. But he had not been heard from since. We said we wanted to go and look for him because he had disappeared and there was no news about him and his whereabouts. The man asked, 'Are there no young men in the house to search for your brother?' We told him that our older brothers had all rebelled and the brothers who had remained at home were only children and that we were much older than them. That was why we decided to go and look for him. The story seemed real and believable as we told it that way."

Another big lie which miraculously worked was when they told an old half blind man that they were going to visit a grandmother whom they had never met as they were born and raised in the North, in Khartoum, and had not been to the South. What was astonishing was that they mentioned the name of their grandmother as Nyandeng Kon and the old man said he knew Nyandeng very well. He even saw resemblance between Awuor's sister, Awuor Abul, and one of Nyandeng's granddaughters of about the same age. Awuor Abul took the lie a step further by stating that the other granddaughter was indeed their aunt's youngest daughter.

Awuor tells the story with a sense of humor. "We found an old blind man with his daughter at the station. He was not completely blind. He could still see things, but not clearly. We asked them, 'Where are you going?' …The old man answered, 'We want to go to Ayod.' … 'We are also going to Ayod …We have a grandmother in Ayod … Our family left

Ayod a long time ago. We were both born in Khartoum. And we have never been to Ayod.' The old man asked, 'Who is your grandmother in Ayod?' Praise be to God, Mading, Awuor Abul gave him a name, and the old man said that he knew her. God put a name on Awuor's tongue. She said that our grandmother was called Nyandeng Kon. The old man said, 'Nyandeng Kon? I know Nyandeng Kon very well. My child, indeed I know Nyandeng Kon very well.' His sight was weak, but he had not completely lost his sight. He repeated, 'I know Nyandeng Kon; and you look like her granddaughter.' When Awuor lies, she does so with seriousness; she does not laugh … Awuor responded. 'Yes, she is her last-born granddaughter.'… I do not know how to handle such big lies. I was about to laugh, but told myself that if I laughed, I would destroy the plan that was succeeding by the will of God … So, I turned away and went to laugh somewhere far away. Then I came back and joined them. The old man said, 'My children … I will personally take you to her house and hand you over to your grandmother.' This was an extraordinary coincidence."

They say that once you start lying, one lie leads to another lie. The challenge now was how to get out of this lie, should the old man take them to Nyandeng Kon and she says she does not know them. Of course, they had to avoid that situation and that required getting rid of the old man at the right time. The time came as they were about to enter the destination where Nyandeng Kon was.

As Awuor recalls, "We were preoccupied with thinking about how we would get away from that old man because of the story of Nyandeng Kon. If he took us to Nyandeng Kon and she said she did not know us, what would happen? It would of course reveal our lie. We were worried and we were walking and thinking about what we would do. The old man had described a nearby village, after which we would reach Duk. We said to ourselves, 'Well, we will think of a trick to get us away from the old man.'"

And indeed, they thought of a lie that was less ominous, except that it reflected a degree of betrayal of the old man with whom they had established a very close, almost affectionate relationship. "When we arrived in the village before Duk, we went to one of the houses … We went and they gave us water. We drank. Then we said to the old man: 'Father, you stay and rest here. We will move on because we are young and strong.

We have the ability to walk. You are an old man and there is thirst in the land.' The old man responded, 'My children, I will hold up to walk on. We cannot come this long distance together and not go with you for me to hand you over to your grandmother Nyandeng Kon. I must take you to her; I will hold up.' He insisted. But we too insisted. We told him, 'No, you will not go with us. You will find us there in the evening when you arrive.' Somehow, we persuaded him. Then we left him. They never saw him again. They at last reached their destination and connected with SPLA forces in the area, the Zindiah Battalion, through whom they achieved their goal of joining the rebellion.

What was particularly remarkable about the story of the two Awuors was that every turn they were confronted with a formidable problem that threatened to block their way, something happened to remove the obstacle and facilitate their march forward. The sisters interpreted this as God on their side. This is how Awuor put it: "When we got to the station at Ayod … we stood at the station just waiting. Suddenly we saw a man. God always brought to us people who would help us. As we reached our final destination at Ayod, we stood wondering what to do, where to go; but God always brought someone to help us."

What follows is Awuor's full account of her remarkable story of Fighting for Respect, a saga that began as a personal reaction to insult, but quickly linked to the wider cause of gross injustice against her people, which had triggered the liberation struggle she was determined to join and which she indeed joined and pursued with great personal and collective sacrifice. A girl whose intellect and shining class performance promised a bright future deliberately sacrificed that for the cause of justice in her society and country. The question that poses itself is how one assesses the outcome of the struggle in terms of the extent to which the motivating grievances have been addressed and resolved. While the record is at best mixed on both the cause of Abyei and the wider challenges of peace, security, stability and nation building in South Sudan, Awuor ends with what seems like both a prayer for divine justice and an unshakeable faith that God will indeed eventually deliver justice. Throughout their tortuous journey to join the rebellion and the equally traumatic experience of the liberation struggle, God was the reassuring source of support that guided and protected them against serious existential threats.

The word God (or Our Lord) was recurrent in Awuor's recollections and in her concluding reflection: "God will bring out and grant all the rights of the people of Abyei. We are South Sudanese; and we will continue to say that we are South Sudanese ... And that is why we joined the war of the People's Liberation Movement." In another context, Awuor argues, "If we were not South Sudanese, nothing would have taken us into the war of the South against the North. We would not have pursued the war for all those years, that is twenty-one years, during which so many of our young people from the South, including from Abyei, lost their lives. It is our One South Sudan that brought us together." Whether they were young men or women or wives with their husbands, they all joined the struggle, and many fell as martyrs in the war in South Sudan. And God will bring out our right and give it to us. God will reveal and resolve the grievances that compelled the sons and daughters of Abyei, soldiers from Abyei, and heroes of Abyei, to come and fall in the war in South Sudan. For their sacrifice, God will grant their rights and the rights of their people and generations of their children in the future."

All this tempts me to invoke the principle of reconciliation before full resolution of conflicts, to acknowledge the legitimate grievances of a people, to make a firm and credible agreement to address them, and to avoid the massive loss of lives and destruction of war and replace it with the pledge to cooperate toward a framework of peace with full justice, security, stability and dignity for all without discrimination on any ground. I now turn to the story of Awuor in her own words.

The Trigger of Rebellion

I was one of those who rebelled. The reasons for anyone joining the rebellion are not always clear. Some people might have heard that so-and-so and so-and-so have rebelled and follow them without clearly knowing the reasons for their rebellion. There are those who heard of the rebellion and joined in imitation. They joined the rebellion simply because they saw or heard of others having rebelled. But everyone has a personal story that drove him or her to rebel. I am telling the story of my rebelling so that it is recorded as part of our history, to become a legacy for posterity. I didn't rebel because I wanted to imitate others; I rebelled on the basis of important principles. And I pray to God that the principles for which I rebelled will not be lost. I want them to be upheld and written down in our history.

We were living in Khartoum, in the neighborhood of Jebra, in the house of Charles Biongdit Deng, Biong Adit. That was in the year 1985. I was in the second grade of junior high school. There was no place for me in the school in Jebra, but we found an opportunity in a school in Al-Haj Yousuf in Al-Radmiya. Mustafa Biong Mijak was living in Al-Haj Yousuf Al-Radmiya. Charles Biongdit spoke to him and told him that I had found an opportunity to study in Al-Haj Yousuf, and that he wanted me to attend that school and live in Mustafa's house. Mustafa agreed, and I went to his house. There I found Nyanthith Biong Mading, who was also living in Mustafa's house and going to the same school. We used to go to school together. That was Al-Zahraa School for Girls, in Al-Haj Yousuf Al-Radmiya.

We were in the second grade at the school, Nyanthith Biong and I, but we were in different classes. I was in the second grade (A) and Nyanthith was in the second grade (B). There were no South Sudanese girls in the school; so, Nyanthith Biong and I were the only Southerners among Northern Sudanese. And of course, I was the only South Sudanese in my class, and Nyanthith Biong was also the only South Sudanese in her class.

I liked literature and poetry. I used to enjoy the class. When the teachers came into the class to teach us, my morale was always high. I liked literature and poetry so much that if we were asked to memorize a poem, I always made sure that I memorized it in the morning before entering the class. I would walk around the school reciting the poem to memorize it. I would walk two rounds reciting the poem to myself and would memorize it. That was my favorite class. Our teacher of literature and poetry was a woman by the name of Insaf. And that was where the roots of my story started and generated the reasons that pushed me into rebellion.

As we were discussing a poem in the class, I raised my hand and asked a question. The poem was titled "The Arena of Power." The surprising thing is that the teacher reacted to my question in a way that embarrassed me during the discussion of the poem. A verse in the poem said:

I shall live in spite of malady and adversity like an eagle on top of the highest mountain.

I would later find that the message of that poem mirrored the life we were leading in the bush. We lived like eagles on mountaintops despite the intense suffering we were experiencing. The poem was written by Abulgassim al-Shabi. In the middle of the poem, there was a word whose meaning I did not fully understand. So, I raised my hand to tell the teacher, Insaf, that there was a word which was not clear to me. The word was '*ghuzlan*.' I wanted to know whether it was a plural for '*ghazala*' the singular for deer, or a plural for the word '*ghazal*', the word for flirting with love. So, I raised my hand and asked her: "What does *ghuzlan* mean?" She said to me, "Don't you know it?" I said, "No, I don't." She shook her head disapprovingly. Again, I asked, "Is it a plural of the word *ghazala* or a plural of the word *ghazal*?" She said, "No, but that's the level."

She deliberately embarrassed me in the class that way. She was surprised that I did not know the meaning of that particular word. She knew that I was smart in the class, and that my level of knowledge was progressing well. Why would I not know that word? When she said: "No, but that's the level," she meant something derogatory. We were of course living in Northern Sudan, and we knew Arabic well. We knew the way things were said. An expression like that was meant to embarrass someone. I lowered my hand when she said to me, "No, but that's the level." She was unable to give me the correct answer. And I wanted to know the correct meaning of the word.

So, the story ended with awkwardness; she did not answer my question. I put my hand down. That incident shocked me. I was very angry. I did not continue to follow her class. I opened my drawer and took out my literature and science books. I occupied myself with reading and did not pay any attention to her. I was just holding on to my nerves and waiting for her to leave the classroom to her office. I wanted to go to her and ask if I had done something wrong so that I would not be tempted to ask her again in the future. When the class was over, and after she had gone to the office, I followed her.

Francis, this is very important for you to hear, because things like this are what you ought to write down in your books on the Sudan; it was a clear manifestation of racism. I went to her office. And in the office, I found a student carrying a notebook to be marked. I stood behind that student because she was ahead of me. After she finished correcting the student's notebook, it was my turn. I took a step toward her desk. And I talked to her, "May I have your permission!?" She said, "Yes, please!" I said, "I want to ask you a question." She said, "Yes, go ahead." She was sharing the office with two other female teachers who taught other classes. There was also a male teacher in the office with them. His name was Hatem. He did not teach our class; he taught other classes. There were four teachers in the office, three women and one man.

I said to my teacher, Insaf, "I raised my hand in the class and asked you about the meaning of the words *ghazal* and *ghuzlan*. I guessed the meaning to myself; I told myself that *ghuzlan* was probably the plural for *ghazala* or *ghazal*. But I was afraid to remain silent without asking to know the exact meaning." I explained my position to her. "I want to know because those words might come up in the exam, and I could fail the exam if I did not know their meanings. I asked you if *ghuzlan* is a plural of the word *ghazala* or a plural of the word *ghazal* and you said that it was not. You asked me if I did not know the meaning. And you told me that my guess was wrong, 'But that's the level.' I know there is no level of comparison between you and me because you are my teacher and I am your student. If you were with me in the class like my classmates, it would have been possible to compare our levels, but the difference between you and me is great. I know that when parents bring their children to school, they want them to learn things that they do not know to add to what they know. I asked you because I was afraid that you would ask me later about the meaning of this word, when I do not know the correct meaning. I wanted you to verify to me the relationship between the words *ghazal*, *ghazala* and *ghuzlan*. That was my question to you, but you did not answer my question. And I want to know if I was wrong in asking you the question so that I don't raise my hand in the class and ask you again in the future."

Before Insaf could answer my question, Mading, the male teacher, Hatem, who was in the office with the female teachers, got up. He was holding a horsewhip in his hand. He said to me, "You girl, get out of the office. The way you are standing is not the way a student should stand in front of her teacher; you fool, you are a varmint." He rebuked me and he went on, "You are, you are, you are …" The three teachers in

the office were stunned, but they did not respond to him. They were all
mute. They should have told him that his behavior was wrong. Even the
teacher to whom I was speaking did not respond. The man kept barking
and barking at me. It was at break time. Everything was quiet. Students
were doing their homework in the classes. The three female teachers
were silent, and he remained standing with a whip in his hand. I just
looked at him, calmly watching him until he cooled down. The tone of
his voice lowered and the intensity of his speech went down.

I then asked him, "Ustaz Hatem, have you finished talking?" He said
"Yes." And he repeated, "Yes, I have finished". I said, "If you have finished, then please go back to your seat." He responded in another rage,
"You Southern girl, telling me to go back to my seat!?" I said, "Yes, I
am a Southerner; a thousand Yes, I am a Southerner, Father and Mother.
But you Hatem, the way you look, who would know where you are
from? From your looks, who can tell whether you are a Southerner or
a Northerner? You, Hatem, bring your hand next to mine; which of us
is lighter than the other. Hatem, you are darker than most Southerners.
You have correctly identified me as a Southerner, but you Hatem, anyone looking at you, and even I as I am now looking at you, no one can
tell where you come from."

I went on to say, "Hatem, the way you intervened in this matter is
not the way of a person who wants to find a solution to a problem. You
have added mud to the mix. That is why I am telling you to go back to
your seat. When I entered the office, I did not talk to you. And I did not
talk to anyone other than my teacher to whom I directed my question.
I was standing politely and talking with respect as a student. My teacher,
Insaf, and I did not exchange any hostile words. That's why I am telling
you to go back and sit in your chair." I said to him. "The best thing is
that you do not teach me any subject. You have never entered our class.
And Hatem, let me tell you that if there was any subject in which you
taught us, I would never attend your class. I would take that subject with
another teacher. And I challenge and assure you that I would pass the
exams in that subject without attending your class."

I said to him, "I used to respect, appreciate and value you as a teacher
even though you were not teaching in our class. I saw you as a teacher
who had studied in the College of Education. But from your behavior today, I do not see in your behavior any evidence of training in

Education as a teacher. As you stand talking to me, I see you like any person from the street. But if you were a man in the street, I would have excused you. But my problem is that you are a person who has studied at the College of Education, and yet you behave in this very racist way. You are the one who is supposed to be a mediator and solve problems if you find children fighting as a result of racist behavior among them. You are supposed to be the Sudanese elder who should know that these children are all Sudanese; but you are a racist, and there is no pedagogy in your mind and mannerism. I will no longer respect you, because I see you like a street man." I believe I was about seventeen years old, quite young.

He said, "Don't you respect me? If you do not respect me, you should leave this school". I told him, "Hatem, this school is a Sudanese school, and I am a Sudanese. This school is not yours; nor does it belong to your father or grandfather. I will continue studying here, whether you like it or not. You are the one who will leave this school if you do not want me in this school; but I am not leaving. I will soon prove my disrespect to you, and you will know that I no longer respect you; if we meet in the street, I will close one eye and look at you with one eye because you do not deserve to be looked at with both eyes. I see no need to look at you with two open eyes. You will see this very soon: I will do it."

I left the office without anyone telling me to go out. Hatem quickly got up and went ahead of me and entered my class. When I reached the classroom, I found him standing in the classroom in front of the students with the blackboard behind him. He was holding an insect in his hand like someone who was giving a science lesson. When I came and saw that he was the one in the class, I looked at him and I saw that there was a space between him and the blackboard and he was standing in front of the desk. He was not our teacher, but he entered the classroom to test what I had told him that I would never respect him again. I entered the classroom, passed through the desks and sat. And when I was seated, I paid no attention to what he was doing. Everyone else was attentive and followed him explaining to the class parts of an insect, but I didn't pay attention to him. I did not care about him and the lesson he was trying to deliver to the class. I was waiting for him to tell me to raise my head to follow and participate in the lesson, but he did not. Then it was time to go home after the end of the school day. I had always gone to Nyanthith Biong in her class, and then we went home together.

On the way home, Nyanthith said to me, "Awuor, our school Headmistress called me today, and told me about a problem that occurred between you and a teacher. She asked me to bring our guardian with us tomorrow to solve the problem." Nyanthith said this to me as we were walking on the road. "Never speak to anyone in the house about it," I told Nyanthith. "What they are doing is not right; it is colonialism. It is not fair for them to be angry with me and they are the ones who started the problem. This teacher had no problem with me and the teacher whom I asked did not answer my question. This teacher is racist, and I don't want our guardian, Mustafa, to waste his time with them. They are the ones who started the problem and are now requesting the presence of our guardian. If you talk to someone in the family about this, I will be angry with you." I threatened Nyanthith. After I threatened Nyanthith, we went home.

In the evening, at about six o'clock, I went to a nearby shop to buy something, but the inevitable destiny that God had put in place was to be fulfilled. I was about to realize what I had told the teacher that I would not look at him with both eyes. On the way leading to the shop was a street, a small alley. I saw Hatem in front of me after I bought the thing that I had gone to buy. I did not know whether he lived in the neighborhood. I looked at him to make sure that it was him. I knew that it was indeed him. He was on the left side of the alley. So, I closed my right eye and let my left open. He saw this and was furious. He was apparently surprised at a young girl who did not change her words. I told him those words during the day, and I met him in the evening the same day. I believe that God did not like what he did and arranged that coincidence to prove to him what I told him during the day. God brought him in the evening to prove the validity of what I said to him during the day. This means that what he did was not fair, and God wanted to show him that he was the wrongdoer. He saw me and went away angry.

Although he was obviously very angry, he did not say anything, because he knew me, and if he had said something, I was ready to also say something back to him; and the problem would have escalated and grown. Then he would have exposed himself to scandal on the main street in the community. The teachers know the students who speak out, and they avoid them. He decided to leave school, when he was the one who told me: "You will leave this school if you do not respect me." And he was the one who said to me, "You, a Southerner, you tell me to go and sit in the chair?" There was racism in the schools at the time. And when they saw a Southern school girl or Southern Sudanese students clever and participating in the class, they would look for ways to distort their minds in an attempt to suppress intelligence in them. They create psychological problems in the students; their psyche is put in a bad mood and made tense. The students then forget what is in their minds.

As I said in my description of Hatem, he was a black man from Ja'aliya tribe. He was very black. You couldn't believe that he was a Ja'ali for he was too dark. He might have been from Matama, Shendi, or anywhere else in the North. Hatem went on his way, and I also went on my way, and my mind relaxed, because what I told him during the day that he would soon see that I no longer respected him, was practically proven to him by God.

When I got back home that evening, I learned that Nyanthith had told Mustafa the problem while I was out shopping. She took advantage of my absence and told the details of the problem to Mustafa. Later that evening, Mustafa called me and said to me: "Awuor, I heard that there is a problem between you and your teacher." I said to him: "And who told you"? "I received the message, and it is true," he replied. "Yes, there was a problem," I said. "I had gone to the office to ask my teacher, but that other teacher intervened and aggravated the problem. His way of speaking indicated that he is a racist. I didn't like the way he spoke; it made me disrespectful of him. What that man did is one of the behaviors that create problems here in Khartoum. You should not waste your time by going to them. Let them do what they want to do." Mustafa said, "Because of my responsibility for you as your guardian, I have to go; so let's go."

The three of us, Mustafa, Nyanthith Biong and I, went to school. When we got there, Nyanthith entered her class, and I went to the office with Mustafa. In the office, the Headmistress called Hatem and he came to the office. Hatem came and sat down. The Headmistress then started speaking: "Awuor, this meeting is called for, because of the problem that occurred between you and your teacher, Hatem, yesterday. What happened yesterday should not have happened. You reproached the teacher and insulted him. I was told that you were very rude to him. That was why I asked your sister, Teresa (Nyanthith) Biong, to inform your guardian to come." Nyanthith also had the name Teresa. "You made a mistake, and you must apologize to him, because he is your teacher. You must apologize to him. Even if he is not giving you lessons in your classroom, he is still a teacher in the schoolyard. We want you to apologize to Teacher Hatem."

Let me say this to you, Mading, when the Headmistress was speaking in her introduction to the problem, there was something simple that preoccupied my mind. I was thinking, "Why is the teacher not made to feel guilty and I am asked to apologize to him? And if I apologize to him, will he not continue to commit his mistakes?" Mustafa had advised me at home how I should speak. I had spoken freely in front of this teacher before. I was hesitant between an apology and a non-apology. But I said to myself: "If you refuse to apologize, that will put you in trouble with your brother with whom you did not have a problem before. You have to ostensibly accept what they are saying. So, I said to myself, I will do what they are asking of me."

After the Headmistress's introduction, I went to the teacher who was sitting on the chair near the door of the office, and I said to him, "Maleish" which means "Never mind." I felt that the word 'maleish,' did not seem to make him believe that I had apologized to him. Everyone was astonished at my behavior. Mustafa will tell you more about this story. I gave up a lot of words I said at home and came out with only one word 'maleish.' Maleish is a simple word, and it is a word a child could say to another child who knocked him down while playing in the street.

It is a word of a dumb person who cannot speak. It is a simple word any person can say. Children can say 'maleish,' and then the matter is over. I approached him, and I used that simple word, 'maleish', and then I went back to sit in a chair. People were surprised, including the Headmistress. They didn't know what else to tell me. The Headmistress became furious, because she felt that I was provocative and scornful and had crossed the line. Hatem was the one who prompted me into provocation. At that point, the meeting came to an end.

We then got up and walked out. Mustafa was very angry with me. We got out of the office. Mustafa then went to the bus station for transportation to his workplace. I entered my classroom. My mind was relaxed. Why should I apologize to Hatem? I became very comfortable. I felt that I had intransigently dealt with them. The Dinka say, "So and so has

surrendered to whatever happens." That was me, I was prepared for anything that might happen.

They could do anything that they wanted. I went and entered my
classroom and participated in the lesson. There was a teacher in the class
delivering a lesson. Her name was Afaf. She used to teach us science. I
liked teacher Afaf. I do not know what Hatem had meant by coming
into the class with the insect and started to explain its parts to us. I did
not know whether he wanted me to feel that I was in the pleasant imag-
inary atmosphere with Afaf, whom he knew was my beloved teacher. I
don't know what Hatem had in mind. During the day, they decided that
I be punished with fifteen lashes with a leather whip. They decided on
that punishment. I didn't know that because I thought the matter was
over. We went home in the evening, with me thinking that the problem
had been resolved.

When we returned to school the next day, we stood in line in the
morning parade. They had asked teacher Afaf, the woman I liked, to execute the punishment of lashing me. She was assigned the task of beating
me because they knew that if Afaf was the one punishing me, I would
know that it was not her decision, but that of the school. I would therefore not hold any grudge against her. That was why they preferred that
Afaf should execute the punishment. They could have asked someone
else, but they were afraid. They might have asked one of the three teachers in the office, Hatem himself who was the source of the problem,
and the other two teachers; seemingly they also refused to execute the
punishment because they were afraid. They all refused. They were scared
by what they had seen with their own eyes. Afaf came and stood in front
of us in the morning parade with a piece of paper in her hand, and then
she said: "Girls, something new has happened that is not acceptable and
cannot be tolerated. A problem occurred yesterday between one of your
sisters and teacher Hatem. She insulted the teacher leaving nothing out.
Therefore, the administration has decided to punish her with fifteen
lashes."

Teacher Hatem was standing at the end of the parade in the place
where the female teachers were standing. He was looking at me. Of
course, beating with a leather whip was a very painful thing, and when
the Northern Sudanese girls were beaten with a leather whip, they
would struggle with the pain and even fall and crawl down on the

ground due to the intensity of the pain. So, Hatem was standing there probably wondering how I would respond to the pain of the fifteen lashes. He felt satisfied that I was being taught a tough lesson. I got out of the line and stood in the middle of the parade, and I extended my left hand. Teacher Hatem was standing there intensely looking at me. I paid no attention to the lashing; I was looking at Hatem. By looking at him, I intended to tell him that fifteen lashes were nothing; and that they would pass, but my disrespect for him would endure.

I extended my left hand and did not change my hands. Mading, because I was intensely angry, I stood in the same place, with my hand extended. I received the fifteen lashes on one hand, without moving or shaking. I just kept looking at Hatem. Everyone in the parade was astonished. My Northern Sudanese classmates became terrified of me until the day I left the school. They used to say, "This girl is dangerous." So, I was beaten; I received fifteen lashes; but I did not pay attention to the punishment. My attention was focused on the teacher who had caused the trouble. Fifteen lashes ended and I remained standing there even after the beating was over. I thought they had not ended. Teacher Afaf was astonished. She said, "Awuor, the number of lashes decided for you are finished, why are you still standing here?" I said to her. "If you still have more, go on, lash me." All the girls were still standing; the parade was still in place.

The girls who were my classmates were amazed. They used to say: "No, no, fifteen lashes, this is unbelievable." The leather whip with which the students were lashed would twist and wrap itself around the hand at each stroke. I was so angry that I couldn't feel the pain of the whip. After I went back to the classroom and thought about it, I saw that those people were mistreating us and that what they were doing was colonialism. I cried in the classroom because my heart was burning with the pain of anger. My heart was extremely burning inside me.

I went home in the evening. For four days I did not see Hatem in the school. He disappeared under circumstances I did not understand. I don't know where he went. He might have requested to be transferred from our school to another school. Or he might have decided to leave teaching. I do not know what happened to him. Hatem completely disappeared from the school. That was in April, no, in March 1985. The schools were about to close in April. It was around mid-March, on the fifteenth or twentieth day of the month. I was very angry.

Planning for Rebellion

At that time in 1985, the Sudan People's Liberation Movement (SPLM) had been founded in 1983. It had been founded two years earlier. At that time, we were always listening to the SPLA radio, and the girls of the Koryom battalion who entered the training fields had graduated, and we heard them singing patriotic songs of the SPLM/SPLA. Listening to the SPLA radio in those days was not an easy thing that one could do openly. But still people listened to it secretly.

Because of what happened to me at school at that time, the idea of rebellion popped into my mind. I had until then taken my education seriously, because I wanted to take secondary school exams and go to the university. But with Hatem's incident, I thought about rebelling and planned for it.

At that time, Awuor Abul was living in Jabra. When the school was closed for the summer vacation in late March, exactly on the 31st, I went back to Jabra to Biongdit's house. I began to plan with Awuor Abul. One day I went out of the house with Awuor Abul and Nyanthith Biong. We were the younger generation group. We went to the market. At that time in the evening, we watched Egyptian soap operas on television and night performances by singers. Singers used to sing after the news bulletin. We cared much about those TV programs and took them seriously. Even if you walked out of the house far away, you had to come back quickly before those programs started. Biongdit was aware that we were interested in those TV shows. That evening, we returned home late. Biongdit asked, "Why are you girls late? The soap operas you normally watch are over and the singers: Zidan Ibrahim and Abu Arki Al-Bakhit have already sung in your absence." Nyanthith replied, "With Awuor Nyanuer we always have to fight first before returning home." And she was right. We always fought with the Northern Arab boys who often attempted to flirt with girls walking on the streets. We narrated the story of our quarrel with them, and everyone laughed.

During the holiday, I went back to Jabra; and in Jabra, Awuor Abul and I drew up a plan. To this day, I do not know the reason why Awuor Abul thought of rebellion. I don't know the reasons for her rebellion.

But I know my own reasons for rebellion. So, I planned together with Awuor Abul. In the evening, when the TV was turned on, the beds were put in the courtyard of the house, and water was sprayed on the ground to make it wet. The beds were spread inside the fence, and with the TV turned on, we would then sit and follow the news.

As mentioned earlier, President Nimeiri at that time described the leaders of the Sudan People's Liberation Movement (SPLM) as "dogs of the world" and we would laugh upon hearing this statement. We were with our brothers Mijak Mou, Noon Deng, Kuol Fog and Arop Chol. We used to laugh when we heard President Nimeiri describing the SPLM leaders as "dogs of the world" but we used to say: "We will be with those people whom they call the dogs of the world soon."

So, Mijak Amou said: "What nonsense! How are you going to be with them? Do you think that the men and youth in Khartoum do not wish to revolt? And you girls think you will be the ones who will find the path that leads to rebellion here in Khartoum?" We said, "Mijak, you will definitely see this happening." We told them that the young men in Khartoum were of two minds; they did not really want to join the rebellion because they were wavering in their opinions and therefore will not join the rebellion. But if you want to rebel, you will rebel, even if it means passing through the den of an ant, as our Dinka people say, you will pass through it. These people have not decided to revolt, but you will see us soon. We will do what we tell you here in Khartoum. We will go out and join the rebellion, but they didn't take our words seriously."

Determined Journey to Rebellion

Charles Biongdit was appointed Advisor at the rank of minister in the regional government of Kordofan in 1985. He was moving to El Obeid. He distributed money to us, the girls, so that we could buy bags, clothes or shoes or whatever we needed in order to get prepared for the trip. Here we saw the opportunity for us to join the rebellion. We said to ourselves "Perfect! We will use the money for travelling and joining the rebels." I remember my mother, God have mercy on her, was visiting. I don't remember the name of the neighborhood where our father's wives used to live. They were in an area which I can't recall.

My mother had just come. One evening, I told her, "I will go out early in the morning and I would like to wear your toub." Awuor Abul and I had washed our clothes and ironed them and put them in the bags with cassettes and song lyrics books. We arranged our belongings, leaving only one garment outside the bags for each of us to wear. Awuor had taken a toub from her mother, and I had taken that of my mother. We wanted to cover ourselves and hide our faces, because our features were known to everyone who knew Deng Majok, and they could object to us on the way and request us to go back home. They would know that we were daughters of Deng Majok. We intended to cover ourselves with toubs in order to disguise our faces and hide our features and characteristics.

We got out of the house early in the morning and left my mother who was already up. She had brushed her teeth and was having tea. That was the last time I saw her. I never saw her again; she passed away in my absence. We had the money that Biongdit had given us to buy the things we needed. We went to the popular market, Al-Souq al-Shaabi, and entered a store that sold pants, T-shirts, shirts, jeans and Adidas shoes. We realized that joining the rebellion did not require women's clothes, but strong types of jeans and Adidas shoes. We bought all the things we needed.

Awuor Abul bought herself a travel handbag. I also bought a handbag. And we filled them with clothes. We wanted to board the express buses for which we had to purchase tickets. Express buses traveled from Al-Souq Al-Shaabi in Khartoum to Renk town. We bought everything we needed. We bought our tickets and were waiting for the buses. As far as I can remember, the buses used to travel at 9:30 am. When we got to the station, we met our cousin whose name was Alor; I believe Awuor still remembers him. He came passing by in front of us. We were walking and carrying bags. It was early in the morning. Awuor Abul said to me, I can see our cousin. "Where is he?" I asked her. "He is over there," she said.

He was just passing bye, but he saw and recognized us. He said, "Girls, what brings you to the market so early in the morning?" He looked like he had come from Ishish, from the house of late Ambassador Kuol Alor, who was living there, or from one of the houses of our relatives who were also living there. He probably went to the bus station to go somewhere else. He was surprised and therefore asked: "Girls where have you come from and where are you going this early in the morning?"

Of course, girls do not get out early in the morning, unless there is a problem. We told him that we had come to buy some items, for we are getting prepared to go with Charles who was being transferred to El-Obeid. "So, we came early in the morning to buy our items." He understood us right away, because it was known to all of them that Charles was arranging to travel to El-Obeid. As the time for departure had not yet come, we went to a cafeteria with him and ordered soda and engaged in a conversation. He drank his soda with us and then he left.

After that, we got onto the bus and left. We drove and arrived in Renk at seven o'clock in the evening. We didn't know where to go because we had not traveled to Renk before. So, we stood at the station. And while standing, God brought a man from Ngok, with scarifications on his forehead. We knew he was from Ngok because of the Ngok scarifications on his forehead. He came crossing in front of us. So, we called him and greeted him: "How are you doing? How are you doing?" And after a while, he stared at us, and said: "Are you daughters of Deng Majok?"

He recognized us by the toubs we were wearing. We wore toubs to cover our faces in a way that would not allow anyone to know us. Nevertheless, the man seemed to recognize us and asked: "Are you daughters of Deng Majok?" We replied, "Yes, we are." He asked, "Where are you going?" We played the game of Bulabek Angui, God have mercy on him, as our cover up story. If you will recall Mading, Bulabek Angui organized a party in your house in Riyadh after his graduation from military college. He organized a party in your house for the whole family in Riyadh after graduating from the Officers College. We had the party in your house. The entire family gathered together there in your house. After the party, he joined the rebellion. By organizing that party, he meant it as a farewell party. We thought it was a party for his graduation ceremony at the Officers College. He intended to join the rebellion. So, he was bidding farewell to the family. A week later, Bulabek disappeared. People searched for him. It became clear later that he had joined the rebellion.

We took advantage of the story of Bulabek to deceive that Ngok man. We told him that we had a brother who had graduated from the Officers College in Khartoum. After his graduation ceremony, he was sent to Malakal. But he had not been heard from. We said we wanted to go and look for him because he had disappeared and there was no news about him and his whereabouts. He asked, "Are there no young men in the house to search for your brother?" We told him that our older brothers had all rebelled and the brothers who had remained at home were only children and that we were much older than them. That was why we decided to go and look for him.

The story seemed real and believable as we told it that way. He told us that it had fallen dark and that we should go with him to his house. He said we could then return in the morning to cross the river by boat. After crossing the river, there were lorries that would take us to Malakal. He said we should go with him to his house, and he would introduce us to his wife. He said we should spend the night with them and he would bring us back in the morning to the river port to take the boat across the River and then continue to travel by lorries.

I believe the man was from the Mannyuar section of Ngok tribe, but I am not sure. He was probably doing business in Renk and lived there with his family. We went to his house. His wife was a good woman. She welcomed us, and then he introduced us to her: "These girls are daughters of Deng Majok, and they have a brother whom they are going to search for in Malakal. They will sleep here with us and in the morning, I will take them to the port to cross the river and then travel to Malakal by lorries."

His wife prepared food for us and we had dinner. We woke up early in the morning and had tea. Then we went to the port and found the boats. We boarded one of them and crossed to the other side. He then returned to his house. In Renk and Malakal, they make shelters, similar to the ones the Baggara tribe used to make in the goz areas, where tea was served. As the lorry was scheduled to leave at 12:00 noon, we sat under a shelter, and ordered tea and engaged in a conversation. When the appointed time for travelling came, we got on the lorry, and then we drove. Gai Tut had appeared at that time against the SPLM. Before we got on the lorry, we were warned that there was fear of attacks on the way. Despite that, we got on the lorry.

There was a Nuer man with us on the lorry. He told us that the road was not safe. He said that we might meet people on the road and if they talked to us, we should refrain from speaking. But God, praised be to Him, made us pass safely; we did not meet any of those people on the way. We reached Malakal without incident. We arrived in Malakal in the evening at around 7:30 pm. We had never traveled to those places before, neither to Renk nor to Malakal, nor to any of those areas.

We stood in the marketplace wondering what to do; we did not know where to go; we were looking around to see if we could see a hotel nearby, so that we could go there to spend the night. A young man named Chotkier from Nuer who had been with us on the lorry came and asked us, "Are you Dinka?" We said, "Yes, we are Dinka." He asked, "Whose children, are you?" We said, "We are from Deng Majok's family in Abyei." He said, "We know your family well. We know Dr. Zachariah in Juba, and we know even your sisters who were in Dr. Zachariah's house." He said, "I have my sisters at home, Terio and Thiyang, they are colleagues of your sisters." He went on to ask, "Where do you intend to go?" We told him, "We have a brother who graduated from the Officers College and came to Malakal here. We have not heard any news about him since he came. So, we came to look for him."

He spoke to us the same way the Ngok man we found in Renk had spoken to us. He said to us, "We will go to our house where my sisters are to spend the night and, in the morning, you can go to search for your brother." We accepted his offer and went with him. When we arrived home, we found his sister Terio, who was a friend to Achai Arop and Akuet Anyiel, and his younger sister Thiyang. We were well received and honored in a good manner without any shortcoming. Terio was working and had a son called Ladgor and another one called Wuor. Ladgor was the youngest.

Terio got married and went to Lebanon with her husband. They lived there in Lebanon and then returned to Malakal. Her husband then joined the rebellion soon after they had arrived. His name was Peter. I do not remember his second name. He had fallen in a battle. So, she returned to her family and was living with her mother. There were two beds in her room. She gave us one bed in which we slept. Her children slept with her sister in the other bed. Her mother was a very kind woman. I met their cousin, who was the wife of the late Dr. Justin Yac's driver.

We went to Chotpier's family house. I met Chotpier recently and I still have his phone number on my mobile phone. We went and stayed with them. His sister was suffering from a bad psychological disorder because her husband had rebelled, leaving her with two children. One was weaned and the other still of the age of your grandson whom you named after your maternal grandfather. The child's name was Wuor.

We stayed with them and helped in creating a positive atmosphere for her, because we found her in a difficult psychological condition and in very low spirits. We used to go to the riverbank in Malakal. We would go there after she came back from work in the evening. We recited many poems and told stories about life to lift her spirits.

We were able to improve her condition. We lifted her spirits. We helped take care of her child. We became like sisters to her. She would tell us: "My daughters, you have relieved me of the burdens I was carrying. You have become like my sisters." We acted as if we were looking for our brother, but we were not; we were actually looking for the path that would lead us to the Anya-Nya. One day we asked her: "Where is Achol Benjamin's house?" Of course, Achol Benjamin was in Juba. She was a friend to our sisters. We heard that she had been married to a Nuer. So, we assumed that the Nuer who would go to her house in Malakal would know the way for us to take. There might be people among them who were against the SPLM/SPLA. And there might also be some who were supporters of the SPLM/SPLA. We learned that there was always a gathering of young men in her house. Her husband held a high position in the government in the regular Sudanese army.

They took us to Achol Benjamin's house one day. We went to the house and greeted Achol who introduced herself to us. We also introduced ourselves to her. We then told her that we were looking for our brother. "Which brother are you looking for?" she asked. We explained to her. Generally, the first day was a day for introducing ourselves to one another and getting acquainted. The young men we found in the house were divided into those who supported and those against the SPLM/SPLA. We decided that we would get the information about the way leading to the SPLM/SPLA through these young men. We were acting as though we hated the SPLM and did not like what they were doing.

We then returned to Chotpier's family house. We told each other that it was in the house of Achol that we would find the way to the SPLM/SPLA. We just had to pretend. We should not disclose to anyone that we wanted to join the SPLM/SPLA. That was why we returned to Achol Benjamin's house two days later. We asked about the route that would lead to the SPLM. We were told that the people who joined the SPLM

used to take the way through Nasir. But many of them were killed on
the way to Nasir. Some of them were killed in the river. So, they had
stopped going through Nasir.

So, we asked which way they took if they had abandoned the way
through Nasir. We said we understood that they were still reaching safely.
Which alternative way were they taking since they were being killed
on the way of Nasir? One young man said, "These people cannot be
stopped by anyone. They are tough people, and they have searched and
looked for another way. Now they go to Ayod, and from Ayod, they go
to Duk Padiet and from Duk Padiet they go to Bor and then they go to
Ethiopia." From there we took the information; it was the information
we were looking for.

We went back home. We stayed. Awuor and I agreed on a plan. Awuor
had a dream the night we got the information about the route. She said
that she saw an old man walking with a large number of people. He
was walking in their midst. We were running after him; but as we kept
running, following him, he would turn to us and say: "Children, please
go back, go back to your people, since you have not found the way you
are looking for."

I told Awuor, "The man you saw in the dream is our father, but he
did not reveal himself to you. It used to be said in the past that when a
dead person prevents you from following him, then you will live. But if
he accepts that you walk after him, that means you will die. The man you
saw is our father. And his appearance in the dream to you alone means
that he has given you due consideration, as you are older than me. You
were born first. You saw the light of the sun before me. The one who
appeared to you is our father without revealing himself to you." I told
Awuor that we should not ignore such matters. Those were among the
ways by which God helps people in such situations. The issue of Nasir's
route that we talked about is in the dream you saw. Nasir's route which
we decided to take is dangerous. We should not take that route; we
should not walk on it. I told Awuot, "If you insist on taking that route,
you will have to go alone; I will not go with you. I would rather return
to Khartoum than travel on Nasir's route. The best thing for us to do is
to inquire about Ayod's route and travel to Ayod."

I discussed the matter with Awuor. And we agreed to travel by the
route through Ayod. We told ourselves, "Well, today we will go to the

lorry station, the lorries that travel to Ayod, in order to do our booking." A few moments later, Chotpier's older sister, Terio, came to us, and told us, "Girls, we have a wedding tomorrow, and my sister and I would like to wear your two pants with their T-shirts; we want to wear the same colors." We agreed immediately because we were planning our travel program to Ayod, and we did not know how to leave them as they used to stick to us. We were looking for an opportunity that would separate us from them. That opportunity came with their plan to go to the wedding.

We had taken our plan as a secret. We did not want to reveal it to anyone, because there was no guarantee that we would not get exposed. An enemy might pick it up and use it to expose us. So, we did not want to reveal our plan. The only person we told the truth was their brother, Chotpier. We told their sister that we had no problem. We said that we would go straightaway and give them the pants. We got into the house, opened the bags, took out the pants and T-shirts, and gave them to them in identical colors. We told ourselves that it was wonderful that God had arranged for them to go to the wedding the following day.

They told us that we were invited to the wedding. But we told them that we were tired and would like to sleep during the day. We would therefore unfortunately not be able to go to the wedding with them. We gave them the clothes and then we took permission from them; we told them that we were going out to take a short walk.

When we got to the market, we found an old blind man with his daughter at the station. He was not completely blind. He could still see things, but not clearly. We asked them, "Where are you going? Why are you at the station here?" The old man answered, "We want to go to Ayod." They were from Duk Padiet. We asked, "When are you going to travel to Ayod, are you going tomorrow?" He said, "We were supposed to travel today, but the lorry left us because it was full, but we will travel tomorrow."

We told them, "If you will travel tomorrow, we are also traveling to Ayod and we will travel together. We have a grandmother in Ayod. We will travel early in the morning. Our family left Ayod a long time ago. We were both born in Khartoum. And we have never been to Ayod." The old man asked, "Who is your aunt in Ayod?" Praise be to God, Mading, Awuor Abul gave him a name, and the old man said that he knew her. God put a name on Awuor's tongue. She said that our grandmother was called Nyandeng Kon. The old man said, "Nyandeng Kon? I know Nyandeng Kon very well. My child, I know Nyandeng Kon very well." His sight was weak, but he had not completely lost his sight. He repeated, "I know Nyandeng Kon, and you look like her granddaughter." When Awuor lies, she does so with seriousness; she does not laugh. The old man said, "I see that you look like her youngest granddaughter." Awuor responded, "Yes, she is her last-born granddaughter." The old man said, "She looks very similar to you."

I do not know how to handle such big lies. I was about to laugh, but told myself that if I laughed, I would destroy the plan that was succeeding by the will of God, to make Awuor mention the name of Nyandeng Kon whom the old man said he knew. So, I turned away and went to laugh somewhere far away. Then I came back and joined them. The old man said, "My children, I am so happy that you are the children of Nyandeng Kon. We live close together. My house is close to her house. I will personally take you to her house and hand you over to your grandmother." This was an extraordinary coincidence.

Awuor said a name and it worked. She said our grandmother was called Nyandeng Kon. I told her that she did very well by thinking of a name known to the old man. We planned to leave in the morning. So, we bought our tickets and went home to spend the night. We were so happy that we would travel the following day. In the morning, we didn't tell the girls that we were going to leave. They put on the pants we gave them and went to the wedding. We went to their mother in the kitchen, and told her that we were traveling. She said, "My children, where are you going? How can you leave when Thiyang and Terio are not here? Why do you want to leave by surprise? Why didn't you tell us early?" We told her that our trip came suddenly because we were told from Khartoum to return, if we did not find our brother whom we were looking for. We said we had no time to wait to tell her children.

She said, "No, no, you cannot leave without them knowing." We ran and speeded away. The old woman sent her young son to her daughters. She told him to go and tell his sisters, "Awuor and her sister are traveling." We ran and reached the station. The little boy ran and managed to tell his sisters about our leaving. When they got home, they asked their mother, "Where are they?" She said, "They ran to the bus station to go back to Khartoum." So, they came running after us. They wanted to go to the bus station for Khartoum. But they met us at Ayod lorry station, which was not the way to the Khartoum station. They found us already in the lorry. And buses, not lorries, went to Khartoum. When they arrived, the woman whose husband had joined the SPLM/SPLA, immediately knew in her heart that we were going to join the rebellion. "Why are you in this lorry? Where are you going? Didn't you tell us that you were returning to Khartoum? Why are you in this lorry." She was inquiring. We had no way to escape. So, we told her that we were going to where that lorry was going. When her younger sister, Thiyang, heard these words, she remained calm because she was a brave girl. She stood looking at us. But her older sister, whose husband had rebelled, was crying. She knew that we were seeking to join the rebellion.

We were afraid to let her know because if we had done so; she would have told us that she would go with us. And she would not have been able to go with us. She might have exposed us. And there was also the issue of the children. If she took them with her, that would have been a mistake. And if she had left them, that would have been a mistake as well. So, we kept the truth from her. The lorry took off and left.

The day before, we gave them the pants in the morning and we left in the evening and went back to the house of Achol Benjamin. We told her that we wanted to talk to her privately because we wanted to tell her the truth. We spoke to her inside her room. We told her that what we had said earlier about looking for our brother was only a way of disguising ourselves, and that we had in fact decided to rebel.

Achol Benjamin cried and said, "I am crying not because I will divulge your secret. My husband is a Nuer, and I will not tell him about this. I do not want any bad thing to happen to you. But what makes me cry is your passage here and having seen you and the pathway of rebellion is a path that is between death and life. Maybe you will die and maybe you will live. My little brother had rebelled and the rebels of Gai Tut (Nyigaat) shot them in the river." She told us that her little brother, Machar, did not know how to swim, but he had to enter the river, so he drowned. "This is what makes me cry, and not because I am going to disclose your plan, with the great trust that you have placed in me," she said.

We spent the night and then we traveled in the morning. We were in the front seat. The driver was a Shilluk. The bags that we were carrying

were large. He told us that people were being looted by Gai Tut's supporters who were on the road and would take the luggage. So Awuor
put her bag under her seat, and I also put my bag under my seat. She sat
on her bag, and I also sat on my bag. When we sat on the seats, the seat
seemed high, but God covered us, they were not taken. We went some
distance. And there was a Nuer man who had told us: "When we travel,
those rebels will come out from the trees in the forest on the way. They
have a problem with the Dinka. If they come, be silent, because you will
not be able to speak the Nuer language. And if they know that you are
Dinka girls, they will kill you. Be silent. And I will talk to them on your
behalf. I will tell them that you are my nieces and that you are going to
your grandmother, as you have lived in the north for a long time. I will
save you."

The old man spoke to us with great kindness. On the way to Malakal
and Ayod, the Nuer sold milk. So, we would buy buttermilk, and consistently gave the old man some milk. So, he was happy with us because
we took care of him. We proceeded to travel. At four o'clock in the
afternoon, the rebels (Nyigaat) came out from among the trees carrying
long guns that were called File. They intercepted us on the road. They
ordered the lorry to stop. Then ordered the people in the back seats to
get down. And they took the bags of the people. Then they came to us
in the front seats. One of them said, "Why have we taken the bags from
the others and not from these girls?" Then the Nuer man who spoke
to us about not talking came and said: "These young girls are coming
from school hostels and are carrying nothing. They are going to their
grandmother, who is my mother. They are my nieces. Please leave them;
they have nothing."

We got away. And they went on their way. And after they took all
the things they wanted, the lorry set off. After the lorry advanced some
distance, it broke down. The driver was very anxious about us. He said to
himself, "These other people's children will be killed. What shall I do?"
He was very concerned about us specifically. Most of the passengers on
the lorry were Nuer and the Bor Dinka from Duk Padiet. The Dinka
spoke the Nuer language and could not be distinguished from the Nuer.
We were the only people who stood out as different. That was why the
driver was very anxious about our safety.

Then another lorry came from behind us. That lorry stopped where we were. They got us onto that lorry. There was space in the front seats. Some of the passengers were moved and we got onto the lorry. The blind old man with his daughter remained behind in the other lorry. We had no choice. We told them that we would wait for them at the station at Ayod. When we got to Ayod, the lorry stopped at the station. We stood at the station just waiting. Suddenly we saw a man. God always brought to us people who would help us. As we reached our final destination at Ayod and stood there, we wondered what to do, where to go; but God always brought someone to help.

In the lorry that took us to Ayod, there was a man called Maduk. He was in the lorry that came behind us and took us. So, we travelled in the same lorry that took us to Ayod. When he saw us standing, looking bewildered, he asked, "Girls, why are you standing here?" We told him that we wanted to go to Duk, where our grandmother was, and that we did not know anyone or where to go in Ayod. He said, "My brother's house is here." His brother was a high-ranking officer in the regular army. He had gone to Khartoum for security work. He said, "Well, this is what will now happen. My brother's house is here in Ayod. I will take you there." He took us there. It was a desperate situation. If you knew that a Dinka was a high-ranking officer in the government army, you must go to his house. But of course, you had to be careful not to expose your intentions and reveal what you intended to do. We had no choice; it was better to go to that officer's house than to go somewhere else to strangers.

Madut took us and we got to know his brother's wife, Rasha. She was a Bor Dinka from Duk Padiet. He said to his brother's wife, "Rasha, these girls will spend the night here, and they will go to Duk Padiet in the morning." Duk Padiet is an area that belongs to the Ghol section of the Bor Dinka. It is located on the borders between Bor and Nuer. The People of Duk and the Nuer interact and have intermarried. They are mixed. He said to his brother's wife, "Prepare beds for them and make them dinner." It was a hot season in April, and the beds were outside in the courtyard of the house. The woman prepared dinner for us. I remember she prepared a *shermout* (dried meat) sauce with thick porridge (*asida*) that night. His brother's wife used to make wine called *sukusuku*. She used to brew the local alcohol called *aragi*. Members of the regular army would come to drink at her house.

William Nyuon Bany had not yet come at that time to launch an offensive to capture Ayod. The regular army of Nimeiri's government was present and still in control of Ayod then. It had not yet been taken by the Sudan People's Liberation Army. We went and slept. In the morning, we saw the soldiers coming to the house. They were coming to buy and drink wine. They were wearing military uniforms. Awuor and I were surprised, but we knew how to cover up our story. They came and greeted Rasha: "How are you doing, Rasha? We can see that you have guests today. Where are these girls from? They look like girls from the city?" "Yes, they are my sisters," Rasha replied. They asked again, "Where have they come from?" "From Khartoum," she answered. "And where are they going?" they asked. "They are going to Duk Padiet to see our grandmother," she responded. These soldiers used to sleep in the trenches and only get out at nine o'clock in the morning.

Rasha told them that we had our grandmother in Ayod and that we were going to her. The soldiers inquired of us, "Girls, did you come from Khartoum?" We told them that we did. We later learned that these people became very angry when they learned about our rebellion. They said, "How could the girls rebel right in front of us without our knowing about the story of their rebellion?" At that time, they told us, "Girls, we have heard from your sister Rasha that you are going to Duk Padiet. We have lorries coming tomorrow to deliver supplies to Poktap." The army was in Poktap in Central Bor. "You are city schoolgirls. You cannot go on foot to Duk. You will travel in those lorries." Imagine, those lorries were going to deliver supplies to soldiers who would exchange fire with us. We told them, "Very well," and remained silent.

After a little while, a Dinka man came to us. I think he was told that there were girls from his community who had come. He was from Aweil. He was a soldier. He came and greeted us. And then greeted Rasha. Northern Arab soldiers came and left. The Dinka soldier then asked us, "Girls, where are you coming from and where are you going?" We told him that we had come from Khartoum and were going to Duk Padiet to our grandmother. The strange thing is that the Dinka man knew that we wanted to join the rebellion just by looking at us. As they say, a man knows how to slaughter his chickens. Although we covered up the matter and denied it, he did not believe us.

He told us not to be afraid. "I am your brother, and despite my presence in the army, I do not like it. It is only a means of livelihood, just to sustain myself." He said, "Our Dinka brothers came and crossed from here, and I helped them to pass. I did not object to what they were doing. I will not expose you. I ask you to respect and trust me." He actually persuaded us, but we refused to reveal the truth to him. He insisted that he knew we were going to join the rebellion. "Do not be afraid to tell me the truth," he pleaded. I do not know why he wanted to help us. He even wanted to give us money, but we told him we have enough money. We left the matter hanging; we did not reveal to him our plan for rebellion. And he did not believe that we were not going to join the rebellion. He told us, "I know you want to join the rebellion and you should not be afraid of me."

We went back to the lorry station to wait for the old blind man and his daughter, the man who had said that he knew our grandmother Nyandeng Kon and his daughter. We met them and brought them home. We told the woman of the house that the old man and his daughter were traveling with us. So, they were accommodated in a room. In the morning, the soldiers came and the Dinka man from Aweil told us again, "You want to rebel." The Northern soldiers told us, "You will travel in the pick-ups when they come." We said, "Very well" and kept silent. We were privately amused by the paradox of travelling in the enemy's lorries carrying the supplies to those who would fight us and perhaps kill us? In the evening, we revealed the truth to the old man and his daughter; we told him that we would travel in the morning at around four, while the army would still be in the trenches. We explained that if we travelled by day, we would be followed because the army knew the way. We told him that we would travel early in the morning, actually around two in the morning. He decided to go with us.

We would of course carry our bags. We decided to carry them on our heads. It was two o'clock in the morning when we left. We went to the old man and woke him up. He was leaving with us with his daughter. His daughter was a married woman and she led him with a stick. We did not tell Maduk who brought us to his brother's house the truth about our plans. We only told him that we were going to our grandmother and that we would leave early morning the following day. We went to the old man and his daughter and woke them up. And we left with them. We were carrying a jericana, a jar of water which we had covered with sackcloth and which we sprinkled with water to keep it cool. We carried with us roasted peanuts and cakes. When we felt hungry, we would sit under a tree, eat and drink water.

The old man was walking slowly and lagging behind with his daughter. We were much faster in walking. The trees in the forest between Ayod and Duk Padiet were dense with climbing plants and intertwined up in the branches. We walked bending over because of many trees. We sat under a tree at the edge of the road, waiting for the old man and his daughter. As we were waiting for them, two rebels came from behind us and were carrying a File rifle. We were sitting under a tree. When they arrived, they looked around and wanted to move on. But one of them stopped.

While we were in Malakal at the house of Chotpier's and Terio's family, we learned a few words of the Nuer language as a precaution that could enable us to answer simple questions. One of the men stopped and asked in Nuer language: "Where are you going?" We told him that we were going to Duk Padiet. We were wearing lawa and tied slippers with a rope, to look like poor people. Looking that way, we thought that we would be ignored if people saw us as poor. Our new clothes and shoes were in the bags.

"Where are you coming from and where are you going?" the Nuer man asked. We told them that we were coming from Malakal and were going to Ayod. Basically, they expected everyone walking that road to be joining the insurgency; and they would shoot them dead. We told them that we were going to Duk Padiet. Then the other man who was in front called him and said, "Come on, let us go." So, they left. Then the old man came with his daughter. After they sat, we gave them roasted peanuts and cake to eat and water to drink. We told them of the two men who had just come and crossed the road, armed with a File rifle. When the old man heard that, he was terrified and began to shudder. He said, "My children, these are the Nuer rebels; they are the ones who kill people here. When did they cross here?"

The old man was a Dinka, from Duk Padiet, and he knew that the Nuer rebels of Gai Tut were in that forest. "Where did they go?" he asked. We told him that they had gone on along the way. Awuor Abul was laughing at him and saying, "Uncle, why are you so afraid? If you were here, we would all have been shot. It is good that you remained behind. And we hoped to disguise ourselves through you. If you get so afraid in this manner when you were far behind, we would have been shot dead if you had been here with us. Why are you so afraid?" The old man said, "O my daughters, these are the ones who kill people." We told him, "Yes, we know they are the ones who kill people, but God has saved us, and they have now gone away."

We asked them to eat their roasted peanuts and cakes, the only food we had, and that after eating we should keep on walking. They did and we left. We walked. We arrived at a nearby home and sat under a tree. As we were sitting there, a woman came and clapped her hands and said: "My children, my children, get up and leave; if you stay here for five more minutes, you will be killed in this house. Please leave."

She was a Dinka of Duk Padiet, but I think she was married to a Nuer. She told us to go because, she said, "These people do not want the Dinka and they will kill you; and I do not want a curse on my house." We did not even sit to rest. We were still standing and we left immediately. The old man told us that we should press forward and that we had only a short distance left for us to come to a village after which we would be in Duk Padiet. There he said that we would find water. It was a dry season and there was thirst in the land. We were preoccupied with thinking about how we would get away from that old man because of the story of Nyandeng Kon. If he took us to Nyandeng Kon and she said she did not know us, what would happen? It would of course reveal our lie. We were worried and we were walking and thinking about what we would do. The old man had described a nearby village, after which we would reach Duk. We said to ourselves, "Well, we will think of a trick to get us away from the old man."

When we arrived in the village before Duk, we went to one of the houses. The old man told us that he knew the people in that house and that they were his relatives. We went and they gave us water. We drank. The amount of water was small and so we carefully shared it. Then we said to the old man: "Father, you stay and rest here. We will move on because we are young and strong. We have the ability to walk. You are an old man and there is thirst in the land. The water we just drank is not enough for us." The old man responded, "My children, I will hold up to walk on. We cannot come this long distance together and not go with you for me to hand you over to your grandmother Nyandeng Kon. I must take you to her; I will hold up." He insisted. But we too insisted. We told him, "No, you will not go with us. You will find us there in the evening when you arrive." Somehow, we persuaded him. Then we left him. After we left and entered Duk, we found some government buildings that were destroyed during the fighting with the Northern Arab army. When we approached, we saw a large number of the SPLA soldiers under the trees. There was no government army in the area. The SPLA force in the area had just graduated and began to deploy. It was the Zindiah Battalion.

Zindiah was a branch of Koryom Battalion. Its commander was Peter Panom, a Nuer who was a loyal leader and fought fiercely. He was the commander of Zindiah. The Zindiah battalion had just come from Ethiopia and was going to engage in battles. They had just arrived. We found them under the trees. We greeted them and sat down. We knew they were our people. So, we became relaxed. Peter Panom saw us. He looked at us intensely. And then he called for us. So, we went and sat near him. He asked us, "Where did you come from?". We had entered homes that were partially demolished, changed our clothes and put on Adidas shoes. We knew that those people were our comrades and we felt free. "Girls, why do you come and sit down? Where are you going?" Peter Panom asked us. We told him that we had decided to join the rebellion. "What rebellion?" he asked. We told him the SPLM/SPLA rebellion. "And how did you know that we are SPLM/SPLA? Maybe we are against it?" he said. We responded, "We do not know for sure, but God showed us that you are our comrades; that is why we came to you."

The SPLA soldiers were surprised; where those girls came from and where they were going. In those days, if you were well dressed, you could be accused of being a traitor (Nyigaat). If you came in shabby clothes, then they would know that you were from Anya-Nya. But if you were very clean, and said that you just came to join, they would feel as if you were just getting off the plane and wanted to spy on them. The army was astonished and suspicious. So, Peter Panom told them, "These are military orders. These girls have come and joined us. None of you is allowed to ask them questions. It is me who will be talking to them." They were deterred by military orders.

Then Peter Panom asked us, "Have you really accepted the rebellion?" We said yes, we had accepted the rebellion. "You are coming from the city, and the conditions of the city differ from the conditions of the jungle," he told us. "And you know the mosquitoes in Khartoum do not bite people, because they are fought with medicine and mosquito nets. The mosquitoes here in the bush eat our blood for food. There are no mosquito nets, no medicines, and we do not have houses. We sleep in the open space under trees. Will you be able to resist mosquitoes?" he interrogated. "Yes, we will be able to resist," we replied. "Secondly, we do not have vehicles; we do not have lorries, taxis or buses. Our legs are our means of transportation," he said. Then he said, "We are now in Sudan, and we travel from here to Ethiopia on foot. Would you be able to travel on foot?" he asked. "Yes, we will, because if you decide to rebel, you first have to be determined and resolute and then rebel. If you do not make your decision with determination and willpower, you should not go and join the rebellion. That is why you see that some people do not come, because they cannot make such a commitment. But we have accepted and will be able to live up to the challenge." He told us, "If you will be able to resist all the circumstances, we have no objection."

There were some women who had gone to Ethiopia, like the batch of Koryom, who had been trained. Some women were with their husbands, and they decided to rebel together. But there were no women where we were. That was an army that had graduated and was going out for operations. It had arrived and sat under the trees. But there were women in the neighboring areas. And there were neighborhoods in that area.

Peter Panom called one of the officers of Arok Thon Arok. Arok Thon was the one who would be notified of the arrival of new recruits and joiners to register their names. He called one of Arok Thon's bodyguards called Monycuei, God have mercy on him; I learned that he has passed away. He said to him, "Monycuei, you will now assume the responsibility for these girls. You are responsible for them from here in Duk until you hand them over to Arok Thon." He gave orders to the officer to deliver us to a house in Duk Padiet, which is the village of Nyanthon Awuor's husband. Nyanthon is married from the people of Duk, but he did not know that we were related to them.

When we went there, the officer told us that people from our area, including Bulabek Monychok, Kuol Suuk, and Wuor Jok Abyei, that group, had passed through that area and had stayed in the house of the in-laws of Nyanthon Wuor. We went to the house and were well received. Food was served and they hosted us well. They knew that we were their in-laws. Then they told us that a number of people from our area had passed there recently. In the morning, Monycuei came to assist us. He took us to a place called Kongor, which is a village that also belongs to Bor, close to Poktap. In the morning we began our journey, and, on the way, we met a man with whom Monycuei began to talk. He asked him: "When are you coming? We are waiting for you. When will you join the rebellion? You said that you would come to us and you have not yet come."

Can you imagine, Mading Deng, that man was a spy! He had camouflaged himself and told people that he was going to join the rebellion and that he was arranging things for his children, but he was a spy. The Lorries that the northern soldiers said that we would travel in were the pick-ups that he went to show the drivers the places where the landmines were planted and a map showing where the land mines were, so that they would not pass by and get killed by the landmines.

We were astounded by the fact that someone who had decided to rebel was still at home despite his decision to rebel and was telling Monycuei that he would join the rebellion, but just wanted to arrange some things for his children. We were very surprised by this matter. We thank God for giving us wisdom on the way in those days. After we had walked some distance, we asked Monycuei: "What was that man saying to you?" He said, "He told us he will join the SPLM/SPLA, and that he wants to arrange some things for his children first." We said to Monycuei: "Is this man not doing something else? This man will not rebel. If you say you want to rebel, your heart will not allow time for waiting. If one delays making a decision to rebel for two days, he will not delay for a third day without making the decision. When we decided to rebel in Khartoum, and we delayed for a short time, the days we spent at home planning for rebellion were not relaxed. Our hearts did not rest. This man must be doing something else; and he will not rebel." Monycuei said to us, "Why are you girls talking this way?" We told him: "You will see it later by yourself." Our trend of conversation then changed. We arrived at Baaidit. There was a place for hosting and serving people that had arrived from other places. Awuor and I lived in one room.

We had not yet reached Ethiopia; we were still inside the Bor area. We got to where Arok Thon was at his residence. We arrived there on May 9. We had left Khartoum on April 4 and stayed in Malakal until April 21. And we spent the rest of the days between Duk Padiet and Ayod. We arrived on May 9, which meant that we had spent over a month on the way. When we arrived at Arok Thon's residence he registered our names and wrote our statement for joining the SPLM/SPLA on May 9, 1985.

When we got to the registration site, we didn't find any of our people from Abyei there. The recruits were all from Bor. They gave us a room and Arok Thon sent our names to be broadcast. They were broadcast on May 9th. Our family heard our names in Khartoum on the SPLM radio on May 9th. They were searching until our pictures were taken to the Television. Arok Thon registered our names. Then we stayed. After two days, that man whom we had met on the way with Monycuei and who had said that he would rebel, arrived at Ayod. He was in the truck that was in front of the fleet of government trucks to reveal the places where land mines were laid to the drivers behind him to avoid the mines. He was helping them to pass safely. And they were paying him. This was his business, and he was deceiving people that he would join the rebellion. We were suspicious of him from the beginning, which was why we told Monycuei that that man was doing something else and would not rebel.

We continued walking with Monycuei and reached an area near Poktap. I have introduced Arok Thon in the story, but I have not yet started to tell the details of our meeting with him; it will now come. When we arrived at Poktap, Monycuei told us that we would pass by a house to drink water because there was thirst in the land. So, we went and entered the house of a woman who was the housewife. That woman was looking at us with intensity and what seemed like hostility. Her gaze was that of someone who was not happy.

She was from Bor Dinka and was also a spy. But the SPLM didn't know. We were the ones who exposed all those things. She looked at us bitterly from the time we entered the house. We were closely watching the situation around us whenever we got to a new place. We did not enter any place without noticing something. We were always attentive wherever we went. Our attention and caution always revealed what was going on around us. The woman's gaze at us was unusual. We were annoyed at the way she looked at us. We told Monycuei that we were leaving. He asked why? "You should rest and drink water," he urged us.

We told him, "No, Monycuei, we must go." When we were going on the way, Monycuei asked what happened. We told him, "Didn't you see how the woman was looking at us? She might have looked at you positively, but she was looking at us negatively."

At the time, she was cooking for the soldiers of Nimeiri's army in her house and she was washing their clothes. It showed the way the Dinka do things. Monycuei was telling us that he did not know what had happened. We told him that the woman was hiding something, and that we did not like staying with her. He told us that the house of his uncle was ahead of us, and that we should go there to drink water. So, we walked and there they gave us water. They had hunted that tall animal, the giraffe. The meat was cooking. Then they brought us boiled meat with soup. The soup was black. We asked what meat it was. They said that it was giraffe meat. We abstained from eating it and only asked for water to drink. Monycuei laughed and said: "You do not want to eat giraffe meat when you have made a decision to join the rebellion." He said, "People here eat even donkey meat." We said we would look into that when faced with that situation in the future, but we did not want to take that meat at that time.

They gave us water and sour milk, which we drank. We spent the day in Poktap. In the evening, we walked a long distance until we reached an army area. We spent the night there. We found some women there. In the morning we went to Arok Thon. It was on May 8th, and on May 9th, our names were broadcast on the SPLM/A Radio.

There was a radio station, and Yassir, my husband, Sana's father, later became a radio broadcaster in the Arabic language section of the SPLA/SPLM radio. But at that time, he had not yet joined the Movement. There were the late Dut Kat, the great broadcaster in the old Juba radio station, and Chaw Mayol Juuk, a nephew to Kuol Manyang Juuk, who was also a presenter and was on the radio at that time. Yassir joined the SPLM in 1987, two years after we had joined. We went to the area where Arok Thon was present. And after registering us, he sent our names to be broadcast. We met Nyandhael Nyankor, Biong Deng Alor, Kuol Biong Mijak, who is the brother of the lawyer, Deng Biong, Alor Deng Alor, Arop Haroun, and a large number of the sons and daughters of our area of Abyei. The Ngok daughters were many.

They were living in the same house in which Arok was staying. They had left Abyei since February that year. We were then still in Khartoum. Because they were travelling during the hot season, they spent much more time on the way than we later did. We left Khartoum in April. They were on the way for two months. We met them at the house where Arok lived. We walked on the road. And the journey was really very difficult. It is said that God exists, and it is really true. God really exists. As human beings, we sometimes go through many calamities. There are places which, when you pass through them, you do not know whether you will survive or not. But God makes you live. And there is fate and the final day. If the fate of your life is long, you will not die, because what causes you to die is your life's fate and the end of your days. Neither illness nor danger will take your life if God has not determined your fate and the date of your death.

We walked through very dangerous Nuer areas. At that time, we were being attacked by the Gai Tut rebel forces (Nyigaat) on the way. A number of our students were killed. The sons of Abyei who went before us included Juac Aghol, the brother of Kuol Adol's wife, who was with a group of Ngok students. They had left Khartoum and rebelled as a group. The system that was followed by the Nuer was to gather you and appear to be showing you hospitality; they would gather you as if you were being hosted and offered food. They would ask you to eat. They would then come and shoot you while you are eating. It was a terrible thing. Those before us were deceived that way. People would arrive exhausted and thirsty. They would want to drink water and eat food. Then they would come to you with food. You would sit as if you were eating. Then you would be shot. It was a very bad system.

When our group came, we heard about this horrific practice. So, we did not accept to sit and eat. Even our own food that we carried in our bag, we used to eat it while looking around to watch. You would not eat with your head lowered. We always travelled at that time on foot. I remember once narrating those memories to Arop Haroun. I recalled to him how we walked on the road and the great protection they gave us. I said that it was our duty to reciprocate and that it would be appropriate for us to attend the wedding of every one of those brothers to offer services to them.

Arop Haroun carried sliced dried fish on his shoulder like a gun. We used to buy dried fish that was brought from Bahr el Ghazal. Arop carried on his shoulder the fish that the Ngok used to cut into slices and dried. I have forgotten the names of fish. There were large tilapia fish and mud fish that were cut into long strips. Arop Haroun had come with the strips of fish, and when we sat at a specific point, one strip was taken out and cooked. There was no salt in those days. And I remember when the salt ran out, and I couldn't bear to eat food with saltless sauce which made the food doubly cold. I would rather eat thick porridge without any sauce or broth. People would laugh at me and ask what was the difference? I would say that there was indeed a difference. When porridge without salt is mixed with a sauce that also had no salt it would become cold and tasteless. It was better for me to eat thick porridge alone because it tasted a little sweet, but if mixed with a sauce that has no salt, it would completely spoil it.

We passed through Nuer regions on a road that was very, very tough. We thanked God a lot for having preserved us until we met our brothers and walked together as one family. That was God's plan. And that helped us a lot. We were walking to an area that could be reached in three hours, but we reached it in nine hours. Mading, you might ask me how we walked for nine hours to an area that could be reached in three hours. We would walk to the area we wanted to reach in three hours, and after three hours, we would be shot at and some people would fall dead. And some would turn back, if we met the rebels. So, we were going back to the area where we had come from after three hours. The next day, we would reorganize and walk the three hours that we had walked the day before. All of these were nine hours: three hours walking, three hours returning when we were forced to return, and three hours tracing our way again. And if God would help us and make the way safe, we would walk forward. And we had already walked the distance between Sudan and Ethiopia in three months on foot in the jungle.

I remember that there was an area where we stopped. We were very thirsty. Then we reached a village near a river. When we got to the river, people sat and drank until they nearly fell into the river. They could not believe that they had found water. We met the new recruits. Arok Thon used to wait for more people to come. And then they would travel as a group for protection; they could help one another, if they were many in number.

Once, we were walking with a group of recruits, when one of the men in our group said we should stop to rest in this village because we had girls with us. He wanted people to rest at our expense. They were tired and didn't want to show people that they were tired, but rather because of the girls. So, we said that if the break was because of us, we did not want to rest. One man said: "Where did these girls come from? Girls who do not get tired when men are tired? What kind of people are you?" We told them that we knew they wanted to rest at our expense and said that it was because of the girls. "Let us go," we said.

The journey was really, really bad. Many of us would be shot dead; then we would turn back; and then we would resume the journey again. Mading, the conditions of life, the circumstances of this world, the conditions in the bush, and the quality of life in the SPLM, Mading, all that has completely confounded me. When I hear a person complaining of suffering, I despise such talk; I do not give it any attention. There is no suffering we did not undergo in this world. Even the blessing of marriage cannot erase what one has endured. I got married after having gone through all kinds of troubles, hardships and sufferings that have left deep imprints on me.

Becoming a Woman Warrior

Let me now go back to the story of our recruitment into the Movement. We reached a place called Kongor in Bor which was the recruitment Headquarters of Arok Thon Arok. We arrived there on the 8th of May 1985. Our names were sent to the radio of the People's Liberation Movement. There we met many new recruits from Abyei and all the surrounding areas of Bahr el Ghazal. We met them in Kongor. After a period of two weeks, we left Kongor and travelled through the Nuer area to the military training center in Ethiopia. At that time there was a rebellion against the Movement or against Dr. John, the leader of the Movement. The rebellion was under the leadership of Gai Tut.

We were walking long distances. We were going to Ethiopia. But then we would come to an area where there was fighting. Our progress would be blocked by attacks from the rebels against the Movement. We would be forced to return to the area from which we had left. We would walk back the same distance to go and sleep there. In the morning, we would take off again and walk to where we had reached the day before.

So, we would have walked on foot for three times the hours. We were a large group of recruits. There were also a few soldiers who were trained and charged with guiding and protecting us in case there were problems. The group included our relatives, among them Arop Haroun, Deng Alor and Kuol Biong Mijak. It was a large group. We girls were also many.

Our group of the girls included myself and Awuor Abul and Nyandhel Nyankoor (Achai-Nyandhel). Other girls from Abyei included Abuk Alor Jipur and Aluk Deng Matiok, and Awuor Aleu. It was a large group. We walked and walked and walked all that long distance. We would move on and again come across the shooting. People would be killed, and we would be forced to go back to the area from which we had come. The following day, we would go back again on the same route. But God protected us and gave us a safe passage to move on. It was a period of many, many problems and risks, but God protected us to keep moving on.

We arrived in the area for refugees in Ethiopia after three months. Those were three months filled with life threatening dangers and serious hardships. The refugee camp was in an area called Itang. That was where the refugees were gathered. There were also compounds for the military in the areas called Bilpam and Bongo. Most of the girls who were already trained were taken to Bilpam. There were girls in the Battalion of Koryom (Locusts) who were trained before us. They were taken to Bilpam. They were trained in Bilpam and then taken to graduate in Bongo.

Our group of girls was the second batch. We went to Bilpam in June 1985, and we joined the batch known as Khazug (Disaster). So, we trained with the batch of Khazug in Bilpam. After the training, we were taken to Bongo for graduation. We were in two groups. The group of the Liberation Army consisted of men who had been trained in Bongo and we, the girls who had trained in Bilpam, and then taken to Bongo for graduation. The graduation was pleasant; It was really sweet and beautiful. We sang nationalist liberation songs, revolutionary songs. The graduation was really enjoyable.

After the graduation in Bongo we were taken back to Bilpam. It was a critical war situation with much suffering. The Liberation Army was continuously facing attacks. They would go into battles and soldiers would be injured and there were no facilities for treatment. There were no doctors or hospitals with medical facilities. But the Government of

Cuba came with help. They sent doctors and medical equipment from Cuba. They came and began to train us in providing emergency first aid to the injured. A number of us girls from Khazug were selected and taken for medical training provided by the Cuban doctors. The training was short. The situation was dire, really critical, and required quick action. Conditions were really severe. But God had mercy and made improvement possible. God always makes it possible to get things done.

The Soft Arm of Warfare

We were trained for only three weeks in the medical field. After the training, we were assigned to the hospital in Bilpam. I was assigned the area of injections; I injected people. And my sister Awuor Abul was assigned the area of nursing injuries. And our other sister, Achai Deng (Achai -Nyandhel), was in the area of pharmacy dispensing medicines. The Cubans did their best to get us medicines and medical equipment for the hospital. That helped in providing help to people under those very difficult circumstances. God helped us. We took charge of the hospital. From time to time they would take us into situations of military operations. And we took part in military operations. We would then return to where we were living.

Where we lived was a good area in terms of the climate. The weather was always good. And that helped ease the stresses of the situation. We lived there in Bilpam from 1985 to 1986. And we used to help in providing services and hospitality to visitors and guests of the Movement, including people from abroad. We tried to help in many ways within our capacity. We offered services and facilitation and helped in organizing activities. We stayed in that area for a long time.

And of course, the destiny of life and the end result for a girl is to get married, have a family, and raise children. In this area, Dr. John encouraged the girls. He came and talked to us and said, "You girls, you have fulfilled your responsibility. You have not fallen short of discharging your obligations. If there are among you individuals who want to choose a different path for the future, there should be no problem. If you should decide to get married and have families and raise children, those families and children are part of our liberation struggle. Those children are the generation that will continue what we have started." So, Dr. John encouraged the girls with those words.

And indeed, things began to happen. The destiny of some girls led them into marriage. And then we got families and begot children. Dr. John encouraged us that even if a woman stayed at home to take care of her children, those children belong to the Revolution; they are the children of the Movement; and they are the children of the Sudan. They will be the ones to serve the country in the future. He said, "We need the next generation to continue the mission. We will grow old and withdraw from the face of this world. And when we are no longer here, it will be the next generation that will remain." The destiny of each one of us came and we got married and had children. Dr. John encouraged us in that area.

And now, I would like to tell the story of my own marriage. My marriage was on the 31st of March 1991. It was in the town of Torit in South Sudan. But even after marriage, one does not separate oneself from military service or the service of the nation or any contribution which can help the South and the generations to come and to build a better future for the country. So, up to now, we are still connected to the army; our relations with the army are still strong. We have not withdrawn from the army, nor have we withdrawn from our national responsibility.

Women in the Liberation Struggle

With respect to the role played by South Sudanese women generally and, in particular, the efforts of South Sudanese girls in the Sudan People's Liberation Movement and the Sudan People's Liberation Army (SPLM/SPLA), I would like to go back to the early days when the SPLM/SPLA was founded, and the youth and the people of Southern Sudan began to leave the cities and join the rebellion. The foundation of the Movement was still being established in the Ethiopian areas.

Frankly, women are great freedom fighters. They are strong. They stood like men. There was no distinction between women and men, except in biological creation. You could find a woman assuming many great and tough responsibilities and carrying enormous burdens, despite the harsh conditions that people were living in, and the really bad and difficult conditions in the cities.

Women organized themselves and would hold secret meetings to assist groups of young men who wanted to join the SPLM/SPLA to participate in the liberation struggle. These young people often did not have the means to enable them to travel and needed financial support. I remember that women used to meet and collect donations. Every one of them used to give as much contribution as they could afford. They ascertained the number of those planning to travel and covered the travel costs of the youth. Women would travel to areas of the SPLM/SPLA in Bahr el Ghazal and continue on to Bor and would form women's groups in the countryside to support the struggle.

The women in the rural areas of Bahr el Ghazal did not fail to provide whatever they could contribute. They really struggled in the practical sense of the word. Southern Sudanese women were freedom fighters, whether they were in the countryside or in towns. They stood like men. They worked very hard and contributed whatever they could afford. Women in Bahr al Ghazal were receiving the Southern Sudanese youth who were joining the SPLM/SPLA, and assisted them with great interest, self-sacrifice, and great joy. They exerted themselves to create favorable conditions for the young people who were joining the SPLM/SPLA.

Women also used to hold gatherings to make food supplies, food items that were prepared for the travelers. They included things like dried *kisira* or *injeera*, known as *abre*, cakes, roasted peanuts and sesame seeds. All these things, which women used to make, were prepared for the young people who were on their way to the liberation struggle. Women were committed to organizing themselves and if the young men going to the movement were many, they would divide them among themselves and accommodate them in separate houses. Each house was allocated specific numbers of men to accommodate and host them until the day they (the young men) travelled. The woman of the house would be fully responsible for hosting them from the day they arrived until the day they left.

That was one of the things that women did. Then the youth would proceed to the next area and the same thing was done in that area. This would be repeated in different areas of Bahr el Ghazal until they reached Bor. In the areas of Bor women also met them with joy and happiness and offered them great care. These young people were given great consideration and appreciation. Women knew the conditions that Southern Sudan was going through. It was necessary to stand together as one people and to provide assistance to the generation of the young that would be able to resist and defeat the enemy and restore the stolen rights of our people. Women in Bor did the same thing that women in Bahr el Ghazal did, by showing care to those young men. As in Bahr el Ghazal, those young men were distributed into houses according to their numbers, and the women would take care of them for 24 hours by providing them with food, drink and places to sleep during the period they would spend on their way to the front. Clothes were also collected for those who did not have clothes due to their poor conditions, or for those who left the city in a hurry without preparing to take what they needed.

Donations of clothing were collected by those who had young men at home with clothes they could afford to give away. Those clothes were taken and given to the young men who were heading to the fields of the liberation struggle at the inception of the SPLM/SPLA in 1983. Women used to support them until they entered Ethiopia and reached Itang where they were registered and received training. Some of them received military training in Bongo. Others were trained in Bilpam, an area that was transformed into a training center for young women. So, South Sudanese women contributed much and sacrificed in the liberation struggle.

And as I told you, when we arrived in the area of training, we did a lot of things. We spent six months in training. And after the training, we were able to provide care for the sick and the wounded who were brought back from the war fronts. As they say, joining hands by strengthening one hand with the other hand can throw farther away. That was what happened in Southern Sudan with women, young women, young men, and even the very elderly people. I know of people who are still vivid in my memory. Although they were old even then, their conscience couldn't allow them to be idle. Many elderly people went and joined the SPLM/SPLA and even entered the field of training. Many of them became martyrs in the battlefields. They registered their history in Southern Sudan by their actions.

May God extend the age of those who have survived, for there are those who even though they were senior at that time have survived. I believe they have now grown very old and cannot do anything. But they have exerted their efforts and made history. This is the group of people that Southern Sudan should take care of because they are people who fought for the rights of their homeland. They have the upper hand in the liberation struggle of Southern Sudan. They were the means by which

the independence of Southern Sudan was attained. This group contributed tremendously to the attainment of independence for South Sudan.
These are people we should not forget. Whether they have died or are
still alive, we should not forget them.

Those are the things which happened. I told you, we entered the
fields of training and graduated in 1989. After graduating, we went and
stayed in the refugee areas of Itang and Panyido from 1989 until 1991. In
1991, the war reached its climax. The rebel forces of Eritrea and Ethiopia
staged a coup against the government of Mengistu Haile Mariam in
1989. A new Government was formed by the Ethiopian rebels, which
led to the withdrawal of the SPLM/SPLA from Ethiopia to Kenya.
The reason for the withdrawal was that the new Ethiopian government
thought that their enemies from the former Government of Mengistu
Haile Mariam were being supported by the SPLM/SPLA, led by Dr.
John Garang. The new Ethiopian government said that it did not want
the Sudanese rebels to stay in their country anymore. Those were the
reasons we left Ethiopia and came to Kenya. This was in 1991.

In Kenya, our army was based in a place called Keybes near Lokichokio.
Kebede was another area between Lokichokio and another area in Kenya
called Kakuma. The Sudan People's Liberation Movement's army was
there under the command of Pieng Deng Kuol. He was the commander of the Sudan People's Liberation Army at the time the SPLM left
Ethiopia for Kenya. They were in Keybes. And some of the citizens were
in Narus. Others were in Kapoeta. And yet others were in Chukudum,
Torit and another area called Kadipo. This means that people were scattered in various areas of Southern Sudan regions. I was among those
who were in Torit. That was where I got married. My marriage took
place on March 31, 1991, in Torit town.

The SPLM girls had to meet their destiny. Whatever a girl does, in
the end, she eventually gets married. And as I said, Dr. John had encouraged us in this respect. He told us, "Girls, you did not at all fail the
Movement; you have done your job and the destiny of a girl is to get
married. We need you. And we need the children you will bear and
breastfeed. We will grow and become old. We must have children to
leave behind, a new generation. That new generation is the one that will
assume the responsibility that we are now carrying. Whether we achieve
our goal or not, they are the ones who will assume our responsibility."

The words of Dr. John encouraged the girls. We got married, each one of us according to her destiny.

I think we did not go far after we got married. Most of the girls of Southern Sudan who joined the SPLM/SPLA or went to the training fields are still associated with the army to this day. I don't remember knowing anyone whom I can say left the army from the group of the Koryom battalion that was trained before us. We were the Khazouk brigade. Girls and women in the SPLM/SPLA fought and struggled a lot.

I remember a highly respected woman who was in the SPLM/SPLA. I think she had also been one of the prominent figures in Anya-Nya One. Her name was Ager Gum. She was a woman for whom I had high respect because she fought a lot in the SPLM/SPLA. I believe she died of an illness caused by frustration due to the problems that were occurring within the SPLM leadership. She died at a time when she heard the news of the death of Yousif Kuwa Mekki. She was a true freedom fighter. She loved all the freedom fighters very much and wished that God would keep them for the liberation of Southern Sudan and die as martyrs in the struggle or after the liberation of the South solve all the problems of the country. Her hopes were all in this. In those days, when she heard that someone had died suddenly, she would get deeply saddened. Yousif Kuwa, may God have mercy on him, was from the Nuba Mountains. Dr. John was a patriotic and unionist leader who brought the whole of Sudan together.

John Garang didn't differentiate between the North and the South. He brought all those who had a problem and grievance with the system together in one place and united them. Our problem was a Sudanese problem. It was not a problem that was associated with tribalism. We all looked at ourselves as Sudanese and each one of us was feeling and caring for one another. If you had a problem, you would know that the same problem that you are facing was also faced by the other person. Dr. John wanted to find solutions to the problems of the Sudan as a whole. Ager Gum also cared for everyone in the struggle. She was a person I exceedingly respected, may God have mercy on her. And may God also have mercy on all our martyrs, the SPLM/SPLA martyrs. And on the top of them is Dr. John Garang.

These are people we cannot forget. We must remember them. We must record their memory in history for generations to come. We who are surviving must be strong and continue the march for development in South Sudan. We must take care of each other; we must particularly take care of the wives and children of the martyrs. These are the people who sacrificed their lives and accepted martyrdom for the land of South Sudan. And they brought peace and stability, even though stability right now is not as was expected. But the situation has improved and is better than it was in the past. It is good that people have begun to deal with the recent problems in the country. I hope that they will be fully resolved. It is encouraging that people have started to address these concerns. This will be hopefully accomplished, God willing.

On the other hand, the women's struggle was a protracted one. After staying at home as a result of getting married and having children, earning a living was tough and the conditions were difficult. But despite these harsh conditions, women continued the struggle in their houses as married women. Every one of them had to leave her children and work hard to provide for the family. She got exhausted working to get something for her children to eat. And people struggled to support the education of their children. Despite the fact that there were hard conditions in the bush, every woman tried hard to enroll her children in school. We also used to build houses in the refugee areas where we were living. Children went to schools in spite of the harsh conditions under which the people were living.

Husbands were always far away in areas of military operations. But women never failed in the absence of the men. The only anxiety that women faced was that there were no telephones in those days and there was no way to inquire or ask about their husbands' well-being. And they rarely got someone they could ask about their husbands' whereabouts. Sometimes, they did not even know the places they were taken to. Only God knew the unseen. Women exercised patience and self-control and they were patient enough. They assumed full responsibility in taking care of their children without knowing the whereabouts of their fathers. They took care of the children and prayed to God to keep their husbands safe wherever they were. So, women suffered a lot. But they showed much patience, resilience, strength and courage. Women, children and the aged were the most affected by the hardships that people faced in the bush. If they were not courageous enough, they would have given up, but they did not. Instead, they struggled. As the saying goes:

"Behind every great man, there is a woman."

The Sudanese women at large and the South Sudanese women in particular are strong. Had it not been the strength and the energy that they had, the SPLM/SPLA would not have progressed, nor would it have been successful. And the independence of South Sudan would not have been attained. Much of the credit in this must go to the women. The credit goes to the women for their conscientiousness, their belief in God, and their faith in Him. They relied on God, and they did all the things they could do, leaving to God what they could not do. This is what was happening.

The life of women and young women of South Sudan was a life of liberation struggle. Among them were women who sacrificed their lives and died in battlefields as martyrs. I can recall that in our group, there were women who met their martyrdom in the battles in Bahr el Ghazal. Some of those women who went into action survived and are still alive now. May God keep them, and may God also have mercy on our martyred soldiers and officers, and on top of their list Dr. John Garang. This is what happened.

As I said earlier, we completed our training in 1985 after which we worked in a hospital in Bilpam. We were helping in providing medical services, such as first aid. The situation was very dire. There were no doctors and no medicines, but God later made the situation better. The Cubans came and trained us, and they brought medicines and medical equipment. And with the benevolent might of God, we were able to assist our people.

Two years later, we went to refugee areas in Itang. Next to Itang, there was another area called Panyido. We were moving between those areas. Sometimes we would go back to Bilpam, which was the army center until 1990, when the coup against Mengistu Haile Mariam was staged. He was ousted and the SPLM/SPLA left Ethiopia for Kenya. Some of us went to Kenya and from Kenya, some went to Sudan. I came to Kenya after my marriage. And until today, we are still in Kenya and some of us are in Sudan. This is what happened.

Ours has been a long struggle and great liberation struggle. And we thank God very much for His aid and support for our cause. The rights of human beings cannot be lost before God. Therefore, the rights of every South Sudanese and the rights of every Sudanese were not lost in front of God. This is what I can say.

We, the SPLM girls who joined the army still have our organization up to now in South Sudan. We have our office. Nyankiir Atem, from Bor, is the one in charge of that office. Our promotions in the army are still ongoing. There is also another thing which I didn't speak about. There were women who joined the SPLM/SPLA when they were already married. They joined with their husbands. Of course, we were still girls, not yet married. We had no husbands with us when we joined the rebellion. That is why we were called Katibat al-Banat (Girls' Brigade). But there were women who joined with their husbands, and they went to the fields of the army training. It was necessary for everyone at that time to join the army for security reasons. This was for reasons of coverage and protection. One could help himself or herself in case of a military attack. One could also assist in the evacuation and withdrawal or cover of colleagues from a crossfire and or help civilians who had not joined the military.

These were some of the factors which made people join the army whether they were married women or young unmarried girls, for it was useful. However, the contribution made by girls was greater than the one of the married women. Married women had responsibilities behind them at home. They had children to take care of. They had their own contributions in the army, but they were incomparable with the ones made by girls. Notwithstanding the overall contributions by people helping one another, women made enormous contributions. They stood up like men in the liberation struggle for South Sudan. The brigade of married women that came and joined the training later was given a different name from the one of Katibat al-Banat which comprised young women who went and joined the fields of training as unmarried women. The women who joined the training as married women were called Katibat al-Sheitha (Chillis Brigade). I give this information to differentiate between the women who went with their husbands and got trained and the girls or single young women who went and got trained. The name Sheitha, chillis in meaning, sounds stronger and tougher than Katibat al-Banat.

Katibat al-Sheitha was a very strong brigade; it did not fail in any way. They did as much in the war as they could within their capacity. Whether they had been in the cities or in the countryside, before they formed Katibat al-Sheitha, they did much service even before joining the training and became Katiba al-Shatha.

I thank you Dr. Francis and I thank God for the chance He gave me with you. And I also thank the person who is working with you on this project. I thank God for it is through His divine power that people meet. And it is God who programs events that can endure into the future. No one knew that all these memories would one day be recorded or that the idea itself would come to your mind. I personally did not know that someone would come and give me the positive energy to contribute to recording our important and great history and our struggle that should not go without documentation. This is something very important. And I am very glad and thank God that I have been able to meet with you and work on this project. May God give you a long life and extend your age. We really need to collect these important accounts for the future. We must have a clear and documented account of our history for the future that will continue to be on the tongues of our people. If nothing is written about our history, people will forget it and they will not know what has happened.

This is a very important program. What you are doing now is part of the liberation struggle. There is no difference between the liberation struggle and what you are doing now. They are both components of the same continued struggle. Although the war has now ended in the South, and South Sudan has become an independent sovereign country, we must document our past and the history of our struggle. It is very important to let the future generations learn and know the things that have happened in the past. We hear stories about things that happened during the period of our forefathers. They left those memories and nostalgic recollections to us. We came and found those memories and recollections.

This is the same thing you are now doing. In the past, history depended on oral memories. Now we have the benefit of recording experiences for documentation. All things come in a sequence. In your case, you writers and politicians, and especially you Dr. Francis, your struggle is a long one which I personally very much appreciate. And I don't appreciate you because I am your sister or for any other personal reason; I consider you as one of the leading freedom fighters of South Sudan. When people were in the war of liberation for South Sudan, whether you were abroad or inside the Sudan, you never slept with a peace of mind; you remained awake and felt concerned for us. As we were alarmed and worried in the bush, you were also alarmed and anxious in the places where you were. You were in the cities, but you were not at ease and your conscience could not give you a room for a rest, because your country was burning. As your own country was burning, and as you are a person with conscience, your conscience didn't have mercy on you; it was also burning within you as your country was burning. You have stood with us as politicians and writers; you have never failed to be on our side. And your struggle still continues until today.

I thank God and I pray to Him to keep you in fitness and good health to continue the struggle. And in everything, as they say, "one hand combined with the other hand can throw farther away." All the problems will find solutions and God will give us success. He will also give success to our brothers who are bearing the highest responsibilities for our country. May God have mercy on all the martyrs of the Sudan People's Liberation Army, and on top of their list Dr. John Garang de Mabior.

Bonds of Southern Identity

We appeal to the people of the Sudan or the people of South Sudan after they attained their independence and assumed responsibility for its destiny to get together and unite in one direction for the nation. We need to put our hands together and stand in solidarity to work together to move our country forward. To this day, our memories of our people, our heroes from the liberation army who died in the struggle, on top of whom is Dr. John Garang, have never left our minds. Our hope is that South Sudan will succeed and move forward. And though we have sacrificed beloved ones, on top of whom is Dr. John Garang, and they are no longer with us, we hope that the next generation, including their children and in particular the widows of our martyrs will be taken good care of by our government. Those who suffer the most in war are the children and the women and the elderly. We hope that the government and the people of South Sudan will take good care of those people. We now have people who have aged and have no children to take care of them because of the war that has killed members of the families leaving some of them without relatives to care for them.

Separation that breaks up a country and makes people part ways is not an easy thing. It involves a lot of pain and tragedies. If people do not manage the situation well, they cannot progress forward. But we hope that South Sudan will manage and progress forward. The people of South Sudan have sacrificed a great deal during the prolonged period of the liberation struggle. This means that South Sudanese are people whose hearts are strong. They are capable of building their country. And they can produce the result of the struggle that has gone on for so long and has taken the lives of large numbers of people.

Everyone should look at the needs of his brother and sister and those of fellow citizens. We should all unite and reconcile with one another as one family of South Sudan. We should love our fellow citizens as we love ourselves. This is all I would like to say. But there is no problem that cannot be solved. In a new country, there are always bound to be problems, but they can in the end be solved. Twenty-one years of struggle was a very long time. In the end God brought peace. No one expected that there would be another surprise conflict. But surprise came and it will again end by the will of God. We hope that the Peace that has now come will be sustained and that generations to come will not suffer what we have endured for these many years. But God solved those problems and God will again bring peace.

Divine Light on Justice

I would now want to add that the People's Liberation Army comprises very strong people. They were heroes who cannot be forgotten in the history of South Sudan. They demonstrated their heroism to the whole world. The war they fought was a war of heroes and God will have mercy on them; He will bestow upon them all His mercy. That is why I tell you that until now, we remain connected to the Army. My rank in the Army now has reached that of lieutenant colonel; I am a lieutenant colonel in the Army.

Another thing I want to mention is the case of Abyei. I am from Abyei. And we are South Sudanese. And if we were not South Sudanese, nothing would have taken us into the war of the South against the North. We would not have pursued the war for all those years, that is twenty-one years, during which so many of our young people from the South, including from Abyei, lost their lives. It is our One South Sudan that brought us together. And now, we say that we from Abyei are part and parcel of South Sudan. And God will bring out our right and give it to us. God will reveal and resolve the grievances that compelled the sons and daughters of Abyei, soldiers from Abyei, and heroes of Abyei, to come and fall in the war in South Sudan.

God will bring out and grant all the rights of the people of Abyei. We are South Sudanese; and we will continue to say that we are South Sudanese. And no one can tell us that we are not. And no one can prevent us from being South Sudanese. We are from South Sudan. And that is why we joined the war of the People's Liberation Movement. We came and joined the struggle, boys, girls and wives following their husbands. Whether they were young men or women or wives with their husbands, they all joined the struggle, and many fell as martyrs in the war in South Sudan. For their sacrifice, God will grant their rights and the rights of their people and generations of their children in the future. That is all I want to say.

Nyenagwek Kuol

PART THREE
WADING IN TROUBLED WATERS

Nyenagwek Kuol:
A Fighter Turned Ambassador of Peace

Introduction

A REMARKABLE FEATURE OF a people's liberation movement is that the struggle takes many different forms. Some take up arms and put their lives in peril where the goal is to kill and risk getting killed. That is the ultimate price for freedom in which you are ready to die so that your people can be liberated from various forms of bondage and indignity. That was the path of Pieng in this collection of profiles in the South Sudan liberation struggle. Awuor Deng, with her sister of the same name of Awuor, also chose a version of the struggle in which they also rebelled and joined the armed struggle, trained as soldiers, and served in the supportive role of caring for the injured and others in need of medical attention. Nyenagwek Kuol found herself struggling within the system that she was almost inherently resisting, but in which she paradoxically found opportunities to wade her way through its troubled waters, which enabled her to serve her people, including by redeeming abducted children and returning them to their families. She also contributed to treating former abductees and their families from the trauma associated with abduction and enslavement. She eventually joined the armed struggle toward the end of the war, after which she ironically became Ambassador for Peace.

The factors that provoke individuals to rebel also differ significantly. Pieng witnessed horrific brutalities of his people tortured and killed in gruesome ways by the Arab dominated Government that drove him into a rage of hatred which he admits became deeply ingrained as a prejudice against the Arabs. Awuor reacted to a condescending treatment by her teachers that she interpreted as racially based, and one teacher was actually manifestly racist. She saw their attitude as a reflection of racial discrimination and denigration of Southern Sudanese which led to the armed struggle she chose to join. Nyenagwek was keenly aware of the generalised mistreatment of South Sudanese and the brutal killing of individuals from her area who were recognised by their people as heroes and martyrs. All of them are from the Ngok Dinka of Abyei, an area of South Sudan that was administratively annexed to the North by the British colonial administration, ironically to provide them with better protection against the neighbouring Missiriya Arab slave raiders, the very people with whom they were being affiliated. While the British were in control of the government, they provided neutral and impartial management of the relations between the Ngok Dinka of Abyei and their Missiriya Arab neighbours to the North. With independence, and especially with the civil war between the North and the South that erupted at the dawn of independence, with racial, religious and cultural overtones, the Ngok Dinka were driven into the war as part and parcel of their kith and kin in the South.

Nyenagwek ends with a concluding observation with which I end my comments in Pieng's story, the paradox of so much killing and destruction of war to correct wrongs. After such a long devastation of the North-South war, the South after only two years of independence plunged into a fratricidal conflict that has again caused so much suffering, death and destruction and has profoundly destabilised the country. This drove her into prioritising peace-making over warring, which was recognised and appreciated by Universal Peace Federation by appointing her Ambassador for Peace.

What follows is the story of Nyenagwek Kuol told in her own words.

Background to Rebellion

My name is Nyenagwek Kuol Mareng Maker. My grandfather, Mareng Maker, was a prominent Sacred Spear Master of the Pajok lineage in Anyiel Chiefdom of the Ngok Dinka. He was the Spiritual Father of Mangar – Anyiel age-group, whose two senior and junior segments were initiated with the traditional scarification marks on the forehead in 1953 and 1963. I was born in Abyei town on May 11, 1981. The circumstances surrounding the period of my childhood made me want to be a fighter, and for that matter a freedom fighter. Nothing was easy from the time I was born. I was continuously forced by the harsh conditions that were pushing my generation to the edge to fight back for my rights. This included the right to education as a girl child. I ended up joining the armed struggle staged by the SPLA in the bushes of Southern Sudan at the age of 22 years.

My early childhood was during the most difficult times in the history of the Ngok-Dinka people of Abyei in which political polarisation and security tensions reached their peak in the entire Abyei Area. This was in sharp contrast to the cordial relationship between the Ngok Dinka and their neighbours from the North, specifically the Misseriya – Ajaira, who were said to have lived in peaceful coexistence for centuries as described by Dr. Francis Mading Deng in the biography of his father, the late Paramount Chief Deng Majok[1].

Many trying events coincided with my early childhood. On top of the list of those events was the battle of Maker-Abior in which some notable Ngok personalities were killed, among them the late Bol Agon Arop Biong, who belonged to the Nyangateer age group of Abior chiefdom. The Ngok people were severely affected by the battle of Maker-Abior. It was clear that the government of Sudan and the Sudan Armed Forces took side with the Misseriya Arab nomads against the indigenous Ngok-Dinka of Abyei. The history of what followed Maker-Abior is well known. In short, the vast area of Abyei was reduced to Abyei town, as displaced masses of the population fled from the villages into Abyei town. This triggered the intensification of the armed resistance staged by Abyei youth and the eventual transformation of Anya-Nya Two in Abyei area into the Sudan People's Liberation.

The Army - SPLA

My early childhood had also witnessed the assassination of Luk Yowe[2]; a prominent freedom fighter and one of the founders of the armed resistant in Abyei Area. Late Luk Yowe was serving in the Sudan Armed Forces but took an early retirement in late 1970 and started some military training of volunteer Ngok Dinka youth when he realised the discrepancy and the imbalance of the traditional power between the Ngok Dinka and the Misseriya Arab nomads, following the formation of the Misseriya militia known as Murahleen. The Murahleen were well armed with modern weapons and were escorted by the SAF elements in their seasonal migration to Ngok land and farther South. Late Luk was ambushed and assassinated in early 1983. His body was dragged into Abyei town and displayed under The Court Tree of Chuen-Ayak for days by the SAF to warn any of the Abyei youth who were contemplating armed resistance of a similar fate.[2]

Another important event around my birth time was the oath-taking ordeal in 1982, using the Sacred Spear of Alor Ajing of the Dhiendior lineage of Mannyuar chiefdom. All the age-sets of the Ngok Dinka were brought to Abyei to take the oath by kissing the Sacred Spear and denouncing any future relationship with Anya-nya freedom fighters. These events were inscribed deep in my consciousness and would shape my memory and built the spirit of resistance within me.

Like many families in Abyei, my family composed of my mother, myself, two sisters and a brother were forced to move with many other families to Northern Sudan in late 1986, in search of security and survival. My family was among the first families to be repatriated back to Abyei in 1992, when the government initiated voluntary repatriation and the establishment of what was known as "modern villages" in Todac, Noong and Maker-Abior. But our stay in Abyei area did not last for long because the villages were not prepared to accommodate the returning IDP's. Nor were they secured from continuous harassment from the Murahleen militia. So, we had to flee Abyei again in 1995, back to Khartoum, where some relative security was available to the IDP's.

Opportunity in Crisis

I was admitted to El-Neelain University in Khartoum in 2001 for a diploma program in Business Administration, but like anyone else coming from a disadvantaged family, I was forced to look for a job to help support my family and pay for my study. I was very lucky to be employed as the private secretary to the Director General of the Committee for the Eradication of Abduction of Women and Children (CEAWC).[3] The Director General was the renowned lawyer Dr. Ahmed El-Mufti. The Committee was established by the government in 1999 to respond to the pressures from strong protests, internal and international, against the abduction and enslavement of Dinka women and children within and outside Sudan.

CEAWC was composed of two overlapping entities: The higher national committee headed by the Director General and the Joint Tribal Chiefs committee composed of 22 chiefs of equal numbers from both communities of Dinka and Baggara of Kordofan and Darfur. The government made a concession to accept the return and reunification of abducted Dinka women and children on condition that the Dinka chiefs would not take any legal actions against the abductors or the government.[3]

Two qualifications gave me the advantage to get the job of the secretary to the Director General of CEAWC. The first was that I was among the few of my age-mates at that time to have a basic training in computer and information technology. And the second was that our house was in close proximity to the assembly centre for the abducted women and children located in Riyadh suburb of Khartoum. I also came across the advertisement for the job in good time.

I was fortunate to get two successive promotions at CEAWC based on my qualifications and capabilities. Because of my fluency in both Arabic and Dinka languages, I was promoted first from office work to that of a social worker tasked with interacting with the abductees and integrating them into their new environment. I therefore left my job in the office of the Director General, although the job of the private secretary was more convenient for my university education. My new workstation was relocated to the assembly centre for the retrieved abductees.

My new position gave me the opportunity to become much closer to the abductees in the assembly centre and to hear their terrifying stories and agonies of the many children who were forcefully separated from their families and taken into servitude and harsh conditions. I heard unbelievable stories of sexual exploitation of the abducted women and girls by their abductors. In some instances, the abductor would sexually abuse both the mother and her daughter. To make matters worse, the abductor would rename them both to his name as his children.

My second opportunity came in early 2003 when I was promoted to be field coordination officer. I was based in El-Fula town in western Kordofan until March 2004, when I decided to join the SPLA in Northern Bahr El-Ghazal. My job as field coordinator was full of challenges. On top of those challenges was that I had to travel frequently with male colleagues as well as members of the Joint Tribal Chiefs (JTC) searching for abducted women and children in very remote rural areas of Southern Kurdofan and Southern Darfur among hostile communities and the harsh environment.

Another major unexpected challenge was that most of the abducted women and children were in deep psychological trauma, stigmatised and in denial. The following anomalies were frequently observed by our teams that were involved in rescue, integration and reunification activities[4]:

Some of the abductees were completely alienated from their original Dinka communities and culture and would deny any relationship with the Dinka. Instead, they would identify themselves as Arabs, despite the harsh conditions they were subjected to by the Arabs. That could be the reason taken by some international organisations, such as UNICEF, to down-play these reunification processes, as reflected in their annual reports, such as the report released on January 22, 2005 before the second and largest reunification of the abductees with their families. It was not easy to convince an abducted child or woman that they belonged to South Sudan.[4]

Some of the abductees were not ready to accept their families and go back to them because of the new life they had become used to. Some had already formed new families, despite the hardships to which they were subjected.

Some of the abductees had completely undergone cultural assimilation and were boasting of their new tribal identity as Arabs who were superior to Jenge/Dinka. It was not easy for them to leave the cultural pride they had assumed which made them feel superior to South Sudanese. They were not even prepared to accept food brought to them or cooked by non-Arabs whom they did not trust.

On the other hand, some abductees, who had been subjected to even harsher conditions or sexual exploitation, or had been abducted when they were older, were ready to be reunited with their families in South Sudan.

When I joined CEAWC in 2001, I found another girl, Ajok Wol Atak, who was employed before me as a field coordinator. She is currently a member of parliament in the Transitional National Legislative Assembly of South Sudan. We became a team of two determined girls. The two of us managed to recruit two other girls, Akur Chol Malual and Akiyoy Mou Pajoak. Both of them are currently senior government officials in the security sector. We became four females working for CEAWC in close coordination with the Dinka chiefs under the Leadership of Honourable James Aguer Alic. Honourable James Aguer had voluntarily and singlehandedly initiated the reunification program until the central government in Khartoum was compelled to embrace his vision and established the CEAWC.

In early 2004, we managed to reunite the first retrieved group of over 750 abducted women and children with their families in Northern Bahr El-Ghazal in the SPLA controlled area. That was when we were introduced to Commander Paul Malong Awan, who was by then the deputy commander of the SPLA Third Front and some other top officers in a warm welcoming ceremony.

A Step Toward the Rebellion

From this background, it is obvious that what triggered my decision to join the armed struggle after we visited the liberated areas of the SPLA was an accumulation of factors. There was of course our head-on encounter with the bitter facts of women and children abduction and their exploitation by the Arabs. There was also my early childhood memory congested with numerous instances of the injustices inflicted upon us by the Misseriya militias and the Sudan Armed Forces. Among these was especially the painful collection of live frogs from Nyamora River in 1993 in which I had participated in compliance with the strict orders from the commander of Battalion 131 of the SAF stationed in Abyei town on the grounds that the frogs were disturbing his sleep. Each Dinka person, including children younger than 10 years, were forced to pick at least five frogs a day from the river side and throw them into the nearby Chol Malual forest.

Beside these vivid triggers, I had earlier joined a pro-SPLM student movement called the African National Front, well known by the acronym, ANF.[5] We had already confronted the security forces of the National Islamic Front (NIF) in Khartoum in an incident famously known as the SPLA Flag hoisting in May 2002. My friend, Akur Chol, and I were prominent members of the ANF during the time of SPLA flag hoisting in Khartoum at El-Neelain University. We were well versed in the SPLM vision of New Sudan. Our tour to the liberated areas, bringing with us former abducted women and children, was therefore a golden opportunity for us to compare and contrast the reality we were living in with our perception about our beloved liberation movement. The warm and jubilant welcoming ceremony and the briefing about the objectives of the SPLA were very impressive and motivating for us to make the decision to join the Movement.

One of the painful scenarios that I witnessed myself concerned a young family of a husband and wife, with their children. Most painfully, the couple turned out to be a brother and a sister who did not know their relationship until they were identified by their own mother, when she came to check in the assembly centre. The story was very painful. Among the Dinka, the marriage of people related by blood, however distant their blood ties, is taboo. It was, therefore, shocking to witness the forceful incest of a brother and sister which was inflicted on these siblings as a direct cost of the war between Southern and Northern Sudan.

The Decision to Join the Rebellion

After we returned from the liberated areas back to our duty station in Khartoum, the national security of the National Islamic Front (NI) put us under close observation. We felt threatened and unsafe, given the nature of our work and our frequent travel to remote areas. Our lives were certainly in danger. We, therefore, decided to leave Khartoum and join SPLA. So, we created an urgent follow-up mission. We went and reported ourselves to the SPLA controlled areas after an adventurous journey in April 2004. We went in our double-cabin Toyota four wheels drive. That car proved to be a big asset to the armed struggle in Northern Bahr El-Ghazal.

My short time in the SPLA from April 2004 until the final peace accord was signed on January 9, 2005, was full of exciting activities. But I did not have the privilege of experiencing active combat. We were immediately taken for basic military training at Pariak Military Training Centre of the Third SPLA Front. Four of us were initially the only new recruits. But, luckily enough, some youths joined us, and our numbers grew to more than 500 recruits in the centre. Our group had the honour to be graduated by the Commander-in-Chief, the late Dr John Garang de Mabior, who was on a peace tour to all regions of SPLA controlled areas known as the New Sudan. Comrade Akur and I were given the rank of First Lieutenant and Comrades Ajok and Akiyoy were given the rank of Second Lieutenant after we graduated from the military training centre.

Commander Deng Alor Kuol played a big role in the decision to relocate us from Northern Bahr El-Ghazal to Agok in Abyei Area. We then went from Agok to Nairobi to attend an intensive English language course. I combined a part time job as a journalist for Sudan Radio Service with attending an English language course. I also managed to participate in all the activities of the New Sudan Women Association (NSWA), including their first conference held in Yei town in February 2005 two weeks after my wedding. But as a freedom fighter my only choice was to postpone my honeymoon and attend the national call of duty. I got married to Dr. Ajak Makor on February 12, 2005. I am currently the mother of three beautiful children, a girl and two boys.

I came back to Juba in October 2006 as part of the advance SPLA officers to establish the new Headquarters in Juba. My assignment was an information technology officer in the directorate of logistics until 2008 when I was requested by Honourable Mading Deng-Abot to assist him in his capacity as the Director for Political Organization in the SPLM Headquarters. I was officially seconded to the SPLM and put on the SPLA reserve list. I was appointed in the position of communication officer in the SPLM Southern Secretariat. After that, I was appointed Director of Information and Communication in 2011. My last promotion in the SPLA was in 2009 to the rank of a Captain.

From 2012 up to 2014 I served as the Minister of Information and Communication in Warrap State. I resigned from that state ministerial position on February 4, 2014, in protest against the civil war that erupted on December 15, 2013. I then joined the group of Former Detainees (FD's) and later become a member of the Peace talks until the peace agreement was signed. I represented the FD's in the Independent Border Commission (IBC) and voted for the ten states against the option of the thirty-two states.

My position, which was the initial position of the FD's before they switched sides, was eventually adopted by all the groups and our country reverted to the post-independence status. My decision to vote for ten states had already exposed a deep difference and conflict in our group. I resigned from the FDs on July 9, 2019 and joined the SPLM-IO under the leadership of Dr Riek Machar.

My dream and hope have always been to be a citizen of a country where rights are obtained through merits and capabilities. That has always been my aspiration and commitment, despite all the trying experiences and disappointments that we passed through. Luckily enough, I managed to resume my studies during the recent civil war from 2015 to 2018 and I graduated from Cavendish University in Kampala with a Bachelor Degree in International Relations and Diplomatic studies. I am currently enrolled in a Masters Degree in Peace and Conflict studies at Kampala University in Uganda.

The Paradox of War

My bitter experience of the destructive consequences of war and its heavy toll on social cohesion, especially after our nascent country became engulfed in it for a period of two years post-independence, has changed my perception and belief in the power of the the armed struggle. Instead, it has pushed me to the other bank of conflict resolution through peaceful negotiation and coexistence of diverse cultures. Toward that end, I published my personal proposal on resolving the conflict in the Abyei area through economic cooperation and integrated markets, while maintaining an independent political identity for the Abyei area.

My role in peace negotiations was observed and appreciated by the Universal Peace Federation and I was appointed as an Ambassador for Peace in 2017 in Dakar, Senegal. I am currently involved in bringing peace to my country as well as to our neighbouring Sudan and promoting international peace as an Ambassador for Peace for the Family of Humankind under God.

References

1. Arop, Arop Madut. *Ngok Dinka of Abyei, South Sudan, in Historical Perspective*. Grosvenor House Publishing, 2018.

2. *Slavery, Abduction and Forced Servitude in Sudan*, Report of the International Eminent Persons Group; May 22, 2002, Khartoum – Sudan.

3. UNICEF *Operations in Southern Sudan Monthly Report Dec 2004 / Jan 2005*.

4. Ajak Makor: *The African National Front (ANF); 50 Years of Political Struggle in the Sudanese Universities*.

5. Nyenagwek Kuol Mareng: *The New Deal; Abyei from a contested Area to an Economic Integration Market between South Sudan and Sudan*, July 19, 2019.

6. Francis Mading Deng, *The Man Called Deng Majok: A Biography of Power, Polygyny and Change*, Yale University Press, 1985.

Elementary School,
Comboni Enahoud, Sudan, 1964
Raphael Tikley Abiem

Raphael Tikley Abiem

PART FOUR
THE DEEP ROOTS OF ANGER

Raphael Tikley Abiem: A Child Soldier at Nine

Introduction

THE FOURTH STORY IN THIS compilation tells the same saga from the perspective of a child, driven into rebellion by raging anger to strike back against gross injustice, mistreatment and intolerable indignity, by joining the Anya-Nya armed liberation struggle (1955-1972) at the unbelievable age of nine years. The version of the story included in this compilation derives primarily from a pamphlet by Raphael Tikley Abiem, entitled *Mission to Niagara and Back: The Journey of a Southern Sudanese Boy to Mobutu's Congo to Buy Guns,* published by Africa World Books, 2020. It is reproduced here with the permission of both the author and the publisher.

The publisher's note included the following: "Imagine a baby whose cradle is a mortar and his blanket, the grinding pestle; it is from such tight spot that Raphael Abiem, wiggled out of his father's home in 1965 at nine years of age to join the first liberation movement, Anya-Nya. He had already witnessed enough atrocities at that tender age to convince him that Abyei, his home, was the baby trapped in between two grinding worlds: Arab leaning Sudan to the north, actively crashing on Abyei; while the African Sudan, south, passively lay down and watched. In every sense, Abyei is a natural extension of Southern Sudan, which for regrettable reasons beyond the purview of this book, has been administrated by the north since 1905. The outcome, needless to mention, has been one long litany of misery and distress. The harder northern Sudan had Abyei by the throat, suffocated the population to silence, the louder their voices rang claiming Abyei is theirs to keep."

The publisher goes on to say, "Even at such a young age, (Tikley) saw Abyei as the crack on the face of the physical map of the Sudan, a political Rift Valley of sorts, a point which, should the country fall apart one day, it is there that it would split. He spent two years with the movement, walked a thousand kilometers to Niangara town in Mobutu's Congo and back."

Mission to Niangara and Back is an attempt to rekindle the memories of some of Raphael Abiem's companions whose contributions to the liberation of Southern Sudan would be forgotten if not documented in some ways." The young Raphael Abiem returned home and resumed his education up to the University of Khartoum, where he studied Law, and went on to receive a Diploma in Political Science from Stefan Gheorghiu Academy for Socio-Political Science in Romania, and further on to Harvard Divinity School and Harvard Law School, from which he obtained two respective masters degrees.

But his childhood adventure and the deeply rooted cause that drove him to war at that early age have left in him a fury and a vengeance he pursues with the fiery words of a highly educated scholar with remarkable literary skills and mastery of the English language. Ironically, as he explained to me, he developed these skills as a counterbalance to his hatred of Arabic, which he loathed as the language of the oppressors. This echos what both General Pieng and Chief Makuei Bilkuei said about their resistance to the Arabic language.

The author himself wrote a moving dedication of his work: "This pamphlet is dedicated to the souls of Anya-Nya heroes (Southern Sudan's freedom movement from 1956 to 1972), those I was fortunate to have been with from 1965 to 66. Most of them have long since died, alas, unsung, and unremembered. My aim is to inject their memories into our current discourse and whatever discussions are afoot in the now independent South Sudan about honoring our veterans.

"I would have achieved my goal were it only to serve as a reminder that 'the now' in which we bask, stands on the shoulders of men and women long returned to dust. It is an invitation to be mindful of the grounds on which we stand; the more we know of, remember, and cherish this fact, the more confident we tread, not only on motherland, but also among the population on whose affairs we preside over.

"Some of our departed heroes had led impactful lives for which they are remembered. Some are mentioned here, not with any depth from which additional knowledge could be gleaned. It is the slippery ones, those who did not live long enough to write their own stories, or have their stories widely told, if orally, that I attempt to beckon back to memory; they are one with the dust but it is on their remains we hoist the flag. It is them we offend with every act that defiles and undermines the spirit with which the struggle was conducted, the unity they forged out of a few frail ropes which tied southern ethnic groups together; it is they who, though limited by northern dominated and rationed education, negotiated with their feet the space on which subsequent movements, notably, the SPLA, stood grounds to launch the rebellion that has earned us the nation we call our own … May we all commit to keeping their candles alight.

"For the living among my Anya-Nya friends, should you put your glasses on and read this piece, remember it is from an equally blurry of vision and tortured mind it flows. Memories tend to ebb away with time. I have tried to recover, as best I could, of what I was able to retrieve from a distant past, fifty-four years ago. To you who gave my childhood meaning and purpose, I say: Freedom remains my invaluable motto, my guiding star."

Tikley's acknowledgment of his comrades in arms reflects the same moving passion that drove him to war as a child: "A long silence, followed by plaudits in songs afterwards – a long while after the fact, is the Jieng (Dinka) way of acknowledging a favor well received. Generations would recite it, dance to its lyrics and tune, own and quote it; it is a shared cultural expression and a good legacy for the posterity of the acknowledged.

"Alas, unless reclaimed, the back of Jieng culture is turned, grey and disappearing. But were my will to be done, it is in a song I would acknowledge Jacob Jiel Akol for his contribution to this pamphlet. But if there is no room for anachronisms, conventional English expression of appreciation would do.

"To you, Jacob Jiel Akol, I say, were it not for your gentle prods, your insistence that I help populate the jigsaw, the largely untold story of the liberation of Southern Sudan, this pamphlet would not see the light. No one could have given me advice I would easily relate to than Jacob himself. In the 60's, we traversed the same bumpy road to the Congo, suffered comparable indignities there and emerged at the other end sobered by experiences.

"One thing amazes me: how Jacob Jiel Akol awakened me to the realization it is a service to posterity to leave behind a trail showing the depth from which we come. Thank you. I am set to tell my story of how provocation to anger at an early age, though often sure to traumatize most children to incapacitation, also fuels others, catapults them to distances and paths they would otherwise never dream to traverse.

"My gratitude also goes to Peter Lual Deng of Africa World Books Australia Publisher. One quiet morning, a mail delivery person rang the doorbell, asked me to sign on to a receipt, and off he went. It was a load of books authored by South Sudanese. I did not ask for them, did not pay for it; it was a surprise of a lifetime. Now that I think of it, the gesture was to awaken me to an obvious fact I did not pay attention to; time to share experiences about little known contributions to the struggle for South Sudan. I hope this modest effort, the story of a nine-year boy, will add to the overall picture of the struggle."

Tikley concludes his introductory comments with admirable modesty: "I caution readers, this work is an empirical account of contexts in which I was, people I had been with, activities I participated in and places I had been to. Nothing of historical value except when read as part of a bigger picture missing pieces to make it whole. We all know there is more to the story of Southern Sudan Liberation than 'The Story.'"

A final word of appreciation of what Tikley has done. I have always told my sons who are driven by the same anger that took Tikley to war that there are different ways of fighting, there is the spear now replaced by the gun, and there is the word for advocating the cause and the pen for documenting the cause and the cry for help. My sons have joined me in adopting the alternative to the spear and the gun, in favor of the word and the pen; Tikley has done both. And indeed, by telling us and through us the world of readers, all those whose experiences are documented in this volume have done both, fought and now writing. It is my aspiration and that of Peter Deng, the publisher of Africa World Books, that our people document their experiences for posterity, to be read for generations to come, to learn from the past to pave a better, peaceful, and a constructive prosperous future.

To end this Introduction with a quotation from the message I sent Tikley when I read his pamphlet: "Dear Tikley, I read your booklet, *'Mission to Niangara and Back,'* with great interest. I am delighted to see that you have begun to act on what I have been urging you to do for years. Your brilliant literary merit is very well reflected. The story is gripping. I very much enjoyed reading it. I would urge you to expand the story into a full-fledged book." The response I got indicates that it will be done.

The Context of Chronic Animosity

The anger that drove all the individuals whose stories are recounted in this volume goes back to their childhood; that of Tikley Abiem is different only in degree, having become warrior at an unprecedentedly young age. This also shows that prejudice and the hatred it breeds are also planted in a child at a very early age. Tikley's Arab age-mate could tell us stories about the way his or her people inculcated a negative view of the non-Arab, non-Muslim people, specifically South Sudanese at a very young age.

I suspect that the difference would be that the Arab children only heard prejudiced views about the Dinka but did not witness first-hand any behavior on the part of the Dinka to support the prejudiced accounts. In contrast, Tikley and other Dinka children did witness deeds that reflected that prejudice, not only in insults and disparaging statements, but also through physical brutality and mass atrocities.

Who is to be blamed? The prejudiced child, or the angry child reacting to prejudice? I submit neither. Those responsible are those who nurtured prejudice: parents, elders, and their community. Where does the cure begin, by telling the person hating as a reaction to gross violation of human dignity not to hate his enemies, or by telling the culprits who committed those egregious offenses to stop their evil deeds?

Of course, the question is rhetorical, for the answer is obvious. And yet, unacceptable gross violations of fundamental right and atrocious assaults and murderous acts are repeatedly committed by people who know or should know that a human being worthy of the dignity of humanity cannot accept such treatment and that however long the victims can endure, patience will eventually run out and rage will explode in violent resistance. Then the culprit, often in a stronger position, retaliates with a vengeance that can escalate to genocidal level. Scores, hundreds, thousands and millions perish, and then, only then do we open our eyes to what was glaringly apparent from the start – dehumanizing injustice will ultimately be defeated. Tragically, corrections come when it is too late for millions. Why?

The Anya-Nya war, which Tikley joined at the age of nine, lasted for seventeen years. It cost the lives of two million South Sudanese and untold destruction and human suffering. All the South called for at the dawn of independence from colonial rule was a federal arrangement, but even regional autonomy was rejected by the North as a step toward secession. After all that cost, the North conceded autonomy, and the South, in contrast to the earlier fears, became even more committed to unity than the North. When even that small concession was unilaterally abrogated by the North, not even federation was any more acceptable to the South. Partitioning the country became the residual option. But then South Sudan fell into its own devastating conflict, while the wars in the old Sudan by the marginalized groups against the domination of the center raged on.

To crown the irony of the situation, leaders on both sides, now the two Sudans, are striving to improve their bilateral relations toward some form of a coming back together. The question that continues to pose itself as one reads these Memoirs is: Was all that massive loss of lives, physical destruction and human, worth what has been attained by both sides? Should a wise leadership with foresight and enlightened self-interest not have understood that addressing the genuine grievances of the South was in the mutual interest of all. Even if actually resolving the issues involved might be an incremental process that might take time, the appearance of genuine concern and determination to right wrongs could generate the patience needed to go through the process.

Let us now go to the story of Raphael Tikley Abiem told in his own words.

Victims United by Anger

It was on October 21st, 1964. The University of Khartoum Students Union, in a popular revolution, forced Ibrahim Abboud's military junta to resign. Citizens were elated as they watched them blend in with oblivion's primary colors.

A stream of brilliant, western educated leaders stepped in to claim their share of the power pie. Some wore designer suits, even in the unforgiving heat of Khartoum; others, particularly those who traced roots to established religious homes, dressed in jallabiya (loose cloths), immah (turban) and pants.

Among these seemingly diehard traditionalists were graduates from Oxford, Cambridge, and Le Sorbonne, eager to bridge the yawning educational, perhaps spiritual gulf too, separating them from their political and religious bases. It was democracy cooking but, whether it would smell, taste, and feel to the touch like it when served, was for time to tell.

Doubts that matters would be as good-looking as the new men in charge persisted, especially among Southern Sudanese, the segment of the population historically earmarked for raw experiences whenever changes occurred in the country. But Southern Sudanese misgivings aside, there was no denying that change had brought great jubilation to the country, one if handled well and anchored in good faith by leaders, all considered, could become contagious.

The August 18, 1955 rebellion had turned into a guerrilla warfare Abboud's regime tried to suppress but to no avail. The challenge facing his successor, Prime Minister Sir-el-Katim el-Khalifa, was whether he would succeed where the military had failed. The proof of his success would be to honestly identify the root causes of the conflict and address them. That would end rebellion in Southern Sudan.

Even Southern Sudan, the odd region out, always the country's killing field, never a candidate for development, did momentarily experience some euphoria, though short lived as it would soon prove to be. As far away as El Nahud, a town in western Sudan where I attended elementary school, we sniffed the whiff of jubilation. We sang revolutionary songs, the lyrics of which we did not understand.

The word, revolution, was in every man's, woman's, and child's mouth. Music was a big draw. It spoke in melody of a future free of civil wars and of discrimination based on race, region, or religion, (RRR), the evil trinity that had long threatened to break apart the largest landmass of any country in Africa. Our understanding of discrimination was modest and would demand modesty on the part of the new ruling elites to stoop to and resolve.

Southern Sudanese, especially those that did not know better, my type that was, knew out of experience we would be first to feel the impact of the new dispensation should things go wrong, as they easily did back then.

And so, we drifted along with our northern compatriots mimicking their slogans even when some phrases were regurgitations from the Islamic tradition. We sang the national anthem "Nahnu Junud Allah Junud Al-Watan", composed by Ahmed Morjan (1905-1974) in 1958.

We are Soldiers of God, Soldiers of the Homeland
If called for redemption, we did not betray
We challenge death upon ordeals
We buy glory at most expensive price
This land is ours
May our Sudan live, an edifice among nations
O Sons of the Sudan this is your symbol, carries
The burden and protects your land

The song is much longer. Portions of it glorified a Sudan which was black and African: "We are black jungle sons; do not fear death or be afraid of engagement." The author, Colonel Morjan, though born in Omdurman, had distinct African features, even as he was consummately Arab in language and culture. Perhaps he entered this verse in honor of his ancestors who must have been descendants of some African tribe west, east, or south of the country.

The lyrics were a reminder at long last, the people had regained their land and, therefore, their destiny. But I surmise it might as well have served to spice up the war in Southern Sudan as a fight between soldiers of God and the forces of evil, a theological concept firmly implanted in faith and practice of Islam.

Regardless, the revolution was an occasion for Southern Sudanese to blend in but cautious, timely, the merry-filled moments would dim and set; we would return to our states of minds, firmly locked into our faiths, keen to defend our ethnic and cultural heritages. Our Muslim colleagues, by far the majority in school, would surely get back to what they did before the revolution: call us names such as "slaves" and "fire-wood," a reference to hellfire prepared for non-Muslims who, themselves are the fuel of hell.

There was some truth to their abusive language. Truth was, our mothers, sisters and even some of us, school children, were servants in the homes of some of our richer northern colleagues. Sudan was socially stratified in such a way we thought that was the status quo ante: Uneducated Dinka people were servants in northern Arab homes; sanitation workers were from the Nuba Mountains. At sunset, these employees of the Ministry of Health would walk from house to house, picked up pails filled with human faeces from under dry toilets, and emptied contents in sanitation trucks. As they labored unprotected not even by gloves and masks, jeering hordes of children ran after them shouting: "Neefa, Neefa, Neefa," that is, "putrid, putrid...". In Sudan ran a functional caste system without Hindu spirituality to explain and perhaps soften the bitter reality some people must suffer lowly social status in life.

The Catholic missionary school we were in, Comboni, was mindful of our financial situation; so we were spared payment of back-breaking fees and did not have to work in the homes of our northern friends, at least not during the school year. The missionaries did their best to make us feel we belonged, but there were set boundaries they dared not cross: commitment to keep a strict divide between Muslims and Christians when it came to religious education. Lowering fence in this regard could easily arouse suspicions that missionaries were intent on proselytizing Muslim children. That line was drawn in the sand, which they would not dare transgress.

A couple of years earlier, Abboud's regime had banished foreign missionaries in Southern Sudan and had closed schools for the same reason. With that one act, Sudan arrested any semblance of progress in Southern Sudan in terms of education. In response, young men joined Anya-Nya in their numbers, among them, Christopher Akonon Mithiang from Abyei, who became a prominent commander.

All that considered, Southerners and Northerners alike, heartily saluted the change. The acid test would be the degree to which the government would align rhetoric with policies and actions. If they erred on the side of use of force in Southern Sudan, a strategy that did a great disservice to the military junta, right there would lie their doom. It was common knowledge, should government ignore the conflict burning at the southern edge of the country, they would have inadvertently made a rod for their own backs.

By mid-December 1964, jubilation had run its course. The ball was rolling fast towards conflict. School authorities realized instability had reached a point it looked unavoidable. Southerners in Khartoum had just had a violent brush with Northerners due to rumors a prominent Southern politician, Clement Mboro, might have been lynched. Keeping us in school was growing by the minute a risk the school could not bear. We were sent back to Abyei. We made it home safely. Dinka people who would attempt to come to Abyei through El Muglad after us would not be as lucky as we had been.

January 1st, Sudan's Independence Day, passed uneventfully, but ruling elites would soon reveal they were pseudo-democrats who had long harbored racist views and attitudes towards Southern Sudan and equally revolting, hate nurturing, religious and racial bigotry. Their public pronouncements made it abundantly clear they would do all they could to crush what they termed as: Christian missionary instigated conflict in Southern Sudan. With their state of mind so set, the March 16, 1965 Round Table Conference was doomed to failure from its inception.

The mask of affected respect for the people of Southern Sudan was lifted. Ruling elites no longer needed to suppress their innermost persuasion they were Arab and Islamic. No more would they live ensnared between two opposed world views: the call to enlightenment, the function of received western education, and of hearts desirous to return to Arab and Islamic roots.

As the elites made no secret they would take after their forebears, Southerners too, though unprepared, saw no alternative, but to fish their way away from the north to find their own path, if that were a jagged one. Disaster was in the offing. The country was ineluctably plunging headlong into a war everyone was aware of, yet conveniently wished away. Then the news came from Western Sudan. Seasonal, labor-seeking Dinka farmers and home-helpers in and around the twin towns of Al Muglad and Babanusa, had been attacked. On that day, as laborers prepared to go to work to serve their masters/would be killers, they were rounded up, herded away in chains, and shoved into two large, grass-thatched police depots doused with Kerosene and…set alight. It was no news to whom that must have been a matter of grave concern, the authorities. Whatever had happened in Al Muglad and Babanusa, hardly sounded louder than a child's bursting soap bubble to the ruling elites. Yet, it was hundreds of men, women and children bursting in the conflagrations.

Ten years down the line, as a student in the University of Khartoum, Faculty of Law, I would find and delve into the archives and read perfunctory stories that appeared in the newspaper depicting scenes from that fateful day. Not one story carried a line that showed faint traces of sorrow for the victims. If anything, sardonic smiles (in script) littered the pages, punctuating the news items to highlight government's principled departure from soft approaches to ending war in the Sudan, to use of force.

Southern politicians understood the incident as a bait to lure them unprepared into reacting compulsively so violence could justifiably be unleashed. Suffice, the pain had registered but, grave as it was, hundreds of Dinka men, women and children killed, it was not inclusive enough to marshal Southern Sudanese into unity. The good thing was, ruling elites were now exposed as autocratic to a fault, not the proponents of democratic ideals they had claimed all along.

Abyei was next in line to be cut down. Abyei is the administrative center of Ngok Dinka, approximately 10,547 square miles in area, only 125 miles south of Al Muglad, the scene of massacres days earlier. Reportedly, a horde of well-armed men on horsebacks, backstopped by government forces, in a matter of hours, reduced the entire region to cinders.

The government was tight lipped. When pressed to speak, the refrain was, the incident was the result of tribal conflict, unavoidable when pastoralists rendezvous. Those were the kind of messages that went into historical records; statements to the contrary attracted no attention.

With the Abyei incident also sure to go with the wind, the elites grew ever more confident they could, without consequences, continue playing ventriloquists behind northern characters in the killing fields. They were their cheer leaders, their financiers, and their voice to the outside world. Not once had the government been held to account for their role, if not of directly masterminding the war, at least of ignoring it.

Distant observers of these genocidal attacks were Westerners on whom the elites had pulled tricks as mundane as dressing up in suits and painstakingly suppressing Arabic accent to sound more English all in a bid to show they were worthy vessels for promotion of Western democratic virtues in the Sudan, perhaps Africa.

From the comfort of their exclusive ministerial villas in Khartoum, the 'Ten Homes', government ministers consumed the news capsules of intensifying attacks on Southern Sudanese, in their homes and in northern cities. They did not see indiscriminate killings were quickly bringing South Sudanese together in increased cohesion among Anya-Nya fighting forces. Then, the coordinated attacks on Juba, Wau and Malakal targeting intellectuals from all Southern ethnic backgrounds followed. More than 1700 were killed, 49 government officials. The southern newspaper, the Vigilant, on Sunday July 11, 1965, reported:

"Juba in Blood-Bath, Army Rounds Up Southern Civilians: Reports reaching here from Juba on Friday indicates that the army, the so-called Security Forces of the Sudan Government went out in Juba town on what was described as "extermination operation mission" in the area. All native quarters (Southerners) are reported to have been set on fire and over 200 persons, all residents of Juba town who have never had any connection with Anya-Nya are reported to have been killed by the army and many more wounded, most of them, seriously."

This brought full awareness to Southern Sudanese they were victims together. Southern Sudanese knew precious little about one another at the time, but they were provoked to anger together and so would they fight back as one. Northern Sudan had cast the dye for southern unity. I had already joined the rebellion but decided to return to the area to witness for myself the aftermath of Ngok's destruction. Abyei town was a no-go area; the population was homeless, squatting under trees south of Nyamoura River.

Child Soldier by Choice

I was only nine years old, catapulted to adulthood by experiences. Many children were prematurely weaned of innocence; our eyes were heavily discolored by scenes of bloodshed and attracted to rebellion by the bitter experiences we endured. There was no need for pundits to explain to us what our eyes had seen: pure disregard for our lives.

Many years later, April 13, 1999, I would participate in a discussion panel organized by Yale Law School. The topic was "Children in Combat: How Can We Protect Them?" The stated purpose of the event was to raise awareness of the child soldiers issue within the Yale community, to publicize the campaign going on at that time to stop the use of child soldiers, and to promote dialogue between students, NGOs, UN agencies and people directly involved in the field.

My interlocutor, a UNICEF official, was of the view that all child soldiers in Africa were coerced to join the war. I saw some veracity in what she said, but I thought there was more to that. I had in my mind my own experience, which pointed otherwise. In my context, it was children, mostly those that saw the massacres, that pressured rebel leaders to carry them on their wings so they would grow into and contribute to the war of liberation in any way they could.

In my case, I needed a conduit through which I could express my anger at the gory spectacles to which I had been exposed. Anya-Nya, our rebel movement, availed me that opportunity, a decision I have not regretted.

The first Anya-Nya unit I joined was mono-ethnic, Dinka. The commander was Captain Minyang Apaie, from Panarou. One of his close adjutants was Lieutenant Macham Atem from Twic Mayardit. Signs that Southern Sudanese were uniting were beginning to show. We received, a Lotuka, into the unit; then Paul Mayiel, a Nuer, Moses, the trumpeter, a Ciec, and Alier, a Bor.

Alier said he was Dinka, but when he spoke, I had a hard time figuring out what he was saying. He was heavily tattooed, a square man with a breast the width of a jeep track. He ported the one bren gun with a huge disk for a cartridge. One could put any load on him, but that would not diminish his speed an inch.

I was still in my backyard watching Southern Sudanese mixing in real time. I saw the flower of unity bud, grow into fruit, ripen, and nourish the fledgling Anya-Nya Movement. Nothing could be more encouraging and wonderful to behold. Sharing suffering had earned us unity quicker than expected. I prayed leaders would find a way to maintain and even expand it into a vision that would transcend ethnic lines. Even as a child, I could understand the significance of more people from all backgrounds joining the movement. I could also appreciate the importance of guarding this achievement because failing to maintain its purity would negate its utility, therefore, the weaker Southern Sudan would become.

I could not wait to see more of Southern Sudan, people, terrain forests, mountains, and animal life. In Abyei, the name Kur (stone) is commonplace, but not a pebble is seen in the soil. The first mountain I ever set eyes on was mountain Haidoub, in El Nahud. I could not wait to see more of its kind. Our mountains were anthills. If we wished to experience height, we climbed trees.

I wanted so much to be assigned to a serious mission that would take me far afield, to the deepest-most reaches of Southern Sudan.

The Mission to Niangara

One morning, while attending routine rollcall, the commander of my new unit, Lieutenant Kuot Mayan, called out seventeen of us for a special meeting. I said to myself whatever was held secret from older people may prove too onerous for me to keep my mouth tight about. Then, I recalled, I was a corporal with two stripes, a superior to uncles whom I could command without thinking I was being impolite. I gathered courage and proceeded to where the meeting was to convene.

In the meeting, Lt. Kuot Mayan informed us that we were going on a long trip to Congo and that we would have a stopover in an Anya-Nya camp in Lirangu, a small town in Equatoria Province on the borders with the Congo. There, we would be instructed by Captain Nyiel Abot and his Deputy, Fabio Deng Akol.

A question was raised how seventeen of us, all Dinka, would pass through territories controlled by other ethnic groups and not expect attacks. We only had two rifles, one automatic gun and a limited supply of bullets. Captain Kuot assured us there was no cause for fear. He said, recent killings in Wau, Juba and Malakal, in which educated sons from all ethnic groups were killed, had made Southern Sudanese realize we are one in this war. That sounded convincing. We were all set to go. I heard where we were supposed to travel to, but what that meant in terms of distance to cover, not a genius could have made me understand the implications involved in agreeing to brave the journey.

The next day, before the journey, Captain Kuot called me to his office (under a shade tree) and said my function in the journey would be to carry a small plastic bag he would tie on my back, attached to the skin. I inquired what it was, but he kept silent about it; so, I let the matter rest. He proceeded to tie the bag on me as he had told me. Now, I knew I truly counted as a soldier, not a tug-on, a burden to be tolerated on the way. I was kept in the dark about the bag, yet pleased I had been honored with the assignment, wherever it took me.

I do not recall where exactly we camped when the journey started, but it was somewhere in Rek area, a place I distinctly remember because of its white beach-like sands and lots of Doum Palm trees. Fruits of the Doum tree, I have come to learn, contain a substance believed to be of therapeutic value in the treatment of bilharzia. It was there too that late Kerubino Kuanyin Bol, who later gained reputation as a fearless fighter, if often a controversial one, joined our camp, his point of entry into the movement. He was closer to me in age, a bit older, but we had more in common. He came in a few days before we took off for the journey. I would visit him years later in the Presidential Palace in Khartoum, where he was assigned following the Addis Ababa Accord that came into effect in 1972, which granted Southern Sudan a regional autonomy.

When we took the first steps away from the camp, I felt butterflies flap their powdery wings in my heart and stomach, preaching the gospel of fear of the unknown. But, when I remembered the El Muglad/Babanusa massacres and the reduction of Abyei region to cinders, fear-preaching butterflies quickly got seared out of my system, and consciousness about what I was here for dominated my thoughts throughout.

Our journey to the Congo was circuitous. Instead of travelling straight south to Zande land, from around Gagrial, we travelled towards Tonj. On the way, one attraction I cannot forget was the house of chief Aguer (Aguen Adeel). I must confess his house was an aesthetics architectural marvel. Alas, I saw the building in an abandoned state. The vegetation had already encroached on it and had defaced some of its striking features.

We passed by Chief Aguen Adeel's house. A short distance away, we walked into a swath of wetland I thought would take no more than a couple of hours to cross. It turned out we were up against a much longer wading through the marshes. We walked and walked, from time to time, taking rest on small islands, then up for more ploughing.

When we emerged on the other end of the marshland, I was told we were in Agarland. I was thunderbolt to hear them speak Dinka. My reaction may have been ignorance on stilts, but still spoke to the truth that Southern Sudanese knew precious little of one another; in some cases, downright dangerous lack of knowledge, even within the same ethnic group as is the case with Ngok, my subtribe, and Agar. A few days later, we were in Commander Akonon Mithiang's camp.

We spent a few days there, then commenced our long journey west, past Wau, then south. In Rafili our guide led us straight into what would have been our assured death, a northern army barrack. We were a few feet away when we heard what sounded like a piece of cutlery fall on the floor, followed by a loud laughter. My cousin Ayok grabbed the guide and quickly muzzled him just in case it was his intent to lead us into the trap. One of our trip mates who, throughout the journey, suffered persistent cough, was mouth gagged as well till we were a safe distant away from the army camp.

We walked a mile or so in the bush, parallel to the Wau/Tambura road to Zandeland.

I cannot recall how long it took us to arrive in Lirangu, but it was a journey as torturous as it was tortuous. It was a resilience test, but one I was pleased to have endured. Throughout our journey in Zandeland, people were generous. In all villages we spent a night, we were directed to the house of the village chief who willingly shared with us what little food he had in store for his family.

On arrival to Lirangu, Lieutenant Kuot Mayan and I were called for a meeting to deliver the oddity he had tied on my back the day we embarked on the journey. It must have been an important something. I was instructed to sleep, swim, use the loo, whatever I did, it had to be on my back. My senior cousin, Ayok Deng-Abot, followed on my heels wherever I went, always armed with the only automatic rifle we had. Was the bag the centerpiece for the journey? I wondered.

I would feel relieved soonest that tiny monstrosity would come off my back; breeze would once again fan my back and life would return to normal. Soon, veteran politician, Elia Duang Arop, Captain Nyiel Abot, Lirangu Camp Commander and his deputy, Fabio Deng Akol, walked in. I do not recall if Jacob Buok, an officer, and Robert Mayouk Deng, the two more senior colleagues whose company I enjoyed the most, were in attendance. This story would have been more complete had they informed the content as to the events that took place in Lirangu camp.

Now, the quorum was complete, and it was time to lay the burden down, a task accomplished. I was asked to stand up, so the bag is untied; it had gummed on me and had to be yanked off. A bit of my top skin went with it.

The bag was opened. A hefty bundle of cash, two thousand Sudanese Pounds, four US Dollars to one Sudanese Pound at that time, dropped on the table. It was the largest amount of cash I had ever seen. It was not South Sudan of today. Money was a rarity we saw circulating only in the hands of Arab merchants. If it trickled down to the hands of Southerners, it was a pittance.

But what was the money for, I still wanted to know? Lieutenant Kuot Mayan later confided in me that the money was earmarked for purchase of weapons in the Congo. The Simba, a Congolese 'liberation movement', had been defeated and weapons were reportedly in abundance for sale. He patted me on the back saying, "You are a valued member of the team tasked to accomplish this purpose." I felt uplifted and looked forward for that day of the great transaction.

Niangara the Destination

We stayed in Lirangu for almost two weeks, then, continued the journey to Niangara, a Northern Congolese town on the Uele River, the northern region of Haut-Uele. We arrived on January 1, 1966. It was weekend, so we could not meet with Major Thomas Dhol Theil as was instructed in Lirangu. Niangara was clearly a town reeling under the thumb of a lingering war. It was recaptured from Simba rebels in April 1965 by soldiers of fortune (mercenaries) hired by 'Moboutu' Sese Seko, full name: "Moboutu Sese Seko Ngbendu Wa Za Banga," to fight the war on his government's behalf.

We were told Niangara was a silhouette of what it was. But even as it stood, a ghost of her former self, one could see it was once a small town with a future. Deep trauma had driven the population to life, if life it was, on the edge. Scars of war were on the faces of the few brick buildings strong enough to endure and stand testimony to turbulences the town had been through. So, buildings too could tell stories? I muttered to myself. I recalled when Abyei region was burned down, not a brick was there to speak for the magnitude of the disaster that had befallen unsuspecting communities. It was cows culled, agricultural produce burned, people murdered and buried and grass thatched homes with mud walls, burned down. One rainfall and evidence was gone. With earth leveled, nothing was left to see, but a land that spoke of no atrocities committed. No solid structures were there to bear witness.

But what would all this add up to when reporting conflicts in impoverished communities? Unlike Niangara, in Abyei, only graves of human beings killed stood as evidence; nothing else was there to corroborate claims of extensive losses, human and material. In hindsight, I know now wars are often remembered less about human casualties, and more about material losses sustained. Abyei has never had a solid face which, when scratched, would endure to bear witness to what had happened. It has many times been leveled to the ground but, every time that happened, there was not much evidence left standing, if damaged, to make the news.

Niangara was poor. It had one main street and a few solid structures. That one main street was packed with mercenaries Congolese people with trembling knees, referred to in hushed tones, "Belgians." They ran loose in town looting, imposing order while drunk and chaotic as the traumatized population they sought to control. They roamed backstreets too; along their path, kicked the living and the dead alike; stopped to dally and kiss women they fancied and despised in one breath; shot to death any Simba lookalike mixed with the population. In a word, members of the entire population of Niangara, in fact, Haut Uele Province in general, were to them, suspects and fair game to kill. Nothing differentiated Simba affiliates from the rest of the population as they all hailed from the region and from all northern ethnic groups. Simply, mercenaries were trigger-crazed dogs of war itching to shoot. Uele River was there to receive the dead, a graveyard of convenience. We had a rough night. The days that followed would not be any calmer, a fact of life we could not avoid.

The next day, we met with Major Thomas Dhel Thiel. He told me to join a local missionary school immediately. I did not like what I heard.

Despite my reluctance, several days later, commander Dhel would take me to school anyway. Undoubtedly, that was a show of good intention on his part which, politely, I turned down. My reason, as always, was that I did not rebel to join school in another country, but to contribute to efforts aiming at restoring the dignity of my people. I gave it a try, just in case.

In class, I could not understand a word. Teachers jived as they taught. Children took to dancing with every word and move he made. Were they hearing music so subtle I could not hear? I felt straight jacketed; a captive audience among children I thought were borne dancing freaks. I knew even if I were to endure classes taught in Lingala and French, still I would not be able to understand their way of life. I could not see a sliver of silver lining in Major Thomas Dhel's advice, even though that was the reasonable advice any concerned relative would give a child. But no. I had cast the 'reasoning key' in Nyamoura River when I left Abyei. My mind was locked into the struggle at hand. Four days later, I abandoned school, a definitive rejection of my superior's advice.

With talk about school out of the way, my mind quickly turned to the initial assignment: purchase of arms, a topic everyone had recently been skittish about, since the day the money bag was taken off my back. I looked for clues in the eyes of my superiors, but not a bite worth of information was discernible. Was that corruption at work, I wondered? No! Who the cursed would have known such a word back in Southern Sudan of the 60's, let alone practice it? Unthinkable. We still feared the Most High. He was living among us, not the transcendent God theologians have made Him out to be. Also, our ancestors were evermore present in spirit, seated in large rooms with their backs rested against the walls watching every move we made and apportioning curses or blessings according to our deeds. Totems were witnesses even in their holes. And so, to be moral was not to moralize; it was life lived with consequences, good or bad. We feared the unknown more than clear and present danger that man presents. Conscience never went to sleep. It had to throb at the pace of heartbeats, poised to censor deleterious thoughts which, left untrimmed, would mushroom into the kind of bushes under which corruption evil vine would grow. Not a soul was so lost as to deviate in that way.

Was the silence then a function of utmost secrecy? I hoped that was the case. If it were, I would still see the results, if not here in the Congo, then in Lirangu upon return. I could not hide my frustration but decided not to broach a word till we were back home in Southern Sudan.

Life in Niangara

We spent a month in Niangara. Food was scarce. A small shack near our residence doubled as somebody's bedroom by night and a restaurant by day. Fish was served at four in the evening, a perfect timing. We could afford one meal a day, which was good enough, especially when we did not have to walk distances to find food in a town thronged with death-disbursing mercenaries.

One day, we had barely been through our usual meal when I picked a strange object in the fish. It felt to the touch like fish scale only harder. I stopped eating to have a close look at it. I could not figure out what it was or, perhaps, I was reluctant to accept what I saw was what I had in mind. I passed it on to Lieutenant Kuot Mayan who cast a look at it and mattered in muted, dignified voice: "It is human nail." We pushed the dish aside, still famished, of course, but nauseated at the thought we were one degree removed from cannibalism. We should have known there were too many dead bodies thrown into Uele River every day; that was surely food for fish. I felt living any longer in Niangara was to volunteer for early death for no worthy cause. In my case, nothing other than the cause for which I had to bear the rigors of the journey would make me embrace danger.

I longed to get back to the Sudan to fight my war, even if with bare hands. Returning home with weapons at hand was worth the hunger I had to endure, and the distances I had to walk. Nothing deserved the sacrifice but the liberation of my people from suppression.

The one month we spent in Niangara, other than watching horror in real time and places, was overall uneventful. Food was scarce now that fish was scarce. For a change, I thought I should take a second look at Niangara. Perhaps I would see a thing or two that would impart some color to the bleak portrait I had in mind, a saving grace for Niangara. I decided to take a short stroll around the block of homes where I lived right on Uele River, but hoped I would not catch sight of fish or anything that swam or floated. Just in case, my senses were on full alert ready to delete anything that looked like an aquatic creature. I wanted to appreciate the water which ran crystal clear; dotting the water stream were sparsely paced brown rocks, clean shaved by frothy waves.

On hindsight, now that my eyes have been influenced by close contacts with affluence, I imagined the rocks would be ideal spots for reflection when the town would be safe and people sane enough to think beyond finding food and alcohol.

After some time, I snapped out of my daydreaming, looked around; not a soul was there. I was alone engrossed in unrealistic imagination of the river's potential. Adorned in shades of blue and frothy white, Uele River sped on as if dancing on a long theatre dotted with rocks. It was a wonderful sight for me, a denizen of a region right on the mouth of a devouring desertification. Perhaps not many eyes in Niangara were clear enough to watch the waves gently cat-walk on the rocks as if performing ritualistic cleansing rites waiting for the day Niangara would shake off bad habits, if habits we saw play out, and rise in glory to transform the banks of Uele River into a sight to marvel about.

I could not help sigh in desperation when my thoughts suddenly dashed off to Abyei, my homeland and started wondering, will there ever be hope? I found no room for comparison between Abyei, an arid region, and Haut-Uele, a region, if teetering at the brink of destruction and self-mutilation, still was home to nature. I would not allow my mind to float too long in that direction for fear of conjuring hopes that neither history, nor reasonable prognostication of Abyei's checkered past and threatened future, would confirm.

Instead, I focused more on the nature of the two regions, to show why Niangara appeared attractive despite the gory experiences outlined elsewhere in this story. The magic was in Niangara's sky and her lifeline, the Uele River, both of which spoke of abundance waiting for future intentional generations of Congolese to harvest. But for now, layers of confusing events have blinded that generation of Congolese from seeing Niangara for what it was and will be, a gift of nature.

Abyei was another story altogether; not that nature was particularly repressive, if indeed it often had been, but because of its location in Africa, the line separating Africans from self-confessed Arab tribes, whose life vocation was to covet territories long inhabited by African tribes. Wherever the hooves of their horses stepped, that was the seal they needed to authenticate claims to territories and the right of might was there to back that up.

Abyei's conflict was not and still is not rooted in the mindset of a few evanescent politicians sworn to self-enrich as was the case in the Congo and dogs of war during Mobutu Se Seko regime; it is systemic, rested on political, historical, cultural, and religious depths passed on with varied intensity, from generation to generation; it is a conflict more involved, and its dimensions extend well beyond the borders of the Sudan.

Arab tribes did and still do launch proxy raids today, backed up by all manner of governments that have ruled the Sudan: dictatorships, democracies, oppressive democracies, and theocracies. Their mission, if not stated, has been to cyclically disrupt life in indigenous African communities, Abyei region being one. It has been invaded many times and threats of full-scale invasion remain true.

Musing along Uele River took me a while, but finally jolted back to consciousness only to find I was on the banks of Uele River; still in Niangara, in the Congo, a thousand kilometers away from Abyei and from her ill-hydrated river, Nyamoura or, Bahr el Arab, as Arabs have come to name it in advance of owning it. I had drunk to the fill with my own brew of make-believe peace and lived the illusion I walked on safe shores. But no, I was a few steps away from where I had witnessed many indescribable acts of brutality, the very spot I saw the starved drop dead; diseases ravage communities and white armed men, brandish gadgets of destruction and merrily going about warning the population of more death to come.

Uele River was the true host of Niangara; though much desecrated, it has remained a source of food for the living and resting ground for the dead. For the length of time I spent there, it was with her I communed when I was enraged and frustrated by vanishing hope, that we would ever honor the purpose for which we journeyed to the Congo. It is her I went for audience when fear stricken or chocked with anger about abuses taking place in the neighborhood with no one held answerable. Uele River was my therapist and trusted confidant. I whispered my innermost concerns, and even worries about how Southern Sudanese would fend for themselves when aggressed from the north. I felt she could hear me out.

When it was time to leave Niangara for Southern Sudan, I was fully reconciled with the Congo, and with Niangara, town and region. Then, one last attraction to remember Niangara for, a row of women with elongated heads, I mean long, backward pointing heads, passed by. I was told they were members of an ethnic group called the Mangbetu, indigenous to Haut Uele Province, home to many other ethnic groups, including the Zande.

Mangbetu people believe beauty must be enhanced by human ingenuity. Mothers would not trust nature or genes to determine how their daughters would look in adulthood. From infancy, a girl's head is tightly wrapped in clothes, so it elongates, the longer the head, the more beautiful in the mother's eyes and, perhaps, society at large. Today, I wonder what rights groups would make of such cultural practice. Would it count as another form of human rights abuse comparable to female genital mutilation, or would it be praised as was the practice of tight lacing in which 18th century European women were pressured to wear tight corsets for modified aesthetic appearance?

On this note, I bid goodbye to Niangara, a town I hated, then feared and finally loved; a town whose defining feature, River Uele, was my special counselor who spoke in tongues and sometimes roared, yet I could understand. When I was at the end of my tether in patience with my comrades, my kin, and kith, it was Uele I turned to for wisdom.

To Lirangu on the Way Back

We left Niangara on the first week of February 1966, or thereabout, for Lirangu. The enthusiasm that fueled my tiny body to endure a journey of over 980 km, had ebbed away. My knees were weak. I remembered the biblical story of Samson, how he lost his hair, the source of his power, to a beguiling woman, Delilah who, in the end, handed him over into the hands of his enemies. The parallel was vivid in my mind. Had I been beguiled too by my kinsmen who brought me this far only to line my eyes with more scenes of human suffering?

I remembered the source from which I drew stamina to withstand the perils of the journey: hunger, diseases, life threatening encounters and fear of the unknown. All that was worth enduring if the outcome would be to shake free of oppression. When I learned the money which I carried on my back was for the purchase of weapons, I was ecstatic, and filled with power. I regretted not one step of the nearly one thousand kilometers I walked to the Congo. That was my source of power. Whoever took that spirit away had robbed me of my all. That person was my Delilah.

Now that incentive seemed to have been taken away, I saw no difference being here or there. I fervently prayed my seniors had secretly done the right thing without informing me. I did not have much else to think about or live for. My thoughts shuttled between frustration and artless anticipation. If only I had a choice, I would have stood still in my footsteps and refused to continue a journey I felt was without purpose or destination. Here, the spot in which I stood, was closer to Niangara where weapons should have been purchased. A step further away north felt like abandonment of a solemn undertaking. Never had a journey been so long and yet so fruitless. Meanwhile, the cause for which we walked this far stood evermore threatened.

Finally, we arrived at Lirangu. Throughout the journey, I was drowned in my thoughts and could not spare a thought to check who my road companions were but Lieutenant Kuot Mayan, the only one to whom I turned for avuncular advice.

Lirangu is a town in Western Equatoria region, home to the Zande ethnic group, part of which is indigenous to the Congo's Haut Uele Province and to the eastern region of Central African Republic. It was built around a Leprosy hospital, perhaps the only specialized hospital of its kind in Southern Sudan at that time. Most buildings were made of red bricks, designed, and built during the British colonial administration. When civil war spread to all areas of Southern Sudan, Lirangu hospital was among many facilities that were abandoned.

By 1965, Lirangu had been reclaimed by thick, forbidding jungle only a few would dare casually venture into. It was there, some distance north of Lirangu ruins, that Anya-Nya set up a camp which looked a little Dinka colony, but for the fact that they were there as freedom fighters.

Zande people were accommodating and even generous with the little resources they had at hand. The news Arabs were at war with all the peoples of Southern Sudan, apparently left no room for tribalism. If they harbored thoughts to the contrary, they were concealed; and if at all they had reservations, from all indications, it was nothing they could not tolerate.

I did not understand a word of the Zande language (Pazande), but when I heard it spoken, sentences invariably ended with comforting melodic notes. For instance, "How are you?" *Gini pai* in Pazande, when pronounced, rings musical. It was in the Zandeland I saw, for the first time, musical instruments such as harps, mandolin, sanza, and more, all locally handcrafted. Zande people are also skilled in woodcarving; their music is multipurpose. It expresses joy, sadness, and a system to alert villages of approaching dangers.

Zande people were the human custodians of Lirangu, but mother-nature was the hands-on owner. For years, it had silently been demolishing what remained of man's handiwork and, instead, planted trees and flowers of her choice. She was the uncontested protector too. In her hands, Anya-Nya set up a camp, walled in by fruit trees, including mango, orange, tangerine, banana, pineapple, and oil palm, all mother-nature's gift. Anya-Nya could not have camped in a safer place, nor among more accommodating people. The camp was difficult to access, even by inhabitants of nearby villages.

Attack on Lirangu Camp

Yambio and Nzara, the nearest Northern army garrisons from which danger could come, posed no danger. The forest was too thick for any aggressor to venture into. The sense of security in the camp was such that it could easily slip into complacency. Writing was on trees and leaves, but indecipherable to human eye. Security was lax. All considered, Lirangu appeared a haven walled in by the hands of nature. Life in the camp was secure, but humdrum.

Food was served twice a day. Sometimes, we took hikes in the wild to gather fruits. I do not recall how and from where other kinds of food were sourced but judging from the way Zande people were receptive of our presence, to show solidarity, they must have shared their food with us.

Other than eating, exercising, and attending roll calls twice a day, there was not much to do in the camp. There was no ideology to discuss, no ambitions, besides fighting the war, to pursue and no identified skills to hone. Attending weekly market days held on Thursdays was our only source of entertainment. Even that was strictly regulated. On market days, nearby villages gathered in one location to barter or sell their goods. It was there we had a chance to meet and learn from Zande people about their way of life.

Inside the camp, we spent time telling narratives of close encounters with death and other tales of valor. Our camp was all Dinka, so we told Dinka tales, but precious little about the movement, its present and future challenges, especially how to consolidate unity across Southern Sudanese. From what I heard, most Anya-Nya camps were like ours, not sufficiently mixed to warrant the conclusion and a sigh of relief: at long last, our unity pot was melting. If anything, in some ways, each Anya-Nya camp remained fiercely autonomous. A step on a community's toe could ruin all efforts at forging understanding across ethnic lines and dwarf the idea, "as we suffered together, so must we strive together."

Lirangu was not only home to gigantic trees and beautiful, giving, and protective nature. There were also mean-spirited, tiny freaks of nature, parasites, and other insects, worse among them a worm the Zande people call *Tukutuku*. Elsewhere in the world it is called *jigger* or *Tunga penetrans*. They are tiny worms that penetrate under the toenails and silently suck blood. When it is fully grown, it is the size of a chickpea. My toes are a living testimony to how treacherous Tukutuku can be. In some cases, infection becomes so severe toes must be amputated, an irreversible disfigurement.

There are reports Tukutuku was "inadvertently introduced by humans into sub-Saharan Africa" from Central and South America, where it is indigenous. This may lend credence to claims Africa has been a victim, not only of invading cultures, but also of parasitic humans, such as we met in Niangara.

February sped by, then March. With every passing day, my anxiety mounted. I expected a cache of arms to be handed out anytime during one of the roll calls to those old enough to bare them. But from the way things looked, we were in Lirangu for a long haul. A day in was as good as another just gone. We expected endless days to come our way off God's inexhaustible calendar days.

April, I have come to learn from other cultures, is a month that starts with lies. That night, an April date I cannot recall, must have been the trick night. It created an illusion all was normal; that peace was the inviolable rule, and that exceptions did not happen in the jungles of Lirangu. Our minds were at rest. The combination of lunar influence and April allure had done us in, and we did not know, not till it was too late. With the tempo and monotony of grandfather's clock, unconcerned, we watched days silently peel off the calendar. Amidst this mirage of tranquility, my mind was tempestuous, disturbed about continued lack of armaments with which to defend ourselves in case there were attacks.

One day, I accompanied an older colleague to one market day event in the abandoned ruins of Lirangu. It was a good experience. Items on sale included palm wine, palm oil, plantains, ground peanuts and assortment of bush meats, including monkey meat.

As we were returning to the camp, in the ruins of Lirangu hospital, my colleague asked me to momentarily take custody of his China-made, semi-automatic gun so he could step into the privacy of the ruins to relieve himself. He instructed me to be alert, place my finger on the trigger, but never pull unless there was danger, all of which I committed to heart, perhaps a bit too much. My eyes dilated; my mind, throbbed, geared on high alert, scanning for any danger lurking in the woods, or hidden behind piles of bricks unplugged by bulldozing roots. It was as if the weapons I had dreamed about were in my custody; no, in the palms of my hand. No more fear enemies would attack and flee unharmed.

I was engrossed in another dream, a pleasant one. Suddenly, a loud bang! I had inadvertently pulled the trigger, scaring off serenity of the environment and of my colleague too, who, in a jiffy, appeared from behind the bushes, ash-white with fear. When he noticed it was a false alarm, fear gave way to murderous anger. I could feel it as we walked back to the camp.

We arrived on time for the roll call. The commanding officer asked if there were anything to report. My companion stepped forward and narrated the incident. He had to, because, at some point, he would have to account for the missing bullet. Before roll call was dismissed, the camp commander, Captain Nyiel Abot, asked me to step forward. Ceremoniously, he demoted me to a private from corporal and ordered me detained.

When we arrived at the detention center, I was hand and foot tied. I do not recall how long the detention was supposed to last. But something singularly detestable would soon send us back to Bahr el Ghazal

Province unprepared.

The camp had three entry points: North, East and South gates. I was tied up and detained in the South Gate, the entry-point most guarded as it was also most exposed. The eastern gate was the entrance to the senior officers' quarters. There, Commander Nyiel Abot and his deputy, Fabio Deng Akol, lived. I do not know who else lived with them.

Night hours were growing larger and closer to retirement. Waiting for the clock to strike 12, were new guards come to hold vigil till day-break. It was one o'clock AM… two…three…. Daytime was approaching, but not quite yet. Human mind was at it once again, cutting corners in a bid to self-assure all was working out to his expectation, the usual break in of another day. But what transpired in that serene night made me realize later in life, human beings always walk into the future, remote or proximate, blindfolded. They seem not to understand how an object so close and easily attainable would still be beyond reach if still rested in the hands of time future. That, between a minute and another or here and there, lies eternity packed with undetectable possibilities, still elude human attention. That tantalizing early April morning stands testimony to the truth nothing is in the grip of man which destiny cannot seize and walk away with.

It was four o'clock. The moon shone silvery bright, the brightest I have ever seen. Years later, because of what happened that morning, I could almost appreciate the rational why other cultures have come to celebrate the "April Day of Fools." To me, against the backdrop of my experience that morning, April was, "The month that fools." It fooled us with a night so beautiful in the wild, yet romantic in her stillness. Suddenly, it turned murderous. Ho…, I could not pronounce the third letter. Bang…crack…crack…pow…pow. We were under attack from the eastern gate where senior officers lived.

The guards at the southern gate, where I was detained, immediately fled upon hearing gunshots, leaving me hands and feet tied. I was on my own, waiting for what was in store for me. It was here; yet there; may be, never; all was in future. April had beguiled us with beauty to serve us death. I heard footsteps. Whatever I was waiting for was here. Until it befell me, I would not know. If death were a fellow human, it would be a cat footed thief.

It was a Zande man running west for his life. He saw me and stopped, not minding a minute lost could cost him his life. For what reason, I asked myself, would he, a Zande, stop to rescue me, a boy, a Dinka for that matter? That was a foolish soliloquy; the man was a human being before incarnation to a Zande tribesman. It was from him I learned tribalism is a synthetic thought pattern. It is learned, can be challenged, and if not rooted in reason, trashed as will all things manmade when they lose appeal.

The man untied me quickly and ran his way westward. I followed in his path. I knew I had to run opposite the direction of the shooting. I could not run north because I would pass through the main camp which, by then, would have been occupied by government troops. I was not informed of the secret code of the night as detainees are not supposed to be privy to such sensitive information. Perfectly clueless of where I was heading to, I kept on running west. After an hour, I veered a little to the north in hope I would find a freshly beaten footpath. I walked for half hour more, then veered right; in a zigzag till, luck struck.

I found my people gathered, counting the present, and taking note of the missing, prominent among them, the camp commander, Edward Nyiel Abot and his deputy, Fabio Deng Akol. By the end of the day, only the two never resurfaced. They were marked missing or dead.

I do not recall attempts to verify whether they were indeed killed there and then or, perhaps, captured alive, interrogated, and then killed. That detail, I reckon, may never be known. I still cringe at the thought of walking away, leaving their remains for the elements to dispose of; but we did, not out of cruelty, but because we had no arms to strike back with. The thought they were never given a befitting burial, weighed heavily in my heart, but we had to move on.

The Journey Back to Bahr el Ghazal

That was how our journey back to Bahr-el-Ghazal Province started. We did not plan for it. The first hours were a litany of profound doubts. I felt discouraged and overwhelmed by incidents that dropped on us unprepared. We all wore long weary faces and changed countenances. As more silence prevailed, disheartening thoughts filled in the vacuum making us appear more miserable and disoriented. We sat under trees with scattered minds, heavy hearts, and foggy eyes waiting for an epiphany, something to cast light on the direction and path we should take. With the commander and his deputy gone and no obvious person to take the lead, every step any direction was a serious undertaking.

My mind flashed back on our trip to Lirangu. We had guides that were intimately familiar with both the topography of Bahr el Ghazal and Western Equatoria: mountains, rivers, towns, and villages along the way; and yet they made mistakes that could have been fatal. We followed paths that were not frequently patrolled by government army. Knowing we were too ill-prepared to assume unnecessary risks, we avoided sauntering into roads and villages we knew nothing about. My fear was we did not have someone as familiar with the terrain to guide us through. Water streams presented a danger from which we had to steer clear. Some were infested with dangerous creatures: crocodiles, hippopotami, pythons and even turtles large enough to pose risks to human beings.

I had no idea what thoughts passed through other people's minds as we waited. With no blanket to slip into, I sank deep into my thoughts, regurgitating horrors that had whizzed me off to far flung lands and destinations; and now, here under the foot of a gigantic tree. Who knows how long it would be before we figured out when, how and where to go? I felt empty and gutted; my will, my wheel, as it were, was flat. Should I resign and wait for what comes as I had to this early morning? I said to myself, "If such is the choice, then here I rust, fragment, and be one with the soil."

I would not have hit this low point had it only been for that morning attack and the great losses we incurred. I knew, firsthand, in war, people get killed. However, to choose to fight without weapons, even when there were opportunities to acquire them, was what robbed me of the spirit, the driving force behind my decision to join the movement in the first place. In a state of delirium, I soliloquized and expressed myself to my satisfaction, but when asked questions, I could not speak coherently. I must have appeared to my companions as deeply asleep, so they left me to my musings under a tree I seemed to have hogged all to myself. A boy my age, one with eyes so wide he could see nothing, barged in, and punctuated my horrid daytime dream. He spoke down at me, admonishing me for failing to see what he described as, the "big picture", the reality of liberation struggles. "Up on your feet; continue the journey north," he said in a firm voice. I was convinced he had no clue why we were here under these trees. Annoyed, I answered back: "Walk away and leave behind the remains of our leaders? Walk away and confirm, in this unarmed movement, our duty was to sacrifice the ultimate yet remain persuaded that, somehow, victory was ours?" In a moment of sincerity, I could see myself in him a year ago following Abyei's incineration. I was then upbeat, younger, enthusiastic, and mindlessly daring and, truly angry. I felt I was forged and tested by gory experiences in northern, southern Sudan, and a year of travails on the long meandering road to the Congo, Niangara town. The more I engaged him, the more this young apparition hammered lessons into my sleepy ears and listless soul. I told him I was typical 'him' a year ago, but post Niangara, due to successive disappointments I was no longer the same person. He paid a deaf year to what I said and proceeded: "Wise up; overcome your frustrations and say to yourself, 'nothing is lost.' When death and suffering are met with strong determination, future bends and allows itself to be shaped." In my heart, I chuckled, "What a little brat he must be to even think, let alone believe, future would bend for humans to shape!" I asked, "How would you explain this morning's incident, was it that we did not do enough to influence the course nature should take?" He noticed I was unhappy with his sweeping, idealistic remarks. He continued to rain down advice after advice even as I drooled in that state of pitiful indolence: "Remember," he continued, "the future is as much a giver as it is a taker. This morning, it took the best of us; in exchange, gave us anger, frustration, and inanition. Were these not the very feelings you had in Abyei when you decided to shed the child in you and, overnight, became a freedom fighter? The weights such as we carry this morning, are what would create the resolve needed to take charge of our destiny, which is now firmly rested in the palms of the government in Khartoum." Then as if he never were, vanished.

At that moment, a bee stank me on the right cheek. I wondered if that were my muse's way of ending the conversation, with an awakening pinch that temporarily slammed my mouth shut till our path home was found. Whoever the bee was an emissary for, the task to discipline me was accomplished with excellence. That would be my last time to yield to energy sapping musings. I swore I would face up to all challenges along the way. Unlike trees which cannot help themselves even as loggers clear neighboring trees, human beings are blessed with the power of mobility, the first act of self-defense. As refugees and freedom fighters would say: We voted with our feet, therefore, we are today. The eight hundred mile journey we were about to embark on, would no doubt count as a line in the records of the liberation struggle.

At about four that afternoon, we were asked to stand in line and be counted. We did. It was announced, in half hour, we would be on our way. We rushed to our trees to collect whatever belongings we had. I had none but the rags on me. My feet were bare and perfectly exposed to elements, the most dreaded of which was the tiny man eaters, toenails' nemeses, the tukutuku.

Lirangu is located north of Yambio, north east of Nzara. The forces that attacked our camp may have come from either town, but most likely from Nzara. As mentioned above, much as we needed to pass through villages to purchase food supplies, it was wiser to stick to the jungle tracts and avoid walking along riversides. There were no indications the Zande people would betray us, but it was necessary to exercise caution. From where we left, we headed north making sure we avoided human habitats. We straddled the path between the Sue River (River Bahr el Ghazal) to the west and Ibba River (Tonj River), to the east. We walked for days, eating off the bounties of nature: wild honey, availing ourselves of fresh animal meat; now and then, we would run into small creeks teeming with fish, some species I had not seen before. But again, everything about Western Equatoria was mystery to me. Nature was colorful. Yesterday it was grassland shooting up to a height of fifteen feet; then, as if to give us a short respite before encounter with even more stifling surprise, suddenly, a clear parcel of land appears. The mind is cleared, the heart pulsates at a normal rate, and nature is less intimidating.

The short grass suddenly yielded as we entered probably the thickest, least explored area in the southern region, the great forest Dinka people call (Roor Chol Akol) which, translated, would mean, *the forest in which the sun gets dark*. Perhaps that is a metaphor for trees growing so tall they could block sunlight for days. The British called it: The Southern National Park. In the fifties and earlier, the British employed guards to regulate entrance into the forest, especially by non-natives to the environment. There were even rest houses for tourists one hundred and fifty kilometers north of Yambio at the edge of the Zande side of the park before entry into Tonj, Bahr el Ghazal region. A road paved for that purpose extended from Yambio to the park.

Animal life was beyond my wildest expectations. They gather in large numbers in locations, I have come to learn, to salt licks where, particularly larger ones – buffalos, giraffes, elephants, antelopes, and even white rhinos – gathered to lick minerals essential for health. The Park extends from east of Jur River, to beyond east of Jel River, 7,800 square miles in size. I said to myself, "If only Northern Sudanese knew the land of abundance Southern Sudan was, war would rage on to eternity." Praise be to 'hubris' Northerners were of the mind Southern Sudan was a burden they were better off disowning. Their only fear was, should they let Southern Sudan go, it would fall into the arms of Christian missionaries.

As a movement, we operated without borders in defiance of the country's laws and regulations. I do not know if by 1965, the government still had people to guard the forest. If they did, we did not care to know. So, we entered the forbidding forest anyway. It was intimidating not only to the sight; all about it spoke, smelled, and felt danger was lurking here – maybe, there – anywhere! We were in numbers; therein, we each found courage and strength. I was not all the time mentally gathered to remember the details of the walk through the wild, but we did eventually emerge from that dark forest. I felt relieved. Habitually taciturn faces carried thin smiles, not wide enough to brighten the long journey ahead.

What Took Adhal?

We were, at long last, in Bahr el Ghazal region, home, but not quite. We were relieved now that we were no more hemmed in by gigantic trees. This time around, we shared the vast land with white rhinos (very few), giraffes, buffaloes, and other species, yet we felt safer than when we were in the jungle. Some among us were familiar with the area. Still, we were careful not to disturb villages, preferring instead to trot the wild till we arrived where we felt safe.

All went well till we came to the Jur River. It must have been around June or thereabout, 1966. The river was tempestuous as it looked formidable. Nonetheless, we had to cross.

We had no boats, not trained to innovate and quick to act without weighing the consequences. All these shortcomings, sins of woeful unpreparedness, would become manifest in the way we crossed Jur River. The first to jump into the river were the enthusiasts. They had mighty tussles with the waves, but safely made it to the other bank. The show of power went viral: I almost threw myself into the jaws of the raging waves, but someone grabbed me timely. I do not recall his name, but I owe him my life. Many followed the act; they too crossed safely to the other side. I watched waves after waves of men challenge nature and emerge successful.

Then, before my turn came among the three last to cross, another batch jumped into the water, among them, Adhal, a huge man strewn with muscles, so powerful he could slap the waves flat and walk with ease on to the other side. It was him nature chose to offer to the river gods. As expected, he swam like a hippopotamus, from time to time raising his head to take in air. In a short while, he was a few feet away from the other side. Then, momentarily, he appeared stalled; uttered a loud cry, and went under; then reappeared three times in succession; then, no more was seen of him again. Half an hour later, a giant turtle poked its head out as if to let us know it was the predator. Indeed, we all concluded it was it that claimed the life of our comrade and brother.

Now that I know better, it was unlikely the turtle was the culprit. Turtles are known to pull their victims right to the bottom of the river and lie on them for days until the body rots and are now able to eat up their victim's rotten and loosen flesh. The appearance of the turtle must therefore have been coincidental, probably disturbed by the swimmers and whatever sunk Adhal. The river is known to be home to hundreds of thousands of crocodiles and hippopotami. But, if a hippo were the killer, it would have made visible show of the kill, tearing through the water like a mad bull.

Chances are that it was a crocodile that took our comrade in arms, Adhal. While they hibernate in their dry holes in the three months of dry season, they would emerge very hungry when rains increased and the rivers filled up, flooding their underground holes. At such times, crocodiles are known locally to be extremely dangerous, attacking land animals and humans at any opportunity. Such was the time; and it would be reasonable to assume a crocodile took our formidable brother.

They say necessity is the mother of invention. After the incident, we cut down some trees and made a raft out of it making sure it was sturdy enough to take three of us and the few arms we had. We made it not because we were stronger than Adhal. It is nature's call to preserve whom it will and dispose of others who, in our estimation, should be last to succumb.

New Beginning, Same Struggle

We added Comrade Adhal, commander Nyiel Abot and Fabio Deng Akol, to our individual archives of memories to keep. We marched forth as we had to when we fled Lirangu. Now we have learned from Jur River that, when duty-bound, speed on, no matter what. With that, she rushed to pour her content into the White Nile. Now, we too could not stagnate and sulk in one place. We had destinations to reach, other Anya-Nya forces to merge with and a promise to fulfill. Come what may, as one, we will contribute to shielding the dignity of our people from further abuses.

Invigorated, with sturdy steps, we marched forth on our way to northern Bahr el Ghazal Province. Last year, our camp had spent nearly three weeks around Tonj area. Although I was not familiar with the surrounding, the more distance we covered, the more I could see environing scenes that reminded me of the location where Christopher Akonon Mithiang was in command of a huge, well-armed Anya-Nya base. And indeed, those familiar with the area soon confirmed I was right.

The location of the camp was etched in my memory for reasons, one of which was close to home. It was here August last year (1965), that I ran into two of my cousins, Kuol-chol Alor Kuol and Nicola Adol Mithiang Miyan, who broke the news that our uncle, Lewis Nyok Kuol Arop, who lived in Tonj, was shot dead that morning in his bedroom in front of his wife and daughters by attackers who wore military uniforms and spoke Arabic. They also informed they feared three other relatives besides Lewis, may also have been killed.

Five adolescent young men lived with Lewis Nyok; Kuol-chol Alor and Nicola Adol, in addition to Alor Kwaja, Manyit Daw Alei, and Deng Mijak Kuol. Government security in Tonj was known for heightened surveillance. They kept track of who lived with whom in southern towns. They knew exactly how many people were in Lewis Nyok's house that morning and they came prepared to kill them all, six males in total. Earlier, soldiers had taken a round in town and had killed six men already. This was a little reported incident in which government of the Sudan targeted Southern intellectuals. Most victims were educators who, even with the expulsion of Missionaries from Southern Sudan, would run schools and perpetuate education among the population. It was apparently the government's plan to clear the way for Islamic education in Southern Sudan. As fall back, should Southerners resist proselytization through Islamic education, the government plan was to abandon them to illiteracy till they surrender to Islamic education.

Lewis' house was the last on the list of homes soldiers came to weed of male inhabitants that morning. But miracles do happen. In the end, the five boys miraculously escaped. Dinka people have a saying, "God separates things that must happen from those that are not meant to be." Only two sustained non-lethal wounds. Three hid in a bathroom outside the house, close to attackers, yet escaped unscathed in a moment reminiscent of my Lirangu encounter with my Zande savior. This time, the hero was a man from the Nuba mountains, a northern soldier who came to kill but ended up a savior. What moved him to risk his life in that way, I would understand better many years later when the Nuba people would join Southern Sudanese in the war against Khartoum.

Here was how the future pulled off a miracle, had a trick up her sleeve. The Nuba man was commanded to check the bathroom where the boys were hiding. He opened the window and found them cowering in the corners paralyzed by fear. He quietly urged them not to make moves that would betray their presence. Quietly, he retreated.

With a straight face and sure foot, he joined his group. A few minutes later, the boys heard soldiers' footsteps, marching past the bathroom where they were holed up and out of the compound. They had a close shave with death, salute the selfless Nuba soldier who endangered his life to save children he came to kill.

Lewis Nyok was one of the earliest champions of education in Southern Sudan, an educator whose efforts have thus far been overlooked even by researchers who have gathered a wealth of information on him over the years. Ngok of Abyei is yet to publicly credit Nyok Kuol for being the first Ngok intellectual to stand against efforts, including by members of his family, to permanently annex the area to Northern Sudan. Till his murder in August 1965, it was his unwavering position that Ngok was part of Southern Sudan. Decades into the future, every passing year has spoken of the acuity of his foresight; community's leadership slaughtered, cattle driven away, villagers killed, and villages burned down; even children taken to slavery. No matter what happens, Abyei has remained part of the Sudan, the very dispensation that has for decades sought to destroy the population.

My cousins also informed that before troops came for Lewis, they had already slaughtered six other men in their homes. Bodies of the deceased were hurriedly and irreverently dumped in a pit dug for the purpose well before execution. The soldiers however, retained the body of Bona Bol. The reason was as inexplicable as it was evil; Bol was endowed with a beard so bushy it would be waste, they thought, to bury him with such a priced item on his chin. They wanted to desecrate his body first. According to an eyewitness, a daughter of one of the victims present during the murder, Bol's beard was skinned off his face before he was thrown into the pit along with the six others.

I have asked and continue to find answers for such brutality. Was it out of hatred or something more systemic, inhuman, and degrading? Years later, I would find deeper implication to that seemingly mindless action. To be fair, still I would not dismiss the act may also have been an isolated expression of hatred for Southern people, totally divorced of cultural or religious underpinnings. But history would restrain us from settling for such easy conclusions. There are documented reports in Arab history when shaving beards off men's faces was a recognized instrument of persecution and an accepted judicial sentence for offenders the system deemed fit to humiliate. Arab conquerors of Egypt for instance, reportedly punished and shamed Egyptian men by sentencing them to beardlessness, a life of facial nudity. In that context, no punishment could be more degrading. Perplexing, but perhaps that might have been their way of cutting down on lowlings intent on snaking their way up the ranks of bearded Arab gentry.

The question remains: Was an ordinary, illiterate Sudanese soldier serving in Tonj, a remote region of the Sudan, aware of Arab infatuation with beards? Was the author of the idea an Arab in the first place? There is no denying the allure of hyper masculinity remains visible in today's Arab world. In places several degrees removed from both context and Arab roots, Sudan for example, the culture exists but in pockets.

In some parts of Sudan, beard is taken at face value as an external manifestation of virility and piety, but when the bearded person happens to be non-Muslim, the overzealous are confused about what to make of it. A beard in the face of an infidel is a riddle difficult to square with its association with piety. Perhaps, the originator of the idea to skin the beard off the late man's face, was one such devotee. I entertain doubts a soldier in such context would be privy to esoteric information on beard in Arab and Islamic culture. Bol's case stands out as a glaring testimony of why Southern Sudanese had to reject northern domination and to seek restoration of their dignity through armed struggle.

Those were the thoughts that jammed my mind as we passed by the location where Akonon Mithiang's camp was in 1965. We continued our journey north. Around Gagrial, we stopped for a short while in commander Kuol Amom's camp. Some of our colleagues stayed there. The rest, including me, headed north, to Twic area, where my affiliation with Anya-Nya had begun.

On the way, we passed by areas that awakened strong memories in me. I remembered Ngeny Ater and Bol Arop Diu whom I had been with that night, but in the morning, on their way on a mission, they sauntered into an ambush laid by the Northern army in Twic, Thon area.

I recalled heroes among them: Macham Atem, Kuol Arop Kor, Doldol Nyang, Deng Biong Mading and Arop Deng Majok. I particularly remember Biong Bol Wun-Biong who educated and provided explanations to why we roamed the wilderness away from our homes and towns where Northerners were in control. I witnessed brutalities our people had suffered but could not situate what I saw in a wider, more comprehensive context. He spoke to me about international politics, the West v. Communist East blocks; told me stories about the Czechoslovak leader, Alexander Dubcek, whom he loved; spoke of the tyranny of Franco of Spain and the plot by the Arab world to stand with Arabicized Sudan to Islamize and Arabize Southern Sudan or, if that failed, to depopulate it altogether.

We arrived in Twic, Adiang area, a few miles away from my home, Mijak Manyuar. One midnight, Kuol Arop Koor, an uncle from my mother's side, a senior officer, tied my hands and feet so fast I had no time to fight back. He carried me on his back and repeatedly kept saying: "It is time you returned to school." After some distance, he untied my feet making sure I did not run away as we approached my family's home in Mijak Mannyouar.

He had to drop me there before daybreak, lest he be sighted, and his presence reported to army headquarters in Abyei. When we arrived home, to ensure I would not take to the bush after him, he once again tied my feet and hands, gagged my mouth, and left me right at the center of my father's compound. His task was accomplished. My physical association with Anya-Nya was thus terminated. At daybreak, when people came out of the rooms, there I was after two years of absence.

As I was about to be reintroduced to the very context I had consciously disavowed, I knew my new beginning would be a continuation of how I felt since the day I appeared with my father before the school admission board nearly six years earlier. The two incidents, El-Muglad and the burning of Ngok region, only came to confirm something was fundamentally flawed with the relations between Northern and Southern Sudanese.

One thing was clear, Anya-Nya was only but a chapter in a book that had an introduction and a conclusion; sandwiched in between, a vast array of experiences weaved together by one theme, the strife for enduring freedom, a power second only to everlasting freedom which comes with death.

PART FIVE
REFLECTIONS ON WAR AND PEACE

Warring for a Mirage of Just Peace

Although I have never taken up arms to go to war, no one can doubt the fact that only the most compelling reason would propel one to go to kill and risk being killed. The paradox is that the cause for which people go to war is nearly always quite obvious, and so is the solution to the root causes of the war. What is also paradoxical is that the solution that is obvious at the outset gets negotiated and accepted only after so much suffering, bloodshed, and sometimes genocidal atrocities. Why?

Pieng's experience provides a personal insight into what war really means. I like to watch war documentaries as part of my interest in history. I have seen the documentaries of the two world wars and the American civil war in which victims of mass atrocities lie as corpses that are totally divested of their humanity and significance, except only as unidentifiable statistics. I went to Rwanda only three months after the Genocide in my U.N. capacity as Representative of the Secretary General and witnessed the evidence of that horror in stinking bodies that remained unburied as evidence. While wars are fought with the declared goal of upholding, promoting and ensuring human dignity, foot soldiers are slaughtered in masses and left to rot as skeletons plastered with skins from which birds and scavenging animals of prey feast, the very core of the indignity against which wars are fought. Despite his humanistic care for life, Pieng describes scenes in which soldiers and officers on both sides fall dead by scores, hundreds, and thousands. In one instance, as many as five thousand lay dead and fifteen thousand were captured in a battle. The casualties are regretted as 'unfortunate,' if on 'our' side, and welcomed with gratification, if on the side of 'the enemy.' And where does all that lead in the end? The outcome is bound to be a settlement in which the options and the final resolution were in sight from the outset.

The Sudanese civil war that began in 1955, intermittently fought, halted and resumed until it was once again ended in 2005, led to the loss of no less than four million lives. Throughout, potential solutions centered around four well known alternative models for possible solutions. Even as students in the Secondary School, we learned that the Anti-Imperialist Front, which was leftist, and the communist party, advocated autonomy for the South. I believe most Southerners would have settled for that solution, but it was rejected by the Northern Establishment. The call for a federal arrangement was totally rejected as tantamount to secession and was in fact criminalized as a capital offense for which individual Southern leaders were condemned to death. Each of these models, autonomy and federalism, were eventually accepted. Far from the autonomy under the 1972 Addis Ababa Agreement leading to secession, South Sudanese became much more committed to unity than the North. But that Agreement was unilaterally abrogated. That ruled out any more talk about autonomy as a solution. When federalism was introduced by an Islamic dictatorship, it was seen as too little too late, making what was feared the most, secession, the only residual option for the South. Was it necessary for so much suffering and death to be imposed on the country to achieve what could have been negotiated and resolved with less radical compromises in the first place?

Fanie du Toit's book, *When Political Transitions Work: Reconciliation as Interdependence*, focuses on the experience of South Africa in achieving peace and reconciliation without resolving all the differences associated with apartheid. An innovative, stimulating, and provocative study, the book generically provides an alternative to war as a means for settling disputes. As the argument goes, the first step in reconciliation is for the parties to recognize that peaceful coexistence, mutual recognition and respect, and pragmatic nonviolent cooperation in a process aimed an incrementally reforming the future is the constructive way of avoiding destructive violent conflict. The ideal of solving all the major problems in the conflict should be pursued as a promise that cannot be given a time frame for accomplishment. Arguably, "reconciliation cannot wait for the day when all differences have been resolved before it can begin or indeed progress. Reconciliation is a process that is based on the commitment of former enemies to work together nonviolently, despite historic differences and the unfinished business of the past on the understanding that issues will be resolved over time." (p.138)

The process rests on recognizing intrinsic interconnectedness and interdependence between the parties in conflict. Whereas apartheid in the words of Archbishop Desmond Tutu aimed at what he called "unscrambling the racial omelette," the racial entanglement that cannot be undone, "reconciliation represented a political agenda that, as its point of departure, admitted to the fundamental (unchangeable) and comprehensive (political, economic, social and moral) interdependence of all citizens. Interdependence was acknowledged, not only as a given fact, but as a possible norm for how society ought to organize itself in future, as a promise of justice to come." (p.33)

De Klerk reaffirmed this framework when he reportedly said, "There is but one way to peace, to justice for all: that is the way of reconciliation, of together seeking mutually acceptable solutions, of together discussing what the future South Africa should look like, of constitutional negotiation with a view to permanent understanding." (p.33) Paradoxically, it is usually after an intensive, costly and painfully exhausting violence, what has been described as "mutually hurting stalemate," that the warring parties can open up to more constructive compromises.

As du Toit explains, "Arguing that reconciliation is morally or strategically desirable is one thing, but to convince a divided nation that it is actually possible and practically workable – that a new future is around the corner – is quite another." Post-apartheid government and leaders "set out to put reconciliation into practice in a country that had never before experienced black and white citizens in intentionally reciprocal and mutually beneficial ways." Building trust must be seen to "directly address the wrongdoings of the past and the lingering resentments these have created. Otherwise, peace is likely to be temporary." (p.8)

As du Toit argues, "If a transition is meant to deliver, within a matter of years, the complete erasure and closure of an evil past, then clearly South Africa's transition did not work." He argues, on the other hand, that South Africa's transition did indeed work in that "Political violence was replaced by largely nonviolent political contest action; the apartheid state was replaced by a constitutional democracy with institutions that since 1994 have acted at least partially effectively in curbing executive impunity ... and a vast array of policies and measures have been undertaken to improve the lives of poor South Africans, which has led to the gradual but steady increase in the life expectancy of all South Africans." Although this does not make the case of South Africa simply "a good story to tell," the record "goes a long way to dispel the Afro-pessimism so typical of many 'critical' studies of South Africa." (p.9). It can indeed be argued that despite the gross and unacceptable indignities of apartheid, South Africa averted a full-fledged civil war of the kind many countries in Africa have suffered.

The reconciliation that ended apartheid now seems to be obviously the right thing to have done, but for decades talking to the apartheid regime was strongly resisted by both Africans and the anti-apartheid international community. In the early 1970s, as Ambassador to the Scandinavian countries, which were in the forefront of the international anti-apartheid movement, and later as Minister of State for Foreign Affairs, I persistently spoke out in international fora in favor of talking with the apartheid regime, to probe into the rationale for their racist attitude. If the objective of the African National Conference (ANC) was to create a non-racial South Africa, how could that be achieved without talking to apartheid leaders? The reaction against my position was nearly always unanimous. My views, stated in an African-American Conference we hosted in Khartoum in 1978, were reported by a South African newspaper, which prompted our Ambassador in Tanzania, which was the leader of the frontline countries, to write a report to the Ministry, on what he defensively described as a 'very sensitive development.'

I cannot argue that I was right and those against me were wrong. As du Toit explains, perhaps what was needed was the amount of pressure exerted by a combination of internal liberation struggle, international support for the struggle, and sustained international sanctions that crippled the South African economy for the conflict to be "ripe for resolution." As du Toit acknowledges. "The fall of the Berlin wall in 1989 marking the end of the Cold War in its peculiar radicalized manifestation in Southern Africa, certainly contributed, as did increasing international isolation and condemnation of the regime, as well as sustained waves of domestic protest, pressure, and sabotage from a mix of civil society and other interest groups as well as underground resistance movements." (p.18) But is that not comparable to violently forcing the enemy to the negotiating table? How is it therefore a case of reconciliation to avert violence?

Du Toit however argues that a major factor was that South African "leaders of certain ilk" seized that historic opportunity to lead the country to the desired outcomes, and away from what would have been a far worse violence, perhaps a full-scale civil war. "The inception of reconciliation depended critically on political leadership of a particular kind that came, for better and worse, ... exemplified by Nelson Mandela, and to some degree as well, Frederick Wiley de Klerk." (p.18). According to du Toit, "Mandela ... was no naïve political push over. It was his keen appreciation for concrete opportunities to further the struggle for justice, alongside his hard-fought convictions, which led him to reconciliation." (p.38)

Mandela was well aware of the price that had already been paid in lives lost and the ongoing cost of the stalemate in armed struggle. In his own words, "We had the right on our side, but not yet the might. It was clear to me that a military victory was a distant if not impossible dream. It simply did not make sense for both sides to lose thousands if not millions of lives in a conflict that was unnecessary. They must have known this as well. It was time to talk." (p.22) Du Toit notes that "Both Mandela and De Klerk recognized the possibility of combining realpolitik with deeply held conviction, and, crucially, they acted on it. Each extended an olive branch to his enemy and won the chance of a better life for the majority of South Africans." (p.38)

I visited South Africa for the first time when Mandela was still in prison, but intense international efforts to have him released were underway and the momentum for talks was building up. Former President of Nigeria, General Olusegun Obasanjo, invited me as a Resource Person of the Inter-Action Council of Former Heads of State and Government to accompany him and former Prime Minister of the United Kingdom, Edward Heath, on a visit to South Africa that was a follow up to the 1986 Mission of the Commonwealth Eminent Persons. I remember Obasanjo telling me, after our meeting with De Klerk and his Cabinet, "They must release Mandela. Only he can save this country." I was impressed by the emphatic tone of Obasanjo's statement. But it has always been my view that putting an almost exclusive faith and hope in Mandela, as the international community was doing, risked an inevitable fall into an abyss, once he was gone. While that has not happened, I believe my concern was in place.

I was glad to see du Toit 'humanize' Mandela, and 'saving' him from being idolized and turned into a mythical character. He portrays him instead as a towering leader of his people, but one who closely collaborated with others to do what he did. I was particularly moved by the passage in which du Toit wrote about the idealization of Mandela: "I am unsure which Mandela is being referred to ... the real historical figure, flaws and strengths included, or an idealized, even fictional, figure. Mandela was undoubtedly a giant of his time, but his reputation posthumously seems to have grown even larger, perhaps too much so. He now seems to enjoy a kind of secular beatification that makes it virtually impossible for any contemporary leader to emulate him, far less to improve on his ideas. I believe this would have horrified the real Mandela." (p.7).

I particularly appreciated the way du Toit argues for a degree of parity between Mandela and De Klerk. Although their relationship was and continued to understandably agonize, "a growing sense of their interdependence – the indispensable role of their adversary in realizing the aspirations of their respective struggles – provided a firm platform for cooperation. They were 'in this together.'" (p.32) Du Toit concludes, "Apartheid was an egregious story, even his staunchest critics today must admit that he too played a key role. Without De Klerk, it is difficult to imagine a nonviolent end to apartheid." (p.19)

The pursuit of reconciliation by Mandela and De Klerk was by no means a feat of lofty idealism but the exercise of "visionary leadership. ... It is possible, indeed probable, that reconciliation arose not out of any notion of personal forgiveness but from a pragmatic acknowledgment of the intractability of a military stalemate, and of the power of reconciliation to change things fundamentally." (p.38) As Mandela reportedly stated, "there are times when a leader must move out ahead of the flock and go off in a new direction, confident that he is leading his people in the right way." (p. 22)

I witnessed, under rather fortuitous circumstances a reflection of Mandela's personal attributes that may help explain the shrewd yet humanistic qualities of leadership he displayed in negotiating with the apartheid regime. It was at an intimate dinner in Cape Town, attended, among others by his wife-to-be, Graca Machel, Lisbeth Palme, the widow of the Swedish Prime Minister, Olof Palme, and the Nigerian Nobel Laureate, Wole Soyinka. People were very critical of African leaders generally, and Mandela argued that he had come to know many good African leaders and that lumping African leaders together as bad was grossly unwarranted. His position was dismissed as a reflection of his well-known goodness and forgiving attitude. I noticed that Mandela was visibly getting restless and impatient. Looking at his watch, indicating that he was about to leave, he made his concluding comment: "Every human being, however bad, by virtue of being a human being, has some goodness in him. If you want to cooperate with him; look for that goodness and build on it. That is how you can make the best of the situation." With those words, he got up and left. I was in full agreement with him in the discussion, but it was after he left that I strongly spoke out in support of his position.

Laudable as the South African reconciliation is, considering the economic and social disparity that racially divided South Africans, finding a common ground was a nigh impossible undertaking. When I visited South Africa with Obasanjo and Health, I was struck by the differences between Cape Town, one of the most beautiful cities I have seen, and Cross-Roads, just outside the city, one of the worst slums I have ever seen anywhere in the world. In sharp contrast to my chronic optimism, I concluded that reconciliation could not be possible. No amount of investment to lift up the Blacks would be enough to bridge the gap with the Whites. And any amount of resources taken from the Whites to uplift the Blacks would be too much for them to accept. I am glad that my pessimistic prediction was wrong, and that reconciliation was achieved.

I was impressed by du Toit's account of Mandela's background, born and raised as he was in a cohesive society, regulated by the principles of *Ubuntu*, a concept which embodies the social norms of unity, harmony and respect for human dignity. *Ubuntu* stipulates a framework of shared humanity in which the interests of the individual are in harmony with those of the community. According to du Toit, *Ubuntu* "is a cultural ideal which affirms that people become fully human only through their interactions with other people." (p.53) According to the norms of *Ubuntu,*

"disregarding the human dignity of others fatally wounds one's own humanity." Archbishop Desmond Tutu calls *Ubuntu* the "the very essence
of being human" and "Africa's gift to the world." (p.195) *Ubuntu* has
been credited as the African moral foundation of reconciliation based
on interdependence that led to the eradication of the apartheid system
in South Africa.

Viewed from a different vantage point, it was arguably the denial of
the values and the dignity associated with *Ubuntu* that propelled Mandela
from a free happy childhood in the countryside to an angry and eventually determined freedom fighter. According to du Toit, "Mandela at-
tributed his driving force towards the horizon – his quest to be free – to
his experiences as a Xhosa child growing up in the deeply rural, peaceful hills of Eastern Cape of South Africa. As a boy there, herding cattle
across the rolling fields of Transkei, he wrote of feeling free in every way
– free to swim in the streams that criss-crossed the local village, to roast
mealies (corn) under the stars, and to ride the oxen he guided along the
narrow footpaths." (p.20-21)

As du Toit observed, "Mandela seemed to be able to adopt ever-wid-
ening allegiances and causes, yet it is equally clear that he never re-
nounced the traditional loyalties and deeply held beliefs that first promoted him to join the liberation struggle … By not abandoning his
identity as a Xhosa and an African, and by valuing the universal dimensions reflected in his local identity, he was able to demonstrate how the
universal should be anchored in, and justified in terms of, the local and
the particular. In other words, it is possible to conclude that his embrace
of the fight for the rights of all South Africans while drawing on his
particular identity and heritage to do so, played some role in his decision
to pursue reconciliation as political strategy." (p.11-12)

Du Toit goes on to explain that it was indeed the contrast between
the identity and dignity Mandela enjoyed in his local background and
the indignities of discrimination under apartheid that provoked him to
rebel: "When he moved to Johannesburg as a young lawyer some years
later, Mandela discovered that his boyhood freedom had in fact been
limited to those idyllic childhood days, and that the freedom to be a professional adult simply did not exist for him as he set out to start a career
in law. That began his fight for basic individual rights … In time, after
he experienced firsthand, the intransigence and racism of the regime,

he joined the ANC and eventually turned freedom fighter, beginning a new clandestine life in pursuit of rights for his people." (p.21)

Did the peace and reconciliation Mandela negotiated achieve for his people what he had struggled for on their behalf? The obvious answer is "Yes, but." Since the end of apartheid, I have been to South Africa on numerous occasions and have witnessed conflicting perspectives on what has been achieved. Chatting with taxi drivers, as I generally tend to do, I got two contrasting views that reflected both dissatisfaction with the reconciliation for not having adequately addressed the grievances of the Blacks and acceptance of the incremental approach to peace and its incremental benefits. One driver posed a rhetorical question to me: "Is this what we have been struggling for, only to have some black faces in the government, while we remain in poverty and the whites still control the wealth of our country?" Another driver presented an opposite view: "We know the whites still control the economy, but we also know that it will eventually accrue to us. We will wait patiently; we do not want to rock the boat."

Accommodating conflicting positions that are seemingly irreconcilable, but can and must be made compatible and reconcilable, without being oblivious to their inherent incompatibility, reminds me of my differences with a colleague who is a leading figure in conflict resolution. He argued that conflict is inherent in human relations and that it is futile to try to prevent or resolve it; the most that can be done is to manage it. My position was that the normal state of human interaction, if the moral code of conduct stipulated by the social order is observed, is one of peaceful and cooperative relationship. Conflict, especially if violent, is a break-down of the normal state of affairs; the aim of conflict resolution is therefore to restore the normal state of peaceful and harmonious relations.

I agree with the social restorationist paradigm as described by du Toit that "Human society is not … an arena of danger and violent competition, but rather … a delicate web of cooperation, through which sufficient levels of trust exist, or can be generated." (p.134) According to this framework, "War is … what happens when things go fundamentally wrong in the community of human relations. Unlike liberalism, where violence is often seen as an inevitable, violence is understood as a disastrous denial of how the world does and should work." (p.135) Peace and reconciliation should aim at restoration of the disturbed order.

Two eminent Africans, Wole Soyinka and Professor Mahmoud Mamdani, have criticized South Africa's reconciliation for falling far short of addressing the economic and social injustices of the apartheid regime. Soyinka, referring to the Truth and Reconciliation Commission, asked the question, whether the 'truth shall set you free,' and offered an answer, "Maybe... but first the Truth must be set free." According to him, "Where there has been inequity, especially of a singularly brutalizing kind ... that robs one side of its most fundamental attribute – its humanity – it seems only appropriate that some form of atonement be made, in order to exorcise that past, reparations, we repeat, serve as a cogent critique of history and thus a potent restraint on it repetition." (p.91). He went on to pose a rhetorical question, "What really would be preposterous or ethically inadmissible in imposing a general levy on South Africa's white population?" (p.91)

Du Toit seems to concur: "There can be little disagreement that reparations as a whole have fallen well short of expectations. Importantly though, this failure cannot fully be laid at TRC door in terms of either the design or implementation of its mandate. Arguably, it is more about a lack of political will and institutional capacity, as well as about competing priorities in government, than about the work of TRC as such." (p.104-105) Reportedly, the recommendations of the TRC included proposals for wide-ranging institutional reforms, especially with respect to the role of big business that had supported and benefitted from apartheid. These included a call for the establishment of a Business Reconciliation Fund and the imposition of a wealth tax, "a once-off levy on corporate and private income, a once-off donation of 1 per cent the market capitalization of each company listed on the Johannesburg Stock Exchange, as well as a retrospective surcharge of corporate benefits and of all golden handshakes given to senior public servants since 1990." Such fund "could provide non-repayable grants, loans, and/or guarantees to business-related funding for black small entrepreneurs in need of either ... skills or capital for the launching of a business." The rationale was that business had at least a "moral obligation to assist in the reconstruction and development of post-apartheid South Africa through active reparative measures." (p.105)

Mahmoud Mamdani characterized the South African peace accord as "Reconciliation without Justice." While acknowledging South Africa's reconciliation as commendable, he argued that "the transition failed to transform power relations between white and black citizens beyond the limits of the political elites ... Victims and perpetrators continue to live together in a context in which perpetrators still wield considerable power ... This makes the transformation of historical power relations even more important." (p.92)

Accountability for the crimes committed under apartheid is an issue which du Toit addresses in depth but remains seemingly unresolved because the government allegedly did not implement the recommendations of the Truth and Reconciliation Commission. It is the subject of ongoing debate between the advocates of peace and those for justice. This has often been perceived as a conflict between the African approach, which is more oriented toward forgiveness and reconciliation, and the European approach, which leans more toward punitive justice.

I have always argued that South Africa aimed at bridging the two positions. According to du Toit, "The TRC Act eventually settled on a form of amnesty that depended on the condition that applicants made full disclosure, established political motive, and demonstrated proportionality of the crime to the stated political objective. The conditionality of the South African amnesty provisions meant that no blanket amnesties were granted." (p.69)

Du Toit's thorough analysis of the different theoretical schools of thought on the central themes of reconciliation portrays the complexities of each school focusing on a piece of the puzzle. Clearly each piece alone cannot stand the scrutiny of the cross-cultural world in which we live. As du Toit argues, "It is therefore important, even as differences and contestations are acknowledged, not to give up on pursuing theoretical clarity that at least attempt (sic) to account for what can be expected, offered, and hoped for when societies seek to reconcile." (p.124)

The paradox of fighting to achieve a just peace presents two options. One is to end the violent manifestations of conflict and agree to reconcile, co-exist and cooperate in a process that provides some remedies, while patiently pursuing full redress of the causes of the conflict over time. The other is to continue the violent struggle for change until the major grievances generating the conflict are effectively addressed. In the case of South Africa, the conflict had already gone on for so long and the damage done was so great that the choice was arguably not as difficult as it might sound. While the case of apartheid was admittedly extreme, what happened therefore is what eventually happens in protected conflict situations. Even what is being proposed, ending violence with the understanding that the root cause of the conflict is also often the core of peace agreements, for it usually takes time for the grievances to be significantly addressed as part of the process of implementation. What is new in the proposed reconciliation before resolution is to apply early on in the conflict and before so many lives are lost and so much damage inflicted.

War and Peace in Perspective

I would like to conclude my essay on these four experiences in the liberation struggle with observations in two areas, the cause of Abyei in the struggle of South Sudan and the paradox of fighting for an obvious cause that must in the end be addressed. While these two areas are separate, they are interconnected. The role Pieng and many others from Abyei played in the Southern Sudan liberation struggle and the correlative contribution other Ngok citizens, including the women and even a nine-year old boy, whose stories are included in this volume, made in their various areas of operations makes the linkage of Abyei to the South obvious. The second area of my observations relates to the fundamental question of why it is necessary to inflict so much human suffering and loss of lives to address legitimate grievances that are obvious from the beginning and will eventually be effectively addressed. This is the question Nyenagwek answers in making the shift from fighting to peacemaking. The two areas are connected in that the cause of Abyei as part of Sudan is an obvious one which is in fact recognized as such, even though it is not being resolved for both known and hidden reasons.

Abyei and other Southern areas of the South, Twic and Ruweng, were annexed to the North by the British in order to provide them with better protection against slave raiders from the North. Although these other Southern areas were subsequently returned to the administration of the South, Abyei remained under the Northern administration as a Southern gateway between the North and the South that continued to safeguard the interests of the South at the North-South border. This fact has been well documented and acknowledged by the South Sudanese communities close to the Northern border. It is that bridging and protective role that made the leaders of Abyei to remain in that anomalous position of being South Sudanese in the North.

When the Northern domination replaced British colonial rule and became a form of internal colonial administration that oppressed the South including Abyei, the people joined the struggle for freedom from domination as part and parcel of the South. They did this both by participating in the two wars of liberation and through civilian resistance and diplomatic action in their various areas of work. In this essay, I have tried to document specific instances of correlation between what the freedom fighters were doing in the war Front and what I was doing in my various areas of work inside the country and abroad.

An example here may be apropos. When I was appointed Ambassador after the 1972 Addis Ababa Agreement, I made that peace agreement the basis of our foreign policy. As ambassador to the United States, I used it effectively to reverse a very negative bilateral situation in the aftermath of the 1973 assassination of the American Charge' d'affairs by the Palestinian Black September terrorists. Although they were tried, found guilty and sentenced to prison terms, they were handed over to PLO in Cairo to serve their terms there. This enraged the US and almost broke diplomatic ties with Sudan. I worked very diligently and succeeded in reestablishing close cooperation that made the Sudan third to Israel and Egypt as a recipient of US Assistance. On the first visit by President Nimeiri which I had singlehandedly organized against strong resistance on both sides, I suggested to the President that we include on the delegation representatives of the Southern Regional Government to reflect the Southern perspective, both the President and the Minister rejected my proposal. Nimeiri said to me, "Why do we need a Southerner when you, a Southerner, made all the arrangements by yourself." My only response was, "Mr. President, I thought I did it as Ambassador of the Sudan and not as Southern Sudanese."

When I was in the United Nations as Special Representative of the Secretary General on Internally Displaced Persons, Antonio Guterres, the current Secretary General of the United Nations, who was then the High Commissioner for Refugees, who knew that I was from Abyei, and had discussed the Abyei problem with him on a number of occasions, told me that he dreamt that I, supposedly a Northerner, had been made the Prime Minister of South Sudan.

When I was honored to be the first Permanent Representative of the newly independent South Sudan, and at the time of President Kiir's dismissal of his cabinet, and pending the formation of a new cabinet, my Russian colleague, Vitaly Churkin, with whom I had often discussed the Abyei problem, and who supported the position of the Sudan on Abyei, said to me, "Are you going to be appointed Minister of Defense or of Education?"

These examples show the disconnect between the people of Abyei being recognized as South Sudanese, even as the status of the area remains contested. Some people see this as indicative of the fact it is the land, and not the people, that Khartoum claims, but there is no basis whatsoever for seeing the people and the land as separate. For the Sudan to make such a claim would be utterly absurd.

The main point to emphasize is the extent to which heroic contribution Pieng and other sons and daughters of Abyei made to the armed struggle of South Sudan in which they were motivated by the cause of Abyei, should leave no doubt in anybody's mind that they fought as South Sudanese. For any South Sudanese to hold otherwise would an unfathomable denial of a blood brother. My own correlative account of activities abroad in promoting the cause of the South intellectually and diplomatically obviously complement the heroic role of Ngok Dinka freedom fighters in the war Front. And both are only samples of what the people of Abyei have been doing for decades in their various areas of operation for the cause of South Sudan.

The second area of my concluding observations relates to the paradox of war and peace. Placing the experience of Pieng, the three women, the Two Awuors and Nyenagwek, and the nine year old Raphael Tikley, whose accounts are included in this volume in the broader context of the cause of the South and the wars it has generated for over half a century, and using a cross benefit analysis, the question that continues to pose itself is whether the enormous cost incurred in terms of lives lost and the destruction of the country and its environment was necessary or whether some wisdom and reasoning could have resulted in more constructive results at less or no cost. The South has attained independence, but what does that really mean for the quality of life for the people of South Sudan? Sudan has been divided, but is the kind of cooperation that is emerging between the two countries not a form or degree of reunification, and could a loose kind of unity not have been agreed upon to give the South full self-government within unity and to equitably share power and wealth at the national level? And on Abyei, although the liberation struggle has brought the cause of Abyei to the attention of the international community, the problem remains unresolved. Whatever the final solution, could it be far from what could have been negotiated without so much suffering and blood shed?

The two sets of works, the Memoirs of Sudan's long war by these Ngok Dinka general, women warriors and a child soldier, and du Toit's book on South Africa's Reconciliation, present contrasting visions of war and peace. The Memoir of Pieng in particular documents the horrors of war, told dispassionately with the death of large numbers taken as almost the norm, indeed the objective of war. Awuor also speaks of the horrors of war in terms not only of mass atrocities but also of extreme suffering that still steers deeply agonizing emotions. Tikley as a child of nine who should be shielded from witnessing death was also in the thick of killing. In contrast to warring, the South African study makes an admittedly implausible case for Reconciliation before Resolution of the conflict in order to avoid bloodshed and human suffering.

Although Pieng is well reputed as an exceedingly and even excessively brave commander, who consistently risked his life at the front line, the victims of war are mostly the foot soldiers who are treated as virtually dispensable, not the high-ranking politicians and generals who initiate wars. The call for Reconciliation before Resolution, lofty as it sounds, seems like wishful thinking, a pie in the sky, so to speak. And yet, why is so much killing necessary when in most cases the mutually acceptable end result and the bases for peaceful compromise are apparent from the start, unless one aims at a clear-cut outcome of victor and vanquished, with genocidal atrocities?

This makes me favor the South African dream for peace based on promises for acceptable solutions before full resolution. This means sitting down and agreeing that there are indeed grievances or causes that generate wars, that they must be addressed, and that the available options for addressing them can be agreed upon as a basis for negotiation, and that there is therefore no need for massive bloodshed.

The agreement on principles for peace concluded between the Prime Minister of the Sudan and the leader of the SPLM/A North on

September 4, 2020, is perhaps a good example of the approach I am supporting. The parties agreed to end the violence on the understanding that the causes of the war that has raged for decades will be addressed. This means recognizing the diversities of the country on the bases of full equality, maintaining the forces of the parties in conflict for their own protection until an integrated national army is formed, separating religion and the state to avoid constructing the national identity framework being dominated by one religion, applying genuine democratic principles of governance, and sharing central power and national wealth equitably. This is the essence of reconciliation before resolution, the only problem is that it is coming after decades of war that has caused so much devastation, suffering and death.

The structural problems of agreeing on reconciliation before resolution are profound. War has been an inherent aspect of human experience since the beginning of recorded history. As I said earlier, I like to watch documentaries of wars, specifically the two World Wars, and the American civil wars. And I went to Rwanda in 1994, three months after the genocide, and found bodies with skins plastered onto the skeletons still scattered all over the affected areas. I had to enter a church yard through a gate where I literally had to step over dead bodies. Reflecting on all this, I ask myself how humanity can be so brutish toward fellow human beings. But perhaps it is because, after all, we are animals with inherent animalistic instincts and characteristics. The question that must be asked is: Can humanity avert war in favor of diligent efforts toward a credible promise of a peacefully negotiated just peace or is humanity unavoidably doomed to live in war?

It has always been my principled position that pessimism leads to a dead end while optimism, provided it is not blind but strategically grounded, generates a challenge for action. Perhaps the real question is whether a constructive policy framework for managing conflicts without violence proposed by du Toit can be applied to early phases of conflicts to save lives and end the suffering of masses of the populations. Although the objective of full redress is the normal demand of liberation struggles, most violent conflicts eventually get resolved on the bases of principles that were quite apparent from the start. This means that the suffering and the loss of lives are really unnecessary and morally unwarranted. Nearly always, these conflicts end with compromises that are not far from the framework analyzed by du Toit's book. What might be required is aiming at the best compromises that can gain optimum acceptance and support from both sides at an early stage of a conflict. How such an equation can be developed and how the parties at early stages of the conflict can be persuaded to mutually agree to this more constructive, though not perfect, alternative, is the daunting challenge. Given the element of pride and the need for face-saving in such situations, third party mediation supported by credible carrots and sticks is critically needed to break the deadlock.

CONCLUSION

I would like to conclude with the inherent value of these memoirs as an historical documentation of the war. Years ago, after the signing of the Comprehensive Peace Agreement, I proposed to our friends in Washington that we should begin to undertake or support the documentation of the war by recording the experiences of those who were involved in the fighting. They agreed, although I do not believe anything practical was done. I recently asked Pieng whether any of his colleagues have written about their war experiences. He gave the case of one person whose documentation is an angry account of his allegations against John Garang. According to Pieng, this man is one of the people John Garang had built up and supported. He is, therefore, perhaps understandably a bitter, but shamefully ungrateful individual.

If each of Pieng's colleagues, whom I was told were collectively the core of the SPLM/SPLA, wrote about the war from the perspective of their own experience in the battle front, South Sudan would have a treasure of historical records from which generations to come could learn much to guide their own contribution to the continued building of their nation – the Republic of South Sudan. Documenting the armed struggle of South Sudan is a project that should be encouraged and supported. For now, we have in Pieng's Memoirs a book that documents the role of one man who is universally respected throughout South Sudan, a brother for whom we are exceptionally proud as a family and as members of the Ngok Dinka community. The accounts of the three women included in this volume also document the different ways the shared cause provokes people into rebelling and the varied manner in which they contribute to the cause. The story of Tikley is particularly striking both for his unique status as a nine-year old child soldier and also for the excellence with which the story is narrated.

These accounts are, however, not merely historical records. They represent the documentation of experiences that address critical questions on when to fight, when to talk, and when to reconcile. People go to war when their grievances are not only extreme but are not being addressed and there is no credible evidence that they will be addressed. The warring parties begin to talk when both sides go through what conflict resolution scholars call a mutually hurting stalemate. Often such mutual pain is not only seen but felt by the responsible political and military leaders. It is only then that they make peace and reconcile.

In most cases, peace agreements are based on options that were quite apparent from the start. So, the question that arises is whether with some foresight, moral aptitude, and compassion for the sanctity of life and the integrity and dignity of all humankind war can be avoided by agreeing on the principle of addressing legitimate grievances and cooperating toward that end, even though it may take a reasonable length of time before all the grievances are effectively and fully addressed. This may sound unrealistic, and the history of war indicates that violence may be an integral component of our animal and animalistic propensity that cannot be eliminated, but it can at least be mitigated by aspiring and striving toward that lofty goal.

Finally, for me, since humanity is far from the utopia of peace and reconciliation before the attainment of full justice, Pieng's book and the stories of three women and a child which I have produced in this volume represent a precious documentation of young warriors and a child soldier driven by gross injustice and unacceptable brutality and humiliation against their people to take up arms ready to make the ultimate sacrifice in defense of the dignity and integrity, not only of their people, the Ngok Dinka of Abyei, but also of their people of South Sudan, and indeed of the wider Sudan.

Pieng did that with exemplary valor and humanity throughout the entire territory of South Sudan and up to the borders of the Two Sudans. And he did it with the solidarity of his soldiers from the various ethnic groups of the country with full appreciation of their courage and contribution to the liberation struggle and with no discrimination or favor whatsoever. As a result, Pieng won great respect not only from his

Red Army boys who became soldiers and then the Lost Boys and in the South Sudanese Army as whole. Although a younger brother, with a personality glowing with quiet dignity around him Pieng has already proved himself a legendary hero, and a model of the many war heroes Abyei has produced in the two wars in the Sudan for whom our family and our people, the Ngok Dinka, are exceedingly proud.

But the story of a brave man would not complete the full value of the heroism of our people without also reflecting the remarkable sacrifices the women made, whether directly in the battle front, or indirectly through the delivery of critical services. The determination with which the two Awuors pursued the goal of joining the struggle and the suffering they endured in the process are in themselves acts of heroism which merit great pride from their people. And despite the opportunities Nyenagwek found in the relative comfort and peace of civil service and the relative privileges she received in the system, the yearning for joining the liberation struggle prevailed and she eventually enrolled in the rebel army. The rage which drove a child of nine to go to war is a testimony to the depth of anger and determination to make the ultimate sacrifice by the people of all ages for the freedom and dignity of their people.

It is a great pleasure and honor for me to have had the privilege to put this volume together as a modest tribute to these outstanding individuals and to war heroes in general, both from the Ngok Dinka of Abyei and their comrades-in-arms in South Sudan and the wider New Sudan without discrimination on the grounds of race, ethnicity, religion and culture. May the Almighty God bless the fallen heroes to rest in Eternal Peace.

Major General Justin Deng Biong Mading,
Anyanya 1955-1972
SPLM/A 1955-1973; 1983-2005

Veteran Freedom Fighter, Dudol Nyang Any-Nya 1. SPLM/A

Group of SPLA officers. From left to right: Captain Atem Garang Dau of Shield 2 by then (now Maj. General). 2nd Lt. late Jurkuch Arok Young of Shield 8(killed at the battle of Ashwa). The then Captain (now Maj, Gen, Mou Manasseh Malak). 1st Lt. late Arop Mading of Shield 6, by then. 2nd Lt. Kur Garang Deng of Shield 8 by then. Gen. Pieng Deng Kuol. Back row: Brigadier Gen, Athian Mawien Athian of Shield 7 by then, now Brigadier Gen, of Police. Behind wearing a hat is Fana Amos Ajak Garang of Shield 5 and Majur Kot of Shield 8 next to Athian.

Abyei People's Referendum in October 2013

Abyei People's Referendum 2013

Hon. Nyenagwek Kuol at Abyei People's Referendum 2013

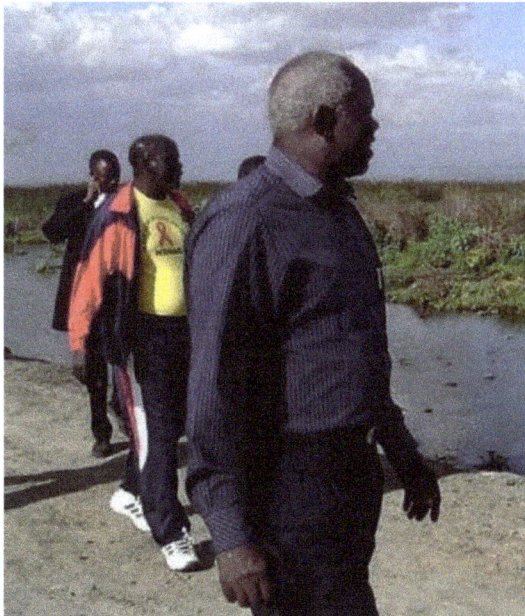

Dr John Garang de Mabior with Edward Lino

Mijak Miyan Kuol, a freedom fighter,
was killed in battle in Kapoeta

UNISFA Solder during Abyei People's Referendum 2013

Cde Arop Mading, Aide Officer to Dr John Garang de Mabior

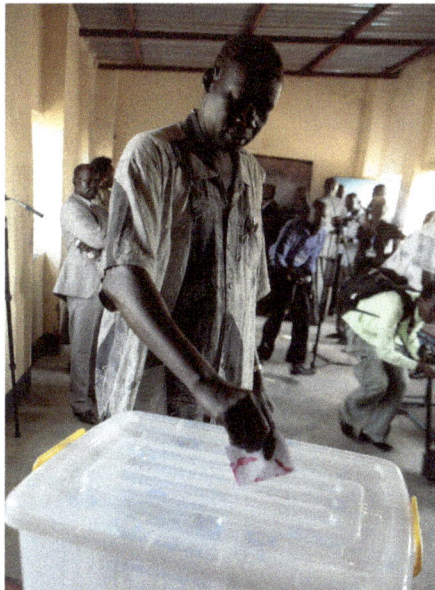

Hon Deng Alor casting his vote in the Abyei People's Referendum 2013

*Veterans journalists Arop Madut and Mustafa Biong
during the Abyei People's Referendum 2013*

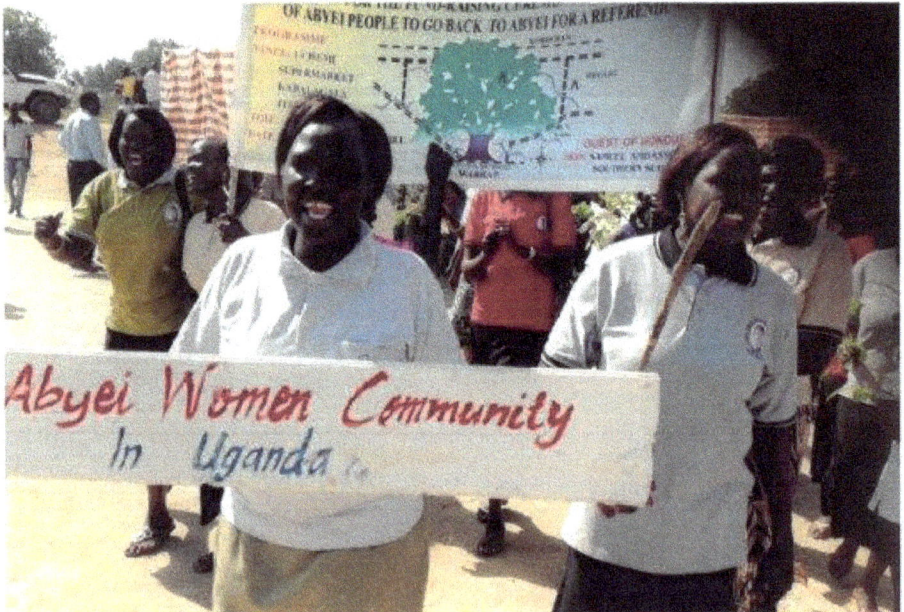

Abyei women in Abyei People's Referendum 2013

Abyei declaration of People's Referendum Results

Abyei Leadership after voting in the People's Referendum 2013

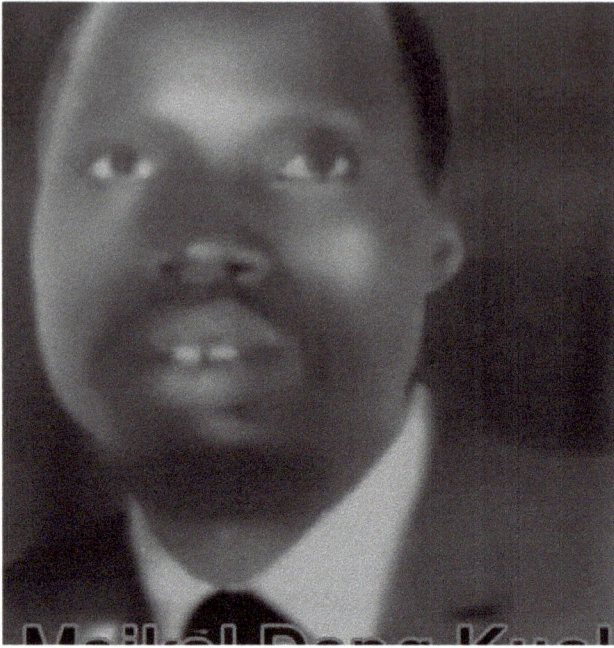

Michael Miokol Deng
Abyei Liberation Front (ALF) leader 1981-1983

General Chol Ayuak Gony
Officer in SPLM/A and Sudan Army

Justin Deng Aguer, first Abyei Commissioner in the 1970s

Silvio Rokdit Ayuak,
First Abyei Community leader in Juba in the 1970s

General Kuol Deim Kuol
Chief Administrator of Abyei Special Administrative Area

Ustaz Lino Ayong Moyom
Assassinated in Wau Massacre by the Sudan Army in 1965

Major General Yussuf Deng Bar, SPLM/A 1983 - 2005

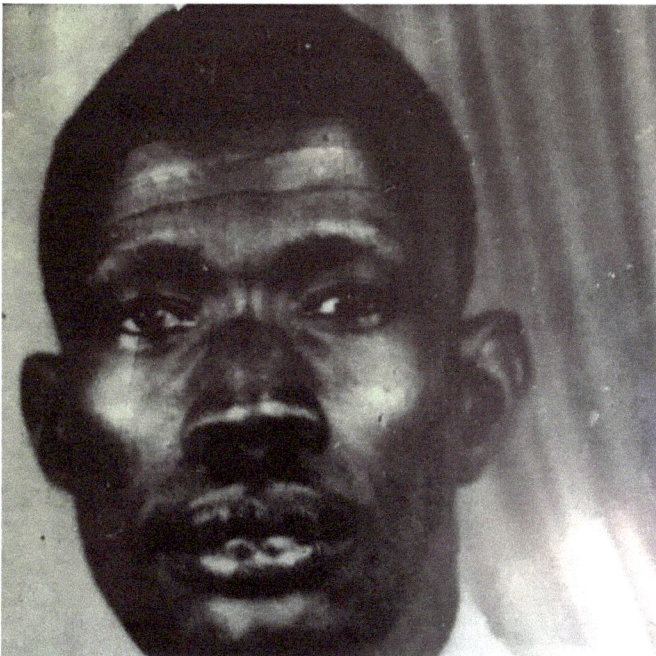

Ustaz. Luis Nyok Kuol, killed by the Sudan Army in 1965 in Tonj

LT Col Akur Chol Malual. SPLM/A

*Major General Edward Achueny Dau Anyana One
1963 - 1972; SPLM A. 1983 - 2005*

Brig General. Victor Kuol Arop Malek Anyanya, 1963 - 1972

Minyiel Row with Dr John Garang

Charles Biong Deng
First Translator of South Sudan Regional Assembly, 1973 - 1983

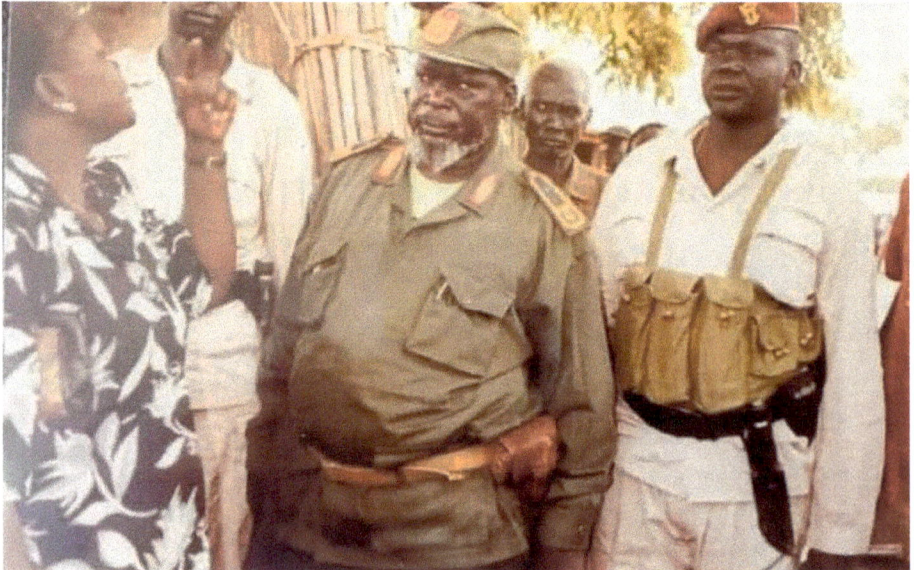

Chol Akuei: Bodyguard of Dr John Garang, Rumbek 2003

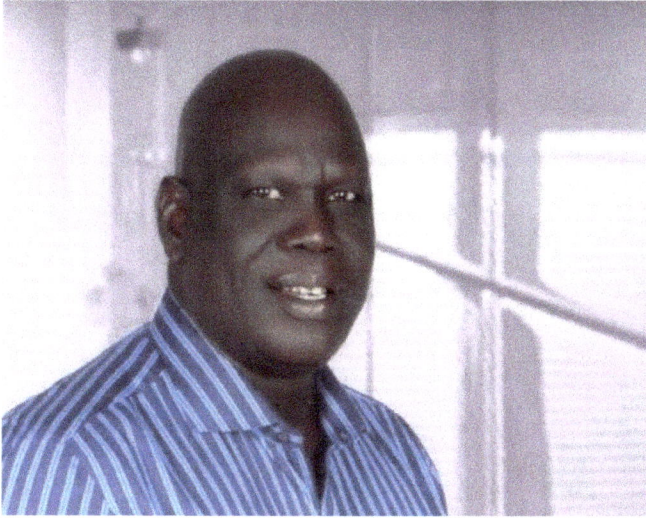

Kur Ajing Ater
Businessman from Abyei

Major General Dominic Kuol Arob Koor Anyanya One
1963 - 1972; SPLM/A 1998 - 2005

*Mark Mijak Abiem, Ph.D Candidate
with the late Dr Agoth Wek, a medical doctor*

Mark Mijak Abiem

INDEX

www.ingramcontent.com/pod-product-compliance
Lightning Source LLC
Chambersburg PA
CBHW052009030426

42334CB00029BA/3150